MASTERS
OF FINANCE

MASTERS OF FINANCE

INTERVIEWS WITH SOME OF THE GREATEST
MINDS IN INVESTING AND ECONOMICS

■ ■ ■

EDITOR: MARGARET M. TOWLE, PHD, CPWA®

Investment Management Consultants Association Inc.

Greenwood Village, Colorado

Margaret M. Towle, PhD, CPWA*, is a principal with Yakima River Partners in Bainbridge Island, Washington. Previously, she served as partner and managing director with HighTower Advisors, where she provided financial advisory services for a select number of endowments and wealthy families. Before that, she was a managing director with Greycourt & Co., where she provided financial advisory services to wealthy families and oversaw investment research across traditional and alternative asset classes. In addition, she was an executive vice president and chief investment officer for Northern Trust Global Advisors. Dr. Towle was selected as a Fellow by the Kauffman Foundation to attend the Center for Entrepreneurial Leadership and was the recipient of IMCA's 2006 Stephen L. Kessler Writing Award. She was nominated and recognized as one of Wealth Manager's "Top 50 Women in Wealth Management" in 2009. Dr. Towle is a founding board member of the Center for Women and Democracy at the University of Washington, and an angel investor in 100 Women in Hedge Funds. Dr. Towle earned BA, MA, and PhD degrees from the University of Washington-Seattle. She began serving on IMCA's board of directors in 2009. She is editor-in-chief of the *Journal of Investment Consulting*, and former chair of IMCA's Advisory Council and *Investments & Wealth Monitor* editorial advisory board.

The interviews contained in this book originally were published in their entirety in the *Journal of Investment Consulting*, published by Investment Management Consultants Association Inc.

IMCA books may be purchased for educational, business, or sales promotional use. For information, please e-mail publications@IMCA.org or visit www.IMCA.org.

IMCA®

5619 DTC Parkway, Suite 500
Greenwood Village, CO 80111
303.770.3377 • www.IMCA.org

Managing Editor, Debbie Nochlin
Designed by Tillie Creative
Cover Image: ©istockphoto
Printed in the United States of America by Henry Wurst Inc.

ISBN 978-0-692-26782-0
This paper meets the requirements of ANSI/NISO Z39.48-1992 (Permanence of Paper).

CONTENTS

■ ■ ■

Foreword VII

Acknowledgments VIII

CHAPTER 1   **Peter Bernstein:** The Philosopher King of Wall Street 1

CHAPTER 2   **John Bogle:** Champion of the Individual Investor 11

CHAPTER 3   **Gene Fama:** Father of Modern Finance 26

CHAPTER 4   **Daniel Kahneman:** Father of Decision Making 41

CHAPTER 5   **Dean LeBaron:** Investment Futurist 55

CHAPTER 6   **Marty Leibowitz:** Wall Street's Bond Guru 68

CHAPTER 7   **Bob Litterman:** Stellar Quant 82

CHAPTER 8   **Burt Malkiel:** Random Walker with a Crutch 95

CHAPTER 9   **Harry Markowitz:** Father of Modern Portfolio Theory 104

CHAPTER 10   **Robert Merton:** Rational Man, with a Big "R," Big "M" 118

CHAPTER 11   **Myron Scholes:** Intellectual Father of the Credit Default Swap 136

CHAPTER 12   **Bill Sharpe:** Godfather of Index Funds 154

CHAPTER 13   **Bob Shiller:** Mr. Bubble 167

CHAPTER 14   **Richard Thaler:** Founding Father of Behavioral Economics 178

CHAPTER 15   **Ed Thorp:** King of Gamblers 188

Index 203

FOREWORD

■ ■ ■

For more than a decade, the editorial board of the Investment Management Consultants Association's *Journal of Investment Consulting* has been conducting interviews with individuals we consider to be Masters in the areas of finance and economics. Our Masters so far have included seven Nobel laureates (Fama, Kahneman, Markowitz, Merton, Scholes, Sharpe, and Shiller) and eight additionally extraordinary investment visionaries (Bernstein, Bogle, LeBaron, Leibowitz, Litterman, Malkiel, Thaler, and Thorp). It saddens me to realize that all our Masters to date have been men, but I believe we will see this change as our interviews continue into the next decade.

Our method was straightforward. We began each interview by asking an open-ended, scene-setting question such as, "Would you tell us what you consider your greatest accomplishment—as well as your greatest disappointment?" Then we opened up the interview to questions from committee members, allowing the conversation to go where it may.

We initially thought these interviews would appeal to investment professionals who were interested in learning about the underpinnings of modern finance and economics, so we published the Masters interviews in the *Journal of Investment Consulting*, starting in 2004. As the project continued, however, we were surprised—and delighted—to find that our conversations with the Masters also provided insight to the human side of the world of investments. In their own words we heard many Masters describe how they survived failure and went on to groundbreaking discoveries and other accomplishments. We learned, among other things, that someday behavioral finance may not exist because all of finance will be behavioral. As I reviewed these fifteen interviews again, I was impressed once more by the Masters' replies and the nuggets of wisdom contained within. Ironically, many of the answers apply beyond the boundaries of economic theory or the principles of finance. I've summarized here some of my own takeaways, and you'll likely expand the list with other points you will find particularly relevant.

TAKEAWAYS

■ Understanding risk is paramount.

■ The desire to learn is a constant and vital to any successful endeavor.

■ Flexibility in thinking and openness in considering other worldviews expand the solution set.

■ Taking the path less followed early in your career leads to breakthroughs later on.

■ Survival in a competitive world requires overcoming disappointment and moving on.

■ Collaboration is vital to innovative solutions.

- Luck happens, go with it.
- Put clients first—no matter what.
- The optimal solution requires a combination of the theoretical and the practical.
- Recognizing that you do not have all the answers is the first step toward a solution.
- Innovation is disruptive; be prepared for opposition.
- Education is of the utmost importance.

This book is a decade-long collaboration of individuals who put time and effort into a project that started with one simple interview, under the leadership of Edward Baker who was the *Journal* editor at the time. It then grew into a whole that really is greater than the sum of its parts. I'm grateful to all who participated, especially the Masters, past and present members of the *Journal of Investment Consulting* editorial board, and the IMCA staff, particularly Debbie Nochlin and Ian MacKenzie, who masterfully shepherded the production of *Masters of Finance*.

— Margaret M. Towle

ACKNOWLEDGMENTS

■ ■ ■

THE FOLLOWING PEOPLE HAVE PARTICIPATED IN THESE INTERVIEWS OVER THE YEARS:

Mark J. P. Anson, Edward D. Baker III, Ludwig Chincarini, Michael T. Dieschbourg, Roger Edelen, Geoffrey Gerber, Ronald N. Kahn, Tony Kao, Matthew Morey, Arun Muralidhar, Meir Statman, and Margaret M. Towle

PUBLISHER'S NOTE:

The interviews contained in this book are edited transcripts of discussions among the participants. Any apparent errors in usage should be considered natural products of speech.

CHAPTER 1

PETER BERNSTEIN: THE PHILOSOPHER KING OF WALL STREET

PETER L. BERNSTEIN

Economic journalist; publisher, *Economics and Portfolio Strategy* newsletter; editor, *Journal of Portfolio Management*; author, *Against the Gods, Capital Ideas: The Improbable Origins of Modern Wall Street*; and *Capital Ideas Evolving*. (1919–2009)

Peter Bernstein's multi-faceted career, which included turns as an economic journalist, investment manager, educator, and historian, shaped a worldview that was dynamic, diverse, and forward-thinking. Bernstein changed the way we think about risk, and he is perhaps best-known as the author of *Against the Gods: The Remarkable Story of Risk.* He was fond of saying, "Risk doesn't mean danger—it just means not knowing what the future holds." Bernstein took the abstract world of risk and applied it to the real world of financial markets, and thus indirectly to our daily lives. In defining risk as a set of possible scenarios, he set the stage for subsequent robust risk measures such as Value at Risk (VAR).

■ ■ ■

EDWARD BAKER: We appreciate having you with us today, Peter. Perhaps you could start by giving us some background on the major factors that influenced your views and helped to shape your career.

PETER BERNSTEIN: First of all, I was fortunate to study economics at Harvard in the late 1930s, when the faculty was trying to learn the theories of Keynes at the same time they were teaching them to us. That was an enormous intellectual experience. Growing up during the Depression also influenced my views. Even though that's now a long time ago, it's still there as an influence. The main thing that experience taught me was a sense of humility and an awareness of the importance of surprise, that is, unexpected things happen. Next, and I say this with some humility, I've tried terribly hard to keep my integrity, control my ambition, and put clients first. I've been serious about that from the beginning. Finally, I've been blessed with more than 60 years of marriage. I was widowed, and Barbara is my second wife. I've had wonderful companionship that has been a major influence on my success. I couldn't have done it any other way.

EDWARD BAKER: We also wanted to ask you what you consider your major achievement. Maybe there is more than one, but if you had to pick one achievement, what would it be?

PETER BERNSTEIN: The greatest joy I've had has to be the books that I've authored. This includes one that came out in the 1960s that nobody knows anymore called *A Primer on Money, Banking, and Gold*, which was in many ways a precursor to much of what I wrote later. These books are not only my greatest joy, but I'm still hearing from people around the world who have read them, so I guess you'd have to say they are also my greatest success.

EDWARD BAKER: I wanted to mention that I used this interview as motivation to go back and read your 1992 book, *Capital Ideas: The Improbable Origins of Modern Wall Street*. I was very impressed with both the quality and depth of the writing. It was very insightful, but entertaining and fun to read as well.

PETER BERNSTEIN: That book is first in my heart too, so that's delightful to hear. By the way, I should tell you that I'm working on a new book, *Capital Ideas Evolving*, which will essentially be volume two of *Capital Ideas*.

EDWARD BAKER: And, to go along with your successes, I suppose we have to ask you what you consider to be your biggest mistake.

PETER BERNSTEIN: I've thought a lot about this, and I'm going to be up-front with my answer. In 1967, we decided to allow my investment counseling firm,[1] which I inherited from my father and which I joined in 1951, to be acquired by a brokerage firm in what was to be Sandy Weill's first deal. We had good motivations for allowing the deal to go through. We wanted to get into the pension fund business and didn't want to take the risk on our own capital. However, it was a world about which I had no understanding, and even though the guys at the brokerage firm were wonderful to me, I could not stand the ethics, the heat, or the conflicts of interest, and I resigned in 1973. Looking back, allowing that acquisition is one step I'm sorry I took.

I should also include under this heading that in 1958, at the bottom of the market, I was a raging bear. I've always regretted that one, too, because I certainly was wrong.

MEIR STATMAN: Did that teach you not to forecast the market or just not to make mistakes?

PETER BERNSTEIN: Unfortunately, nothing teaches you not to make mistakes. But since that forecast, I've been a lot more humble.

EDWARD BAKER: As a consequence, has your orientation been to stay long in equities through thick and thin?

PETER BERNSTEIN: No, that has moved around. My views have changed. I can't say I've never expressed an opinion or a judgment, but I have been more guarded since 1958. The error in 1958 was an interesting one. Business was really bad at the end of 1957. Everyone was expecting the great post-war depression to come, and many of us thought this was the moment. What I failed to recognize was that there wasn't going to be a post-war depression, that this was a world with an entirely different economic structure and liquidity and a different role for the United States in the world—and all of that, certainly in the late 1950s, was going to prevent the return of a depression like we had in the 1930s. To be so focused on a major experience of the past and therefore fail to understand the present, in all of its manifestations, was where the mistake lay. I learned a lot from that, and today it is very important to understand that this is not 1995, it's 2006.

EDWARD BAKER: It's a lot easier to talk about the market in the past than in the present, isn't it?

PETER BERNSTEIN: My sense is this: In the normal course of events, the market will fluctuate, but nothing awful will happen unless one of two things takes place. There are two enormously critical variables on the horizon that one can't time or be specific about, but they are there. One is the exposed position of the U.S. dollar, and I just don't think we'll get by without a crisis there. I think that requires a major hedge. The other is the whole geopolitical situation. I live in New York, and I live in constant anxiety about the state of the world. That's not an economic matter, but it's pervasive in all decisions and appetites for risk and so forth. If the housing boom collapses or business gets weaker—okay, well, we've been through those things before. That's nothing to necessarily make us run for cover. It's the bigger, darker things on the horizon that scare me.

EDWARD BAKER: The geopolitical framework is more important than it has been in a long time, and for the first time people really are developing a global view and thinking globally about their investment portfolios. Do you see investors beginning to broaden asset allocations more globally?

PETER BERNSTEIN: Yes, certainly in the institutional world. I was struck by something I saw in a *Wall Street Journal* article. I don't remember the exact numbers, but a very high proportion of IPOs (initial public offerings) in 2005 and to date in 2006 were made outside the United States in international markets all around the world. In many ways, talking financially, this is a very positive development. It means that we're not going to have a repetition of the Asian crisis of the 1990s. These countries are financially much better based and have more active and efficient markets. That's a powerfully positive element in the world economy.

MARK ANSON: I'm based in London, one of those locations where many U.S. companies are listing. How much of that IPO activity do you think is due simply to regulatory constraints, specifically the Sarbanes-Oxley Act,[2] forcing the raising of capital offshore into other venues, such as London?

PETER BERNSTEIN: I think the motivation behind Sarbanes-Oxley is a very important one. I don't know what chief executive officers read, but I probably read what you read. I said at the beginning about Sarbanes-Oxley that we run the risk that businesses are going to be taken over by accountants instead of risk-takers. I think that reform is an important motivation, but the consequence is very positive. I do worry about regulation. Of course, you have to be in favor of it, but you don't want to kill the goose that lays the golden egg.

EDWARD BAKER: In the United Kingdom, we have more of a principles-based regulatory framework rather than a rules-based framework. That seems to be a much more constructive approach. Do you have any thoughts about that?

PETER BERNSTEIN: No question about it. Sarbanes-Oxley provides so many rules that it becomes extremely costly as well.

MEIR STATMAN: Can you put this in the context of the 1930s, when the Securities and Exchange Commission (SEC) was established? I'm not sure Sarbanes-Oxley is the equivalent of that, but can you talk about the waves of "Let capitalism run" and "Let's rein in capitalism"?

PETER BERNSTEIN: That debate's been going on since the beginning. Back in 1887, we had the Interstate Commerce Commission being established. I recently wrote a book about the Erie Canal, and I got the sense it went on back in the 1820s. It's a story that will repeat itself. The SEC was a more profound development than Sarbanes-Oxley, and much more far-reaching in whom it affected. The SEC established the idea of disclosure and transparency as the core of what regulation and the necessary conditions for good markets were all about. So I think the establishment of the SEC in 1934 was a much bigger event than Sarbanes-Oxley. The SEC was established more than 70 years ago, and it's still an active institution. Seventy years from now, nobody will know what Sarbanes-Oxley is.

■ ■ ■

> The sequence from Harry Markowitz in 1952 to Black and Scholes in 1973—that period of roughly twenty years—is almost spooky, because none of those economists was tuned into Wall Street. They were all in their ivory towers. They were talking to one another, but they weren't talking to investors. Suddenly, almost out of nowhere, there was this great leap, with entirely new thoughts, the biggest of which was that risk is as important as return.

MEIR STATMAN: You were talking earlier about the 1950s post-war period and how the economic structure in the world had changed. That was also the time that the seeds of modern portfolio theory were sown. Did something happen at that time that could explain those two events, or was it just a coincidence?

PETER BERNSTEIN: I think it was a coincidence. The sequence from Harry Markowitz in 1952 to Black and Scholes in 1973—that period of roughly twenty years—is almost spooky, because none of those economists was tuned into Wall Street. They were all in their ivory towers. They were talking to one another, but they weren't talking to investors. Suddenly, almost out of nowhere, there was this great leap, with entirely new thoughts, the biggest of which was that risk is as important as return. Thinking back over the whole history of human thought, there really isn't anything like those twenty years.

In 1968, when I was still in the investment counseling business, my editor at Random House called me and said, "There's a very interesting young man we may be working with, and I'm sure you'd enjoy meeting him. His name is William Sharpe." So I called up Bill, a very charming young man, and asked him to lunch. We sat down and ordered a drink, then without any preliminary, he turned to me and asked, "Do you beat the market?" I nearly fell off my chair, thinking, "Nobody has ever dared to ask me that question. How can you ask me such a question? How could I be in business successfully if I didn't?" This was 1968, and I didn't feel that I was behind the eight ball in terms of my thinking. In fact, I think I was more intellectual than most. Bill and I have often joked about this incident, about how fresh he was.

MEIR STATMAN: Can you say more about the state of the investment advisory profession right now, because it seems like there are two directions. One says, "We are here to beat the market, so don't bother us because we are busy looking for opportunities." The other says, "No, we are here to help you with your life and your life goals, and we are trying to take care of your well-being, not just your wealth." Do you see conflict between those two directions, any balance that needs to be struck, any thoughts you have on that?

PETER BERNSTEIN: I think you're talking about two different worlds: the world of the institutional investor and the world of the individual investor. In the individual investor world, I think it's a terrible mistake to tell people you're going to "beat the market," or find all the mutual funds that are going to do that, because you don't know whether you will be able to accomplish that. To promise something that you don't know whether you can deliver is not only going to hurt the client but in the end hurt you too. I don't have to tell you that investing is a very complicated, very difficult business. It involves a wide range of expertise and thought and, above all, sensitivity to risk and the consequences of being wrong. To promise anything other than "I'm going to try to take care of you" or "I'm going to try to prevent the bottom from dropping out, and I can't even promise that, but I'm going to do my best" is wrong. I think that's obvious. One of the things about the investment advisory business that bothers me is the agency sort of problem, that they go from the fanciest investment committee of the fanciest institution down to the smallest investment advisor trying to entice a client into his arms. I think investment advisors have to be very careful about what they promise, be fee-only, and have everything transparent, or there will be more disasters.

EDWARD BAKER: Why do you think this idea of portable alpha now is all of a sudden catching on?

PETER BERNSTEIN: The driving force was the widespread notion that we're in an era of low expected returns, and so people were scraping at anything. But then I think what happened was that the innate logic of the idea was too strong: Why should I pay the same guy to produce alpha who is producing beta? Maybe I can do it differently. It's not very complex. First of all, most people probably don't really think about alpha seriously enough, but once you ask yourself that question, the world suddenly changes. We also needed the whole derivative instrument business to become much more familiar and easy-to-use. It's a major coming together of a lot of key ideas.

MEIR STATMAN: Is this related to your views on strategic asset allocation, that in some ways we have moved from a focus on, say, a static strategic allocation to the need to look for alpha?

PETER BERNSTEIN: I'm not sure, Meir. I think I might put it the other way. Because the search for alpha now is separate from the search for beta returns, the policy portfolio has a tendency to be more static. I've taken care of that problem; that is, I've got my asset allocation under control because I've got it all indexed. I don't have to think about it. Now I have to look at where I'm going to get the edge. So, to some extent, the focus on portable alpha takes people's attention away from the asset allocation problem. I don't think it's really diverted from the asset allocation problem, but to the extent that portable alpha plays a role in this, it does take some attention from asset allocation.

MEIR STATMAN: And properly so, or is that dangerous?

PETER BERNSTEIN: No, it certainly is not proper. The alpha search, as I don't have to tell you, is somewhat ephemeral, and asset allocation is enormously important at every moment. I have to say, and again this is from research I did for the new book, that where people are really serious about the subject of risk—at places like Harvard, Yale, Princeton, CalPERS, Goldman Sachs—mean variance is still very much at the core of decision making. When Harry Markowitz said that you have to think about risk as well as return, that was the thunderclap, and it still reverberates. Wherever it doesn't reverberate, those people are going to be in trouble, such as the person running the hedge fund who thought he was a genius in buying energy while he had a dreadful risk-management structure. Someday I'm going to write a piece called "The Perils of Brilliance." The times I have been most wrong are the times I thought I was most right. You asked me at the beginning about the things I've learned from all of this, and I have to repeat: It's humility. I think the reason I've been able to survive fifty-five years in this business is because I developed humility, at least after 1958. It's the only way to survive—not necessarily to be the top quartile—but survival is really the name of the game we're playing with long-term considerations.

■ ■ ■

> When Harry Markowitz said that you have to think about risk as well as return, that was the thunderclap, and it still reverberates. Wherever it doesn't reverberate, those people are going to be in trouble, such as the person running the hedge fund who thought he was a genius in buying energy while he had a dreadful risk-management structure.

MARK ANSON: One of the things about humility I've learned in the markets is that the markets can be irrational far beyond my pain threshold. As you look around today, I'm curious if you see one or two valuations or themes in the markets that make you scratch your head and say this just doesn't seem to make sense.

PETER BERNSTEIN: I think that kind of thing is always there, but I would join you in a larger statement. A long time ago, Paul Samuelson distinguished between micro-efficiency and macro-inefficiency. All of the forces in the market are working constantly toward greater efficiency—although they will never get there. Behavioral finance in itself has performed a huge service by drawing attention to an enormous variety of alpha opportunities that people hadn't thought of before. So that process goes on constantly all over the world. But the boom/bust thing is never going to go away; it's going to come back. I see no reason to think that it's ever going to end as long as the system is fair.

EDWARD BAKER: Although variance still is widely used as the primary assessment of risk, we know the use of variance has a lot of flaws and distributions probably aren't normal. In fact, if you move away from stocks, you have important characteristics of distributions with which variance obviously would not deal very well. What are your thoughts about that? Do you think that's a danger? Why has variance stuck around for so long?

PETER BERNSTEIN: Variance has two things in its favor: First of all, it's mathematically very convenient to use. Harry Markowitz came up with the concept, and he was an operations research person, so it was neat. That's the most compelling reason. However, I think it has a more important overtone. Volatility gets you in the guts. There's no question that when prices are jumping around, you feel different from when they're stable. You say to yourself: "What does somebody else know that I don't know? What's going on that I don't understand?" Variance is a proxy for risk, in a gut sense. Now maybe it's too short-term; maybe you shouldn't respond to it. But it's not just the mathematical aspect of it. I think there's a psychological aspect too. Nevertheless, there is no question that the focus on variance (a) makes people too oriented to the short-term and (b) adds all the mathematical limitations that you mentioned. The basic idea is what Harry said in English rather than in math, and that is you have to consider risk as well as return. If you think about everything in the way of implementation that has developed since Harry first talked about this in the early 1950s, and the tools we've developed since then, and yet none of them are really designed to get better returns, because we'll never know how to do that. They *are* designed to figure out how to incorporate risk into the decision. It's knit into the fabric, and we're not going to get it out again.

TONY KAO: I wanted to ask you your opinion about the transformation of defined benefit plans now that people are talking about frozen plans. What is your view on what this has meant to individuals, as well as on what kind of product design needs to be done?

PETER BERNSTEIN: I don't know how to design a product, but I can answer the other part of your question. It's awful, awful, awful. I'm writing a piece now for my newsletter about the background of the equity risk premium, so I've been thinking about this problem a lot. From the end of World War II to the end of the 1960s, the bond market went steadily down, and the stock market went almost steadily up. Looking back, the whole thing looked so easy, but these are such difficult kinds of questions. That period was almost the inverse of what has happened since 2000, and that's what ruined the defined benefit business. The bond market went up, and the stock market went down, and the defined benefit business got into deep trouble. If that hadn't happened,

I don't think the idea of defined contribution plans would have gotten anywhere. That's really the tragedy, and I don't know how you put the pieces back together again. To throw the risk on the individual—I think it's a catastrophe.

TONY KAO: What kind of catalyst do you think it would take to bring back the defined benefit plan?

PETER BERNSTEIN: I really don't know how you would put it back together again. I don't think corporations—to the extent that they recognize the real nature of this obligation—are going to willingly go back into the defined benefit plan.

TONY KAO: What role do you think investment advisors and financial planners need to play as defined contribution plans become a more important part of retirement assets?

PETER BERNSTEIN: Obviously, it's a very important role because individuals need that advice and guidance. I also think the present trend toward life-cycle funds[3] is very beneficial, because these funds help individuals make decisions ahead of time. But the financial advisory profession should also be involved in that. At one end of the spectrum, you have Financial Engines, Bill Sharpe's business,[4] but there are many other ways financial advisors can help individuals frame and design their retirement choices. There should be a lot of opportunity ahead for advisors, because I don't see us going back and re-establishing the defined benefit plan as the typical plan.

EDWARD BAKER: What role should investment consultants be playing in all of this? I mean the people who are advising the individuals as to what to do with their assets, not necessarily the people who are actually running the money, but those who are providing the consulting advice.

■ ■ ■

The difficult thing for the financial advisor and the client—and I learned this when I managed money—is that no one can really identify how he or she is going to react when surprises come along, and yet surprises are inevitably going to come. Somehow investment consultants need to condition people to this fact.

PETER BERNSTEIN: The difficult thing for the financial advisor and the client—and I learned this when I managed money—is that no one can really identify how he or she is going to react when surprises come along, and yet surprises are inevitably going to come. Somehow investment consultants need to condition people to this fact. I give a lot of talks where I stand up and say, "We don't know what the future holds," and I see all of the heads nodding up and down. But people act as if they do know what the future holds, and that's what gets them into trouble.

So it's crucial that consultants try to get through to people that it's impossible to know the future and that surprise is inevitable. As a result, we have to limit the nature of our bets, we have to be obsessive about diversification, we shouldn't try to be too smart, we shouldn't try to shoot the moon. All of these are very simple ideas, and people will accept them ahead of time, but it's hard for them to live with humbly structured portfolios. However, they have to do so if they're going to survive. The main thing that an investment consultant can do is to get through this idea that you can't act as though you know the future if you want to be a survivor. The future may be better than you think, and it's not necessarily going to be worse. But even if it's better than you think, that's also hard to handle. It's that kind of philosophical teaching that consultants have to understand in their hearts, and then get it into the hearts of investors. Once you've got the philosophical grasp, the rest is easy.

MEIR STATMAN: Can we connect this back to your comments about ethics and integrity at the very beginning? I think that one of the problems that financial advisors face is that investors come to them thinking that they are going to get the advisors' services for free. So advisors respond by hiding their fees, and so on. Do you see a way to clarify this situation so that it is more like the relationship between physician and patient? The investor comes in, he pays the fee, and things are reasonably transparent.

PETER BERNSTEIN: I know, Meir, that's the goal; that's the way it should be. When I started in the investment counsel business, the idea that you would pay a fee for advice instead of going to a broker—well, people didn't even know such a thing existed. Now that's regular operating procedure in the institutional world. Individuals just have to learn—and learn the hard way—that if you take on someone to give you advice who's got agency problems and conflicts of interest, then good-bye. Certainly the financial advisor associations are working hard on the ethical problem, and that's good, because the only way the advisors are going to survive is to be clean.

MEIR STATMAN: Has ethical behavior changed over time? Is it better now than it used to be?

PETER BERNSTEIN: No. I look back over the past ten years, and in my memory anyway, I don't remember levels of corruption—to use a general word—everywhere to the degree that it is today. By everywhere, I mean it's in the United States, it's outside the United States, it's in the heart of Congress, in the heart of the administration, in the heart of every political and economic set-up, and I don't know how you get it out. Once it's that widespread, it's extremely difficult to dislodge. For example, as part of a campaign to fight corruption in developing countries, Paul Wolfowitz at the World Bank is trying to restrict grants to countries where there's no corruption, and they can't find anyplace to give money.

EDWARD BAKER: Would you say that's also true of corporate governance practices? Have they deteriorated, or have they perhaps improved?

PETER BERNSTEIN: Maybe there's been some improvement since 2001, and I think there has been. However, the corruption was so pervasive and went so deep. You still pick up the paper every day and there's news of hanky-panky going on. It's very depressing. It was not like this in 1951—or 1961—or even 1971. The 1990s were a marvelous decade in some ways—and a catastrophic one in other ways. There was open greed in a way I don't think existed since Midas.

EDWARD BAKER: Looking at the future, what do you think is in store for us? I don't mean in terms of markets, but in terms of financial or academic innovation.

PETER BERNSTEIN: My sense is that—if you take short selling and portable alpha as the big innovations of the past few years—we are only at the beginning of the process of innovation. And that process will continue as things we haven't even begun to think of today will come about. We have this enormous range of financial instruments with which to play, and enormous goals to make money and to manage and share risk. I'm sure that even just five years from now there will be things to talk about that we're not even aware of at the moment.

■ ■ ■

ENDNOTES

[1]   Bernstein-Macaulay, Inc., which was founded in 1934 by Allen M. Bernstein and Frederick R. Macaulay, was acquired in 1967 by the firm of Carter, Berlind & Weill, in which Sandy Weill, later the chief executive officer and chairman of Citicorp, was a partner.

[2]   The Sarbanes-Oxley Act of 2002, also known as the Public Company Accounting Reform and Investor Protection Act of 2002, which was enacted on July 30, 2002, is a U.S. federal law passed in response to a number of major corporate and accounting scandals. The legislation established new or enhanced standards for all U.S. public company boards, management, and public accounting firms.

[3]   Life-cycle funds, or target-date funds, minimize asset allocation decisions by allowing participants to choose a single investment option that matches their age and retirement date.

[4]   In 1996, William Sharpe, who was awarded the 1990 Nobel Memorial Prize in Economic Sciences, cofounded Financial Engines, a firm that provides online investment advice and management for individual investors. He still is involved with the company and currently serves on its board of directors.

REFERENCES

Bernstein, Peter L. 1968. *A Primer on Money, Banking, and Gold*. New York: Random House.

———. 1992. *Capital Ideas: The Improbable Origins of Modern Wall Street*. New York: The Free Press.

———. 2005. *Wedding of the Waters: The Erie Canal and the Making of a Great Nation*. New York: W. W. Norton and Company.

———. 2007. *Capital Ideas Evolving*. Hoboken, NJ: John Wiley & Sons, Inc.

Black, Fischer, and Myron Scholes. 1973. The Pricing of Options and Corporate Liabilities. *Journal of Political Economy* 81, no. 3: (May/June): 637–654.

Markowitz, Harry M. 1952. Portfolio Selection. *Journal of Finance* 7, no. 1 (March): 77–91.

This interview was published in its entirety in *Journal of Investment Consulting* 8, no. 2, Summer 2007.

CHAPTER 2

JOHN BOGLE: CHAMPION OF THE INDIVIDUAL INVESTOR

JOHN C. BOGLE

Founder, The Vanguard Group; creator, first index mutual fund; pioneer, modern no-load mutual funds; author, *Bogle on Mutual Funds: New Perspectives for the Intelligent Investor, John Bogle on Investing: The First 50 Years,* and *The Battle for the Soul of Capitalism.*

When John Bogle launched the first retail index fund in 1976, he believed it was an optimal structure for retail and small institutional investors. His Vanguard 500 gave them an opportunity to passively invest in the U.S. stock market, something that, at the time, only large institutional investors enjoyed. Underwriters optimistically expected the IPO to bring in $150 million; it raised just $11.3 million—not even enough to buy round lots of each of the 500 stocks in the index—prompting pundits to label it "Bogle's folly." Yet Bogle's pragmatic optimism helped him survive the IPO flop. The Vanguard 500 grew to become the world's largest index mutual fund, and other successful Vanguard index mutual funds followed. Bogle's "disruptive innovation" continues to benefit millions of individual investors.

■ ■ ■

EDWARD BAKER: Thank you for joining us today. We're very interested in hearing your perspectives on the investment industry, especially the mutual fund industry. Perhaps you could start by giving us some background on the major factors that shaped your views and brought you to where you are at this point in your career?

JOHN BOGLE: First of all, the mutual fund industry that I wrote about somewhat critically in my Princeton thesis way back in 1951 unarguably was a better industry than the one we have today. An article I wrote last year for the *Financial Analysts Journal* spelled this out in some detail. Costs were lower, investment thinking was longer-term, and the funds were sounder for investors because they were mostly middle-of-the-road, highly diversified stock funds that basically came very close to owning the market, plus some balanced funds such as the Wellington Fund and a few bond funds that later disappeared. During my first twenty years in this business, portfolio turnover averaged 16 percent per year, give or take a percentage point. Expense ratios were low, and getting lower, running about 70 basis points on average early on and then dropping to 55 basis points ten years later, as the industry grew and we could deliver some economies of scale. The business then was to sell what we made. Today, as everybody knows, it's a business of making what will sell, a very faddish business that has become very expensive for investors. So, it was a much simpler, cheaper industry back then, with the main thrust being very diversified funds with a long-term focus. By and large, in those days, one could hold those funds for a lifetime.

My 1951 thesis was very idealistic; it was all about putting the shareholder first. I called for investment managers to subordinate their interests to those of the shareholders and for mutual funds to be managed in "the most efficient, honest, and economical way possible." Today, in the industry as a whole, we've lost that efficiency, we've lost that economy, and—as we see from recent scandals—we've lost a great deal of that honesty. So that's the ancient background, reflecting the deep-seated idealistic bias that probably any college junior or senior has, followed by—and this is an expression of Justice Brandeis I use increasingly—"the relentless rules of humble arithmetic."[1] In other words, gross return in the market minus the cost of financial intermediation is the net return investors receive. That was the major concept that shaped my thinking beyond that initial idealism and gave me a sense of the appropriateness of running the industry for investors, rather than managers.

If investors and analysts would just stand back and think about how the financial markets work, they would have to conclude that indexing is the winning strategy. However, the strategy for success in the investment business is basically, "Don't just stand there—do something." Trade three billion shares every day. If Alan Greenspan—or now Ben Bernanke—speaks, do something. If General Motors or Adelphia is going bankrupt, do something. If Microsoft isn't getting its new product out on time, do something. Yet we all know that the best rule for investors—the clients of the investment business—is, "Don't just do something—stand there." That diametrical opposition between the interest of the business side and the investors who are its clients gives rise to the great flaws in this industry. I keep trying to think of better ways to say what I'm trying to get across, so I've added one thing to this. The mutual fund industry—and for that matter investing generally—is a field where you not only don't get what you pay for, but you get precisely what you don't pay for. Gross return minus costs equals net return. So the corollary to getting precisely what you don't pay for is this: If you pay for nothing, you get everything.

MEIR STATMAN: Before we pursue those ideas, let's go back for a minute. When you started The Vanguard Group in 1974, it was with a different organizational structure from the conventional industry firm; that is, it was formally owned by the shareholders. Was that a new idea at the time?

JOHN BOGLE: That was a brand new way of running a mutual fund complex.

MEIR STATMAN: So the industry of the 1950s that you were talking about was not as good as it could have been because, with the introduction of this structure, you improved upon it. Would you agree?

JOHN BOGLE: We improved upon it on two levels. First, if you believe we are fiduciaries, the shareholder/owner structure gives us the best possible chance of fulfilling that fiduciary duty. The shareholder/owner approach is not a perfect structure; there's always room for too much greed in any structure, but it's a better structure because philosophically it says, "Our owners are the shareholders, and they demand that the investment managers run the funds in the interests of the shareholders, rather than those of the managers." That's a big step forward in philosophy and, I believe, the correct fiduciary philosophy in an industry where, when I read about it in *Fortune*[2] all those years ago, the words "trust" and "trustee" kept appearing. I think we've lost that notion today.

The second level, which reinforces this structure as an idea whose time has come, is that it produces those very low costs that we now know are essential to delivering to our investors their fair share of whatever returns the markets are generous enough to give us. You could say that the creation of Vanguard was my attempt to "walk the walk" that would justify the "talk the talk" words in my thesis all those years earlier. It was action that reinforced those initial words. This retrospective view of the situation might be a slightly romanticized version, but it's a view that's not without a lot of support. Nothing is quite that pristine, I'm the first to confess.

RONALD KAHN: It's interesting that you look back on the industry in the early 1950s as being so much better than today. That predates Harry Markowitz, William Sharpe, the capital asset pricing model (CAPM), and all the work of academics since then. What do you think academics have added? Have they added anything beyond CAPM?

■ ■ ■

> If we look at the idea of diversification—the fundamental Markowitz theory—and add in Sharpe's theories on the level of risk that you decide to accept in your investment program, all of this leads to investors requiring an intermediator. So investors, with the help of modern portfolio theory or the efficient market hypothesis, began to move to diversified programs instead of trying to do it themselves.

JOHN BOGLE: First, academics can't create a different market return, so the age-old problem is always with us. That is, all of that research, all that theory, even when it's implemented, is not going to give *all* investors above-average returns. Investors, all of us together, are destined to average the market return before costs and then lose to the markets after costs. On the other hand, you could credit academics with the creation of this intermediation—or agency—society that we have today, which I describe, however, as a failed agency society. When I wrote my thesis, individual investors owned 92 percent of all stocks, with the other 8 percent owned by institutions. One assumes that, among them, individual investors would have had great spreads in their returns from one to another, but still averaged the market return before intermediation costs. If we look at the idea of diversification—the fundamental Markowitz theory—and add in Sharpe's theories on the level of risk that you decide to accept in your investment program, all of this leads to investors requiring an intermediator. So investors, with the help of modern portfolio theory or the efficient market hypothesis, began to move to diversified programs instead of trying to do it themselves. I think that's a plus. But can we say that academic research has enabled investors as a group to do better than the market itself? I don't think that's possible.

MEIR STATMAN: In 1960, you wrote "The Case for Mutual Fund Management," the core of which was not passive investing and low costs, but an advocacy of an active, beat-the-market kind of investing that you have since repudiated. What is your view of active management now? If that stands as the contrast to index funds, how do you reconcile the two?

JOHN BOGLE: I still would defend "The Case for Mutual Fund Management" today. It's actually a thorough article; I'm surprised that I was capable of a job that good back then, when I was barely thirty years old and fairly inexperienced. It basically said that in a good mutual fund industry, there wasn't a lot of point to having a mutual fund that tracked a broad market index, in that case the Dow Jones Industrial Average. What led up to the introduction of the first index fund—the First Index Investment Trust, known today as the Vanguard 500 Index Fund—is a story worth telling. The Vanguard Group was incorporated in September 1974 and started operations in May 1975. The understanding was that Vanguard was to limit itself to administration and not get into investment management or distribution; those were to stay with Wellington Management Company. However, for strategic reasons, I decided we needed to be in the management business. I was interested in building Vanguard as a company where we would control the kinds of funds we ran, how they were run, who would run them, to whom our shares would be distributed, and through whom our shares would be distributed.

I thought about the index fund that I had hinted at in my thesis so many years before, which would be essentially unmanaged and so provide a way for me to get back into the investment business. I got out these old Wiesenberger books[3] and calculated the average return of the fifty or sixty equity mutual funds that were in business then over the previous thirty years. When I compared the result with that of the Standard & Poor's 500 Stock Composite Index, the difference was approximately 1.5 percentage points per year in favor of the index, without taking into account index costs. I did calculate mutual fund returns net of expense ratios and turnover costs (but ignored sales charges), which were significantly lower in 1945-1975 than they are today. Then I calculated the two returns—9.6 percent for the funds and 11.1 percent for the index, or market—and compounded them over the thirty-year period.[4] Because I had to persuade the directors that this index mutual fund was a good idea to pursue, I wanted the results to look impressive. So instead of an initial investment of $10,000, I used $1 million and came up with $16 million of final value for the funds, compared with $25 million for the market over that period. The directors thought I was overstepping my mandate by starting such a mutual fund, reminding me that I was not allowed to get into management. I told them that the fund wasn't managed, and—believe it or not—they bought that.

Shortly after the fund was introduced, Paul Samuelson wrote about it in *Newsweek*, saying that his prayers for an index fund had been answered but that "a professor's prayers are rarely answered in full," citing the fund's sales commission. However, it quickly became clear—not only for indexing, but for Vanguard, which was striving to be the low-cost provider—that it didn't do any good to have an expense ratio of 0.25 percent or 0.5 percent if an investor had to pay 8 percent to buy the fund. In less than six months after the offering of the index fund in August 1976, we had moved to a no-load distribution system. When the directors reminded me that I could not take over distribution, I told them that I was not taking it over, I was eliminating it. That was not without a grain of truth, but probably could be considered a bit disingenuous.

By February 1977, we were where we wanted to be: a full-line mutual fund complex providing administrative, investment management, and distribution services on the way to building Vanguard as the industry's low-cost provider, with the elimination of sales charges and the index fund as the obvious manifestation of those benefits.

MEIR STATMAN: That still leaves out the active part, and Vanguard of course has active funds, including funds that used to be managed by John Neff. In fact, I believe you personally owned those funds. How does active management, which is more expensive, live side-by-side with indexing?

JOHN BOGLE: It's not all that complicated. When we had the underwriting of the index fund, Vanguard's assets were approximately $2 billion, of which $11 million was in the index fund. We could, I suppose, have done away with the other funds and been left with an $11-million fund that couldn't possibly operate efficiently. But the other mutual funds already were here, part of our resource base, so my idea was to see how closely we could get them to look like index funds. That meant hiring experienced managers with a special mandate and a long-term time horizon and getting fees as low as we could. We negotiated aggressively with Wellington and made staggering fee reductions that didn't hurt them very much because they were all prospective. If you look at the actively managed Vanguard funds as having no sales charges, expense ratios of around 35 basis points—an 80-point advantage over their comparable competition—and pick up another 50 to 60 basis points through reduced turnover costs, you've got an annual advantage of about 135 basis points. And even more if you count the impact of their sales charges. Even if the active managers are only average in performance, you win, simply by using the very concepts that account for the success of the index fund.

EDWARD BAKER: So do you believe that, in principle, active managers aren't really able to add value, that it's just a wasted effort?

JOHN BOGLE: As a group, active managers are average before costs and losers to the market after costs. It's less a wasted effort than an inability to know what is real—actual net returns earned—and what is illusion—the market returns themselves—what is luck and what is skill, and—equally importantly—what are taxes and what are not taxes. In terms of tax efficiency alone, active managers lose to the index by about 120 basis points a year. That active manager has to be very, very good to overcome the costs of the expense ratios, turnover, sales commissions, and other expenses, such as marketing costs. Even if his performance is good, you don't know that he will be able to repeat it. I believe you can invest in the index in a very satisfactory way for an investment lifetime, that is, for sixty-five years, figuring you're investing from age twenty to age sixty-five and then have another twenty years of life expectancy. You can buy an index fund, forget about it, and get the market return for the entire period, if you're using the Dow Jones Wilshire 5000 Total Market Index or the S&P 500.

To make matters worse on the active side, managers come and go. You mentioned John Neff; he hasn't run the Windsor Fund for the past ten years or so. In the fund industry, the average manager lasts five years, and the average investor owns four funds, so that's four managers in the first five years, eight managers after ten years, sixteen after twenty years, and fifty-two over the entire sixty-five years. What is the possibility that fifty-two managers, coming and going, cleaning out their portfolios time after time, could with remote conceivability do as well as the index? The return you get from holding the market portfolio over sixty-five years—even a modest return—demonstrates the "miracle of compounding returns," and the tremendous impact the cost of active management makes is "the tyranny of compounding costs." The way mathematics works, this tyranny absolutely overwhelms the miracle of compounding returns; to wit, over an investment lifetime the active equity fund investor captures about 20 percent of the return available simply by holding an all-market index fund.

EDWARD BAKER: Do you think there may be more need for active management when you move away from the purely domestic marketplace, e.g., global market strategies or emerging markets or other strategies where market inefficiencies may exist?

JOHN BOGLE: Well, in a word, the answer is no. The same is true of small cap, which is often put into that same category. The reality of investing is that as soon as you have a discrete universe of securities that you can index—let's say, all international stocks—that market has a return that's measurable, and it's measurable by a soundly constructed index. It doesn't matter whether the market is efficient or not. I've often said that the efficient market hypothesis, or EMH, has a lot of truth to it, but the CMH—or "cost matters hypothesis"—is eternally truthful to the last penny. That goes back to our old friend: Gross return in the financial markets, minus the costs of financial intermediation, equals the net return earned by investors as a group. Once you get that discrete group of stocks in the international market—or in the emerging markets subset— and calculate their total capitalization, it will produce a return of x before costs and a return of y after costs. From an intellectual standpoint, I'm inclined to say that in inefficient markets, there may well be greater opportunities for a group of active managers to outperform. However, the reality is that if a small group of managers—say, 10 percent—can outperform by 4 percent per year before costs, there has to be a similar percentage that underperform by 4 percent per year. There's no way around the math.

■ ■ ■

> The reality of investing is that as soon as you have a
> discrete universe of securities that you can index—let's say,
> all international stocks—that market has a return that's
> measurable, and it's measurable by a soundly constructed
> index. It doesn't matter whether the market is efficient or not.

Inefficiency doesn't make it easier for *all* investors to beat the market. That can't be, because smart investors are trading with dumb ones, and the spread between dumb and smart will grow. When you think about it in those terms, it should mean that indexing works *better* in international markets than in the U.S. market. The reason for this is that international transaction costs are higher, tax costs are higher, and nearly all international funds have higher expense ratios, and indexing should work better in markets where the costs of active management are higher. Not that the brightest managers don't have a chance to do better in those markets. I freely concede that they do, although I personally think they're overrated. The record is clear that there is little correlation between past success and future returns. Yes, measuring the returns of all investors in international markets is a fly-by-night, spasmodic thing because the data are hard to come by. But I've been known to say that if the data don't prove my analysis is right, then, well, the data are wrong.

EDWARD BAKER: Let's switch gears slightly and ask you to tell us about your biggest mistake or biggest disappointment, if you can pinpoint one, over the course of your career.

JOHN BOGLE: That's a great question, because I've made a lot of mistakes. One of my life principles is that the only way you can live life is by dealing with what is, and not with what might have been. So that's the way I've tried to deal with setbacks. I'm a rather thick-skinned guy, and I don't lie awake at night worrying about my mistakes—never have, never will. The curious thing is that certainly my biggest business mistake, or strategic mistake if you will, was my utter stupidity, callowness, and unwillingness to learn from the very lessons of history that I was teaching when I engineered the Wellington merger with the Ivest Fund group in 1966. The Ivest managers were what I call "go-go" managers, that is, very aggressive, and I should have known they wouldn't be durable. When Wellington, where I was in charge, announced the merger, I got a call from Bernard Cornfeld,[5] who owned stock in both Wellington Management Company and Ivest Fund, saying that if we let the merger go through, he would sue to stop it. My job was to go to his headquarters in Geneva, Switzerland, and try to persuade him that he was wrong. I was just a kid then, thirty-six or so. He did finally back down and decide not to sue Wellington, but he told me, "Jack, let me give you a piece of advice. These Ivest guys aren't very smart. You'll find that out, and when you find that out, you won't fire them—they'll fire you." And so they did.

The Ivest merger was a bad mistake on my part, not only in and of itself, but also because I let that aggressive thinking creep into the Wellington Fund, which had the worst decade in its history while that merger was in effect. Relative to its competitors, the Wellington Fund was the second-worst performing of all balanced funds; we'd never been in such a position before. It was very close to a disaster. So I'd put that down as my biggest strategic mistake. Yet, a funny thing happened: If I hadn't been fired in January 1974, I would not have had the opportunity to start Vanguard in September 1974. While it was a difficult way to get back on the right track and solidify the things that I knew but failed to acknowledge, my biggest failure led to what was arguably my biggest success.

MARK ANSON: Do you see exchange-traded funds (ETFs) as an extension of index management or as a competitor to index management?

JOHN BOGLE: I look at ETFs and feel like humming a few bars of that old song, "Look what they've done to my song, Ma, look what they've done to my song—well, they tied it up in a plastic bag and turned it upside down." I don't see ETFs as an extension or a competitor—I see them as a contradiction.

MARK ANSON: That's an interesting take.

JOHN BOGLE: ETFs *are* index funds, let's start with that. Many people don't seem to realize that fact. In describing ETFs, I use a little box divided into four squares. The top half of the box is long-term holders, and the bottom half is short-term holders. The left side of the box is total market funds, and the right side is sector funds. Indexing is in the SPDR (S&P Depositary Receipts) or VIPER (Vanguard Index Participation Equity Receipts) box on the upper left—or long-term investments in the total U.S. stock market. (International investors could appropriately put an international index fund there for that portion of their returns.) The box at the top right— long-term holders of sector funds—is empty because investors are buying and trading those; I can't imagine that anyone is holding, say, the technology sector or the Korean market for an investment lifetime. The lower half of both boxes is the short-term sector, and the turnover of Qubes and SPDRs runs to something like 5,000 percent a year. It's difficult to tell what percentage of turnover is accounted for by individual investors. How much of that is brokers' positioning, I don't know, but I'd be very surprised if SPDRs are held to any material extent by investors for long holding periods.

MARK ANSON: On the other hand, if you are a long-term investor, ETFs seem to offer a reasonable way to go because they are more tax-efficient.

JOHN BOGLE: Let's say they *may be* more tax-efficient. I'm not sure that they are. Vanguard's tax-managed (index-based) funds ought to be able to go up against them, blow for blow. Certainly ETFs theoretically have the potential to be more tax-efficient, but both ETFs and tax-managed funds should be highly tax-efficient.

■ ■ ■

> ## Certainly ETFs theoretically have the potential to be more tax-efficient, but both ETFs and tax-managed funds should be highly tax-efficient.

EDWARD BAKER: What about from a risk management point of view? Is there a role for products like ETFs to play when you want to hedge your market exposure for one reason or another?

JOHN BOGLE: There again, I'm the kind of person who knows that I can't do it. I think the idea of timing or hedging is a very difficult thing for investors to pull off. It is in the nature of the human psyche, we are much more likely—this is a behaviorialist kind of argument—to make the wrong choices at the wrong time. We've compared returns earned by mutual fund investors—dollar-weighted returns—with returns earned by mutual funds themselves, or time-weighted returns, and the investors seem to lag the funds themselves by almost 3 percent per year. Fund investors put almost no money into equity funds in the late 1980s and early 1990s when stocks were cheap, and then they poured huge amounts of money into equity mutual funds between 1998 and the crash in 2000. Investors also bought the wrong kinds of funds, that is, in the three years leading up to the crash, they put nearly $500 billion into technology funds, telecommunications funds, and a whole new breed of aggressive growth funds we can describe as "new economy" funds. At the same time, they took about $100 billion out of value funds. Then, after the market crashed, they took money out of those aggressive growth funds and put it into value funds.

■ ■ ■

Overall, investors seem to have an innate sense of bad timing. You can actually measure this. One of the great things about the mutual fund system, unlike the rest of this business of investing, is that every buyer isn't matched by a seller, and that makes it an excellent laboratory for research.

Overall, investors seem to have an innate sense of bad timing. You can actually measure this. One of the great things about the mutual fund system, unlike the rest of this business of investing, is that every buyer isn't matched by a seller, and that makes it an excellent laboratory for research. When you read in the paper that investors today poured money into bank stocks and pulled out of technology stocks, how did that happen? When they bought their bank stocks, didn't somebody sell those stocks to them? When they sold their technology stocks, wasn't somebody buying those stocks from them? By my standards, the market is essentially a closed system. However, the mutual fund industry is not a closed system. We actually can see and indeed measure how badly investors do at timing. They're their own worst enemy. As Warren Buffett says, the two greatest enemies of equity investors are expenses and emotions. You can see the expenses in the gap between the market return and fund returns, and the emotions in the gap between fund returns and investor returns. When you look at data on the origin of these shortfalls, it is staggeringly loaded toward the degree of fund specialization; in other words, the biggest gap between fund time-weighted returns and fund investor dollar-weighted returns is found in technology funds, telecommunications funds, aggressive growth funds. We did a study that covered six years, i.e., the last three years of the up market and the first three years of the down market. With the ups and downs taken together, the twenty-five largest sector funds actually returned about 5.5 percent per year, versus 3.7 percent for the twenty-five largest diversified funds. However, while the typical investor in the diversified mutual funds ran about 2 percent behind the funds themselves, the investors in these specialty funds fell short of the fund returns by about 14 percent a year, which, when compounded over six years, is a staggering shortfall of 59 percent.

MEIR STATMAN: You've talked about expenses and emotions. What about investors' preferences or tastes? What if an investor has a preference for socially responsible stocks, for example? Is that a legitimate choice, or do you consider that wasteful or impractical?

JOHN BOGLE: The record is so clear to me that owning the market at minimal cost gives you the market return, or very close to it, allowing for taxes unless you're in a tax-deferred plan. That's the ultimate strategy, the gold standard.

EDWARD BAKER: Let's shift over to talking about your new book on corporate governance, *The Battle for the Soul of Capitalism*. I've started reading it, and it certainly makes a very compelling argument that corporate America needs a radical overhaul. However, in the end, I didn't find much that was prescriptive in the book.

JOHN BOGLE: Someone wrote to me with that comment, and so we counted the recommendations in the book and came up with 59 "prescriptions," if you want to call them that. The overriding prescription is for a form of governmental participation, or some would say interference, in the system. I believe the root of the problems with our financial system—and leading over into the corporate system—is the loss of the ownership society. President Bush can say that we're trying to bring the ownership society back, but it's never going to happen. We had such a society fifty years ago, when 92 percent of all stocks were owned by individuals. Now it's 32 percent, with the other 68 percent held by large financial institutions, just twenty-five of which own close to 40 percent of the total. So now we not only have institutional ownership, but very concentrated institutional ownership.

■ ■ ■

I believe the root of the problems with our financial system—and leading over into the corporate system—is the loss of the ownership society.

I profoundly believe that these institutional owners, or agents, are not serving their principals. What we need to do, as I say in the book, is establish a federal standard of fiduciary duty that ensures that pension managers and mutual fund managers, in particular, have a duty spelled out in detail in the law to represent the interests of those they serve, that is, the pensioners and mutual fund owners. The problem in achieving this goal is that the institutional agents aren't even real owners anymore; they trade stocks with a fury, with turnover of 100 percent a year and an average holding period of one year. It's now a rent-a-stock industry, compared with the old own-a-stock industry when turnover was 16 percent and the average holding period was six years.

MARK ANSON: I'm not sure that's true of the large concentrated owners. I think it's mainly the large index funds.

JOHN BOGLE: Well, you're correct about the index funds, but that's only 15 percent of all equity fund assets. There's an anecdote that I didn't put in the book about the time I got some of the large indexers together with a few active managers, managers I'd clearly identify as long-term investors. We went over some ideas: taking a stand on issues, establishing a research facility that would be jointly funded, and devising a plan to have these large institutions take a more active role in governing the corporations in which they own stock. At one point in the conversation, one of those in attendance said to me, "You know, Jack, I understand where you're trying to go, but why don't we just leave it to Adam Smith's invisible hand?" I said, "Don't you realize that we are Adam Smith's invisible hand?" And we are. We're supposed to be operating in the interests of our shareholders, but when you stand back from your governance responsibilities, you're simply not doing the job your shareholders have the right to expect you to do.

Part of the reason for that is that governance is not very high on the priority list. Think of the money we spend on marketing, trying to get investors to send us more money, compared with the money we spend on governance. Think of the profits of investment management companies compared with the money we spend on governance. It's a drop in the bucket, and probably not even that. To borrow a phrase from shareholder activist Bob Monks, "Capitalism without owners will fail." Corporations have been allowed to run amok in their accounting, in mergers, and certainly in executive compensation, correctly thinking that few of their shareholders really much care. There's an old saying in the book, "When we have strong managers, weak directors, and passive owners, don't be surprised when the looting begins." We've had some real looting, of course, with the best-known cases being Enron, WorldCom, and Adelphia, as well as incidents that come close to looting, for example, the short-term focus on the price of a stock compared with the long-term intrinsic value of a company.

Another of the prescriptions in my book is a tax on short-term capital gains for taxable as well as tax-exempt investors. Although he now says it was done tongue-in-cheek, Warren Buffett suggested this a long time ago, and it was recently put up as a possibility by Lou Gerstner, former chairman of IBM. These aren't people without credentials. If you have a short-term focus, it's arguable that you shouldn't care about governance. You not only don't care; arguably you shouldn't care. What's the point if you're not going to be holding the stock a year hence?

EDWARD BAKER: Your book clearly underscores some fundamental weaknesses in corporate governance, for example, lack of independence of the boards and lack of separation between the chief executive officer and the chairman. If you were to pinpoint the key weaknesses and improvements, what would you suggest?

JOHN BOGLE: There are actually different sets of circumstances for corporate America—the owned—and for financial America—the owners. In corporate America, I feel very strongly about separation of powers, that is, the boss of the business should not be the boss of the board of directors. It's amazing that system hasn't been changed much more substantially. One of the problems with trying a different approach is that the first thing someone says is, "Prove it works better," and there is no proof. Prove that British corporations, which have independent chairmen, have performed better than U.S. corporations. I don't have numbers to support this, so I have to fall back on a very important idea: *Sometimes common sense tells us what statistics cannot.*

Another recommendation is to have the federal fiduciary duty standard, which I talked about earlier, apply to corporate directors. Much of this reform has to come out of changing our investment system back to the way it used to be, that is, not a system of renters who shouldn't care, but a system of owners who do. A federal standard of fiduciary duty also would require mutual fund managers and pension managers to run their companies on behalf of their investors.

■ ■ ■

> ## Much of this reform has to come out of changing our investment system back to the way it used to be, that is, not a system of renters who shouldn't care, but a system of owners who do. A federal standard of fiduciary duty also would require mutual fund managers and pension managers to run their companies on behalf of their investors.

On the mutual fund side, I totally agree with SEC Chairman William Donaldson's proposal, since supported by his successor Christopher Cox, that mutual funds institute three changes in governance:

- An independent chairman who is not the chairman of the management company. I can't imagine anything that would be more common sense than that.

- A board where 75 percent of the directors are independent. Deep down, however, I wonder what right the chief executive of a management company has to be on a fund board. It's a complete conflict of interest; for example, the board might want to reduce fees, while the management company executive probably wants to increase them.

- Empowerment of fund directors to allow them to have their own staffs or independent consultants to appraise the manager's results, i.e., performance, costs, marketing efforts, cash flows. That makes sense because the manager—even the most honest of managers—is going to view things through the lens of his own self-interest.

In addition to the overarching idea of a federal statute of fiduciary duty, under which agents represent shareholders, by moving past the ownership society that used to exist, beyond the agency society that's failing investors, to a new fiduciary society where investors come first. But investors also have to wake up and get a life. We need a huge investor education effort just to get across what all the experts are saying—every Nobel laureate; people like Warren Buffett and David Swensen; Andrew Lo, who wrote *A Non-Random Walk Down Wall Street* but still owns index funds himself; Paul Samuelson, who called the invention of the index fund the equivalent of the creation of the wheel and alphabet. As we said before, how can all that powerful intellectual wisdom be making such little progress? We must convince investors to look after their own interests.

EDWARD BAKER: How active can we expect index funds to be in this corporate governance oversight role? Doesn't that introduce some relatively significant costs if the funds have to take an active role in all 500 companies in the S&P index, for example?

JOHN BOGLE: I don't think so. Right now the large funds are required to vote each issue and disclose each vote. I don't know how much more work is required. The idea is not to run the companies but simply to ensure that the directors are representing the shareholders. I'm not in favor of institutional investors stepping into the business decisions of American companies. I don't think we run our own business very well, to be honest, and until that happens, we ought to stay out of the businesses of others. So I'm not talking about institutional owners getting involved in business decisions; I'm talking about items that get approved without sufficient shareholder involvement, e.g., the nomination and election of directors; mergers and acquisitions; and executive compensation. They all ought to be the subject of shareholder voting.

■ ■ ■

> I'm talking about items that get approved without sufficient shareholder involvement, e.g., the nomination and election of directors; mergers and acquisitions; and executive compensation. They all ought to be the subject of shareholder voting.

MEIR STATMAN: Unfortunately, our time is running short. Are there some final thoughts you'd like to leave us with?

JOHN BOGLE: One thing is for certain: The mutual fund industry has to change. You can't look at the cost inefficiencies, tax inefficiencies, and marketing focus—to say nothing of the cheating around the edges that we saw in the timing scandals—and think otherwise. Those scandals were all about putting the interests of the managers ahead of the interests of the shareholders. That focus on self-interest is less apparent, but financially much more important, in the other problems facing this industry, including excessive advisory fees, excessive marketing costs, excessive focus on introducing faddish funds at the peak of their popularity, all of which detract hugely from the investment returns received by fund shareholders. I'm a David Swensen guy; I think if everybody read his book *Unconventional Success* and did what he recommends— never buy a mutual fund from a company in business to make a profit—we would start to have the mutualization of the mutual fund industry. Vanguard is still waiting for its first follower. It's so clear that it has to come, simply because the economics—the relentless rules of humble arithmetic—are so compelling.

The outlook for the future of the mutual fund industry will not brighten until investors get sick and tired of it and the industry changes. At the minimum, the outlook is bad for those who are doing it wrong, and better for those who are doing it right. Sooner or later in a competitive field, the competitive norm has to be taking costs out of the system. I don't see how that can fail to happen. Some of these changes require a little help from the federal government in terms of standards, but much of it just entails investors looking after their own interests, if they were only wise enough to do so. I don't know how to get that lesson across. I'm not sure what happened to the attempt at investor education that was to be financed out of the 2002 settlement with Wall Street investment firms. We need that, even though that education will cause controversy because it will lead, finally, to investors being educated that the answer is to own the market and hold it forever. The economics of that are absolutely unarguable, and yet we seem to have a blind spot about this. Essentially, we tell investors to keep trying and if they're not doing well, hire the experts, and if they're still not doing well, hire an advisor to hire the experts. It doesn't work.

■ ■ ■

The outlook for the future of the mutual fund industry will not brighten until investors get sick and tired of it and the industry changes. At the minimum, the outlook is bad for those who are doing it wrong, and better for those who are doing it right.

That's the line of reasoning Warren Buffett talks about in his 2005 annual shareholder letter, and he has this wonderful example of the "Gotrocks" family, as he calls them. The Gotrocks are very wealthy. They own every stock in America, they get earnings and dividends every year, and they're doing very nicely. Then some brokers convince the family that they can outsmart other members of the family by buying and selling certain stocks, so they hire the brokers and trade stocks back and forth. Of course, at the end of the year, the family did worse than they did the year before, because they're getting less than 100 percent of the market-return pie because of those brokerage costs.

They decide they don't know how to pick stocks, so they hire some managers, and the managers go out and vigorously swap stocks around with one another, incurring a lot of additional transaction costs and tax costs for the family. At the end of that year, the family is doing even worse. So now the Gotrocks think, "We know we can't pick stocks, and we know we can't pick managers, so let's pick a bunch of consultants to help us pick managers." And again they do even worse. Warren takes the example all the way up, finally, to using hedge funds, and of course, that strategy can't work either, for it adds costs while having no effect on market returns.

Each time the family incurs more costs, their net returns after costs and taxes decline, and they become more impoverished until they are the "Hadrocks." I see the Gotrocks as the typical American investor. At some point there has to be a realization of the way that costs are diminishing investors' share of the pie produced by the market, and of the fundamental nature of those relentless rules of humble arithmetic. That's the main thing I want to get across.

EDWARD BAKER: Jack, we thank you very much for your time. This has been most interesting and thought-provoking. I think our readers will find a lot in this interview to both believe in and argue against.

JOHN BOGLE: I'd love that. Please let the world know that if any active manager wants to debate these issues, I'm available any hour of the day or night.

■ ■ ■

ENDNOTES

[1] Brandeis (2014) described how the interlocking interests of investment America and corporate America were "trampling with impunity on laws human and divine, obsessed with the delusion that two plus two make five" (p.45). Brandeis, who became one of the most influential jurists on the U.S. Supreme Court, accurately predicted that the widespread speculation of the early twentieth century would collapse, "a victim of the relentless rules of humble arithmetic" (p.45).

[2] See "Big Money in Boston" (1949).

[3] Wiesenberger Financial Services, the nation's first mutual fund tracking service, has provided mutual fund data for more than sixty years.

[4] More accurately, the period was thirty and one-half years; Bogle took the returns through June 1975 in his presentation to the board of directors.

[5] Cornfeld (1927–1995) was a businessman later convicted of selling fraudulent investments during the 1960s.

REFERENCES

Armstrong, John B. [John C. Bogle]. 1960. The Case for Mutual Fund Management. *Financial Analysts Journal* 16, no. 3 (May/June): 33–38.

Big Money in Boston. 1949. *Fortune* (December): 116.

Bogle, John C. 1951. Economic Role of the Investment Company. Senior thesis, Princeton University. In *Bogle on Investing: The First 50 Years*. New York: McGraw-Hill (2000).

———. 2005. *The Battle for the Soul of Capitalism*. New Haven: Yale University Press.

———. 1993. *Bogle on Mutual Funds: New Perspectives for the Intelligent Investor*. Burr Ridge, IL: Irwin Professional Publishing.

———. 2005. The Mutual Fund Industry 60 Years Later: For Better or Worse? *Financial Analysts Journal* 61, no. 1 (January/February): 15–24.

———. 2005. Relentless Rules of Humble Arithmetic. *Financial Analysts Journal* 61, no. 6 (November/December): 22–35.

Brandeis, Louis D. 1914. *Other People's Money—and How the Bankers Use It*. Edited by Melvin I. Urosky. Boston: Bedford Books.

Buffett, Warren. 2005. Letter to Shareholders of Berkshire Hathaway. Inc. (February 28). http://www.berkshirehathaway.com/letters/2005ltr.pdf.

Lo, Andrew, and A. Craig MacKinlay. 2001. *A Non-Random Walk Down Wall Street*. Princeton, NJ: Princeton University Press.

Samuelson, Paul. 1976. Index-Fund Investing. *Newsweek* (August 16).

Swensen, David. 2005. *Unconventional Success: A Fundamental Approach to Personal Investment*. New York: Free Press Simon & Schuster.

This interview was published in its entirety in *Journal of Investment Consulting* 8, no. 1, Summer 2006.

CHAPTER 3

GENE FAMA: FATHER OF MODERN FINANCE

EUGENE F. FAMA, PHD

Recipient of the 2013 Nobel Memorial Prize in Economic Sciences; Robert R. McCormick Distinguished Service Professor of Finance, University of Chicago Booth School of Business; author, *Foundations of Finance* and numerous articles in academic journals.

Gene Fama excels at taking good ideas and making them better. He was among the first to develop a multi-asset pricing model, a direct enhancement of the single-factor capital asset pricing model (CAPM). The new Fama-French model (developed with Kenneth French) expanded the number of systematic factors to three, adding a size factor and a value/growth factor to CAPM's market factor. Fama then applied the Fama-French model to the real world of asset management when he joined the board of directors at Dimensional Fund Advisors, an investment firm founded on Fama's innovative ideas. Others also have successfully used Fama's conceptual framework as a starting point to develop similar multi-factor models, expanding factors and applications to include diverse structures such as hedge funds.

■ ■ ■

EDWARD BAKER: Gene, I think you've had a chance to review the topics we hope to cover with you today. Why don't we just start at the beginning and ask you to give us some background on the major factors that shaped your career and what you regard as your major achievement and biggest disappointment?

EUGENE FAMA: My early career was shaped a great deal by Merton Miller[1] and Harry Roberts[2] and by the topics that interested them and a few others when I was a graduate student at the University of Chicago. After that, I think it was serendipity. I followed several different paths, and many of them turned out to be successful. How exactly, I couldn't really explain.

MEIR STATMAN: Was your early work on random walks (1965)[3] in any way motivated by the claims of those on Wall Street that they could beat the market?

EUGENE FAMA: No, I attribute it to the advent of computers. In the early 1960s, the first computers had been introduced. People like Harry Roberts, who were basically statisticians, were interested in using them, and some of the most readily available data were stock-market data. Most of this work centered around the University of Chicago and the Massachusetts Institute of Technology, where people were groping at the general idea of what you would expect to see in stock prices if the market were working properly. In other words, they were looking at the idea of an efficient market. However, they didn't have any clear concept of what an efficient market was.

Back when I was an undergraduate at Tufts, I had worked for a professor who had a stock market forecasting service. I was very good at devising techniques for predicting past data. The professor, who was a very smart statistician, always had me set aside a holdout sample.[4] The forecasting never worked on the holdout sample, and that made me suspicious of the whole process. Then when I went to Chicago, people were talking about what it meant to say that the market was working properly. The first proposition was the random walk model, which turned out to be a little bit off the mark. So basically, I went to Merton Miller with four thesis topics. I had two children by that time and was anxious to graduate, and he suggested that I pursue the one involving the behavior of stock prices. That's where the story started.

ROGER EDELEN: As your career has progressed, have you perceived any kind of paradigm shift or fundamental change in your views with respect to how you look at things, or do you think it's more of a continuum?

EUGENE FAMA: I think it's more of a continuum. When I started, asset pricing theory, or the theory of risk-return, really didn't exist. It was the mid-1960s before [William] Sharpe (1964) and [John] Lintner (1965) came along with the capital asset pricing model, and it took another ten years before multifactor models took hold. So we didn't really have a good way to think about risk and return when I started. Putting together risk and return stories with the efficient markets theory gave rise to the whole area of asset pricing, which now has grown into a huge area. My views have evolved along with the evolution of work on risk and return, but my view on market efficiency hasn't changed.

■ ■ ■

> Putting together risk and return stories with the efficient markets theory gave rise to the whole area of asset pricing, which now has grown into a huge area. My views have evolved along with the evolution of work on risk and return, but my view on market efficiency hasn't changed.

MEIR STATMAN: If I could follow up on that, we actually had asset pricing models all along. We had asset pricing models for automobiles, for watches, for houses, for example. Why is the market for securities seen as entirely different? To clarify, in a more recent paper (Fama and French 2007) you brought back those considerations that are different from risk. In particular, you mentioned social responsibility and tastes, or preferences. Why in the beginning was the focus entirely on risk, which still may be the only legitimate factor in the eyes of many?

EUGENE FAMA: Taste always has been important in economics. Basically, economics is taste on one side and opportunity on the other. If you go back to Fama and Miller (1972) or any of the other early work, basically it says that people invest in order to consume. We never took into account the possibility that investment itself could be a consumption good. Fama and French (2007) said that you have to allow for the possibility that people have tastes for particular securities. Social responsibility is one example of a preference. There's nothing irrational about that. It's just an expression of taste.

RONALD KAHN: Are you saying that you're not going to be able to find firms that basically have the same cash flows but aren't viewed as socially responsible?

EUGENE FAMA: That's a good example. Take two firms with exactly the same cash flows; one is socially responsible, and the other isn't. If you have investors who want socially responsible products, the prices on the socially responsible ones are going to be higher, and the expected returns are going to be lower.

MEIR STATMAN: In your 1965 paper in *Financial Analysts Journal,* I believe you defined an efficient market as one where price is equal to fundamental value, or intrinsic value, and you defined value as strictly the present value of dividends, or the expected cash flow. It had nothing to do with factors such as social responsibility, to take this example. By that definition, the market where social responsibility is priced cannot really be efficient, is that right?

EUGENE FAMA: Not if you're defining it that way, no. I can look at risk and return and say that the price of risk depends on taste. That's true. So I say, "Okay, but risk isn't the only thing that counts." Maybe, just as an example, social responsibility also counts. Well, that's going to affect pricing. That's perfectly rational. There's nothing wrong with that. Intrinsic value is going to have to take that into account. I'm still saying that price equals intrinsic value is a definition of market efficiency. It's just refining the concept of what intrinsic value is.

RONALD KAHN: Going back to our example of two assets with the same cash flows, where one is socially responsible and one isn't, doesn't that then allow for riskless returns?

EUGENE FAMA: Yes, that's true. If there are investors who look at the two securities and say they don't care about social responsibility, they're going to push the price back in the other direction, and that's going to mitigate some of the price effects of social responsibility.

MEIR STATMAN: That idea originated in behavioral finance, and it's been around since before your work with Ken French. That seems to be a shift that both you and Ken have made, and I welcome it. I think that it is just a question of how different it is from what was accepted before. I don't think that idea would have been accepted by Merton Miller.

EUGENE FAMA: Oh, I think Merton would have had to agree. We're talking price theory here. That's all we're really talking about. So there's another dimension to an asset that has to be taken into account. He couldn't argue with that. No economist could argue with that.

MARK ANSON: Is this the way you also see behavioral finance?

EUGENE FAMA: Much of behavioral finance is about irrational behavior. What we've been talking about up to here is rational behavior.

EDWARD BAKER: Another factor that complicates these socially responsible investing features relative to risk is their lack of homogeneity. You can model risk more easily as a homogeneous characteristic to which everyone responds. I guess that doesn't eliminate your perspective as being wrong. It just makes any attempt to model it or capture it in a framework more difficult.

EUGENE FAMA: It's very complicated. It may be a reality, but you're absolutely right. I mean, model-wise, it's kind of a horror story. You're opening up a big box, and a huge amount of stuff could pop out of it.

ROGER EDELEN: One way of possibly interpreting all of this would be that in your earlier work, you never said that there wasn't an expansion of the model, is that right? You were just saying that if we start with the notion of basic risk and cash flows, we have this model, but other dimensions could be out there.

EUGENE FAMA: Right. If you go back to the first statement of what market efficiency meant, it wasn't in my doctoral thesis. It was in a review paper I wrote in 1970 in the *Journal of Finance*, and even that had some mistakes in it. It wasn't until *Foundations of Finance* in 1976 that I arrived at one clear statement of it.[5] Basically, it said that you have to put aside intrinsic value. You've got a basic communication problem here. You have to tell me what you mean by intrinsic value, and then we can work from there to decide whether the market sets price equal to intrinsic value. The model for intrinsic value is totally aside, totally separate from that.

ROGER EDELEN: So you never said that the model excluded factors such as taste or social consciousness?

EUGENE FAMA: No. But Meir's right. My thinking was restricted in those days to the thinking of, basically, Irving Fisher.[6]

EDWARD BAKER: But there were attempts to generalize the framework, were there not? That is, there were attempts to make utility of consumption a starting point of the theory. However, somehow that never caught on. I guess it was just too difficult to do anything meaningful?

EUGENE FAMA: That's the way Fama and French (1993) phrase the whole thing. That is, it's all driven by the utility of consumption, but it didn't say that investment itself could be a consumption good.

ROGER EDELEN: One follow-up on the question of asset pricing, going beyond the securities markets and cutting to the chase in housing markets: I guess there are securities on mortgages, but overall it's a nonsecuritized market. What is your view of market efficiency with respect to these pure assets as opposed to securities?

EUGENE FAMA: I would think housing has to be a very efficient market, in the sense that people commit large amounts of their current and future expected wealth to a home purchase. For most people who own houses, it's by far their major asset. They take that purchase very seriously, doing lots of investigation into information such as comparable prices and the like. I would think that market works very well.

ROGER EDELEN: In the context of behavioral factors that might be more on the irrational side, one could argue that if a purchase is really major, these factors would dominate decision making. However, it sounds like you would take the opposite viewpoint and say that people are actually more careful in cases like this?

EUGENE FAMA: I think that in this case, they're probably very careful. One of the major shortcomings of finance is that there isn't really any very good real estate research, because the data are so difficult to get. Work on securities markets, where you have quoted information on prices, gains, whatever, is much more advanced than that on real estate markets.

MEIR STATMAN: If you look at the current situation, where we've of course had quite a decline in the housing market, would you say that this is just a matter of the economy heading into a recession, or of people's changes in taste? What happened to cause such a run-up in prices and now this decline?

EUGENE FAMA: That's an interesting question. When the prices were running up toward their peaks, real interest rates were very close to zero. When real interest rates get very close to zero, prices can do almost anything. So the real question is what in the world would push real interest rates to zero? I don't know the answer to that.

ROGER EDELEN: What's your view of commodities as part of an investment portfolio?

EUGENE FAMA: I don't see them. I don't know what they produce. Where do you expect to get a return?

MEIR STATMAN: Well, obviously people hold them as part of a portfolio. Take gold, for example. I imagine people expect capital appreciation to provide the return, rather than dividends.

EUGENE FAMA: Right. But who are the natural buyers and sellers? And do the natural sellers of risk want to be short or long? That's the whole issue. There's an ancient theory of commodity prices, but it all hinges on who's going to be the net buyer and who's going to be the net seller. Who's trying to lay off the risk, and who's going to assume the risk?

MEIR STATMAN: That's an interesting question, because there's no anchor. Typically, dividends would serve as an anchor so that prices cannot go beyond a level that is reasonable relative to the cash flows you can expect. For gold, it must really just be a matter of the eye of the beholder.

EUGENE FAMA: Not really. Again, there are risks in commodity prices, and there are people who use commodities as input. The question is do they want to lay off that risk, or do they want to bear it?

ROGER EDELEN: To the question of whether commodities should be a natural long portion of a typical investor's portfolio, it sounds like your answer is "probably not."

EUGENE FAMA: Yes, probably not, but I don't have enough information to really tell. That's a complicated economic question about who is bearing the risk, and who is willing to pay for bearing the risk.

EDWARD BAKER: Well, I'll ask another question then. When I was a student, I really enjoyed *The Theory of Finance*, the textbook you wrote with Merton Miller in 1972. I wondered why it was not more widely used, and why you have never come out with further editions.

EUGENE FAMA: It's very simple. I think that book sold maybe 5,000 copies. It was much quoted and never purchased. If you look on eBay and ever see it, it sells for a very high price. One thousand dollars is not uncommon.

EDWARD BAKER: I thought your discussion of stable distributions was especially forward-looking, but again, that's a topic that somehow got lost in the shuffle of time. Why do you think that is?

EUGENE FAMA: Well, because basically the evidence says that—and Benoît Mandelbrot[7] has spent his life pushing this—all probabilities or real outcomes are fat-tailed,[8] but stable distributions say something more specific. They say that as you add these things up, the distribution doesn't change; it remains the same stable type. When you look at stock returns over longer periods and you add them up, they look a little more normal than they do over shorter periods. You wouldn't expect that with stable distributions. So people lost interest, and I think they've lost interest to too great an extent. Many of the market tragedies that you see are the result of extreme events in the markets that people take to be unusual but that really aren't that unusual.

■ ■ ■

> ## Many of the market tragedies that you see are the result of extreme events in the markets that people take to be unusual but that really aren't that unusual.

EDWARD BAKER: They become complacent with their assumptions of normal distributions.

EUGENE FAMA: Right. So there's almost no interest at this point.

EDWARD BAKER: I think interest may be coming back in that area. The hedge fund world has certainly showed very clearly that nonnormal distributions are a matter of course, at least as far as hedge funds are concerned.

EUGENE FAMA: Once you become levered, it becomes much more important, right?

MEIR STATMAN: It seems like the hedge fund industry didn't really get the point of fat tails because they got themselves in trouble. Perhaps you could take it from there and speak about the hedge fund business. It seems like it's a booming business with great demand. Do you think hedge funds provide real value, or is it also a matter of just satisfying some tastes that have nothing to do with returns?

EUGENE FAMA: I know you like the taste story, Meir, and that's fine. But here's my take on active investing. Before costs, it's a zero-sum game. Let's take a simple example. Suppose everybody is an active investor, and there are no passive investors. Then you know that, if there are some active winners, there have to be active losers. In aggregate, there are neither winners nor losers. In the actual situation, you have some passive investing, but one can't claim that active investors gain at the expense of passive investors because the evidence says passive investors basically get the returns they sign up for. That means again that the active investors who win have to win at the expense of other active investors. So before fees and expenses, active investing is a zero-sum game. After fees and expenses, active investing is a negative-sum game.

■ ■ ■

> So before fees and expenses, active investing is a zero-sum game. After fees and expenses, active investing is a negative-sum game.

EDWARD BAKER: But that's in aggregate.

MEIR STATMAN: So why do people play?

EUGENE FAMA: That's a good question that I've never been able to answer.

MARK ANSON: Do you think there are skillful active managers?

EUGENE FAMA: Possibly. However, there are also active managers who are systematically bad. There have to be, in order to make up for the ones that are systematically good. On average, they have to come out to zero.

MEIR STATMAN: The question of why people play has to be a puzzle, given that you've already talked about your opinion of the taste theory. Then again, it seems that taste also could be an answer to the question, that is, people play because they enjoy playing.

EUGENE FAMA: If they enjoy the play, would they pull their money out very quickly when things go bad?

MEIR STATMAN: Maybe, if they get the point that they are losing. I think that most investors don't even adjust for the market. They think that if the market goes up, it is their genius rather than the market. So even the idea of basic adjusted returns, where you subtract the market, is foreign to most investors, it seems.

EDWARD BAKER: You do see that kind of withdrawal behavior among hedge fund investors, though.

EUGENE FAMA: They pull out very quickly when returns go bad. Even if faced with the reality that most of the variability of returns is just chance, they still move quickly. If we're all driven by taste, you wouldn't expect that.

RONALD KAHN: What do you think of the trend among academics to focus on market inefficiency, and then many of them go into the active management business?

EUGENE FAMA: Yes, the lure of the 2 and 20.[9] It's hard to turn down. What would be really fascinating would be a study that examines the performance of academics versus that of nonacademics in the hedge fund industry.

MEIR STATMAN: What would be your hypothesis?

EUGENE FAMA: I think the academics are probably worse. From personal experience, I know some academics who have gone into the hedge fund business based on statistical phenomena that, in my opinion, were marginal at best. They were going to lever that up, but that doesn't make it any less marginal. They were betting on something happening that had happened on average in the past but without much statistical reliability. So the chance that these people get blown away is rather high.

ROGER EDELEN: From the investment consulting point of view, do you think there's a reasonable amount of effort spent trying to identify that ex-ante?

EUGENE FAMA: There's no evidence that anybody can pick a good active manager, as far as I can see. Ken French and I (2008) are finishing a study of the mutual fund industry where active managers as a whole basically hold the market, and investors lose by the amount of fees and expenses they pay, almost right on the money. If you look at persistence, there's a bit of persistence, but it depends on how you measure it, and it's very short-lived. If you try to do a general study where you take account of the fact that there are so many funds out there that lots of them are bound to win or lose by chance—we've constructed a way to do that, too—then you find no evidence at all that there are any winners out there.

Meir asked a good question: Why do people continue to play? This is where I think behavioral finance has a lot to say about individual behavior that's irrational. I'd never deny that. I can't argue with the studies that have been done on individual behavior. They're typically well done. There's lots of evidence that individuals behave irrationally much of the time. The implications of that for market prices, though, are more difficult to ascertain.

ROGER EDELEN: You made the distinction between putting an irrational label on an individual as opposed to the pricing effects of that behavior in aggregate. To me, that gets at the notion of liquidity. If there's ample supply counteracting the "irrational" subset, then it's not going to make its appearance in prices. Do you think there are some asset markets where the supply offsetting the "irrational" forces is inadequate, so you actually do see price distortions, but you could think of it as providing liquidity to the irrationals?

EUGENE FAMA: I think you may be mixing two concepts. I don't see where liquidity has anything to do with any of that.

ROGER EDELEN: I'm thinking of the basic concept of the informed trader versus noise trader. When noise traders [those who make trading decisions without the use of fundamental information] come into the market, they push the price, and informed traders [those who have fundamental information] trade against it. The informed traders basically are providing liquidity to the noise traders, but there is a price distortion.

EUGENE FAMA: That's a theory of liquidity, but my problem has always been finding those informed traders. I've never been able to identify them.

EDWARD BAKER: One place where you can see those distortions is in panic-selling moments, when everyone wants to sell and there are limited buyers. You could argue that then there are moments where prices go further than they reasonably should.

MEIR STATMAN: There's generally a problem with volume. Many people have commented that trading by itself is a puzzle in a world where people are rational. Surely the kind of volume that we see is puzzling. Is that simply another facet of the behavior of irrational investors?

EUGENE FAMA: I'm not sure, but I do agree that we don't understand trading. The statistics now are getting a bit more distorted. Ken French recently wrote a paper (2008) on the cost of active trading that basically documented the huge increase in trading that has taken place. Much of it is due to hedge funds, churning and churning and churning. Rational or irrational? Well, it's very cheap now to make a trade. The other part of it—the actual total amount spent on trading as a portion of aggregate stock market capitalization—hasn't changed very much over the past twenty-five years or so, according to his paper. I have no explanation for volume, unfortunately.

EDWARD BAKER: Changing the focus a little and looking forward, what do you think are some of the major questions we will be confronting as we roll forward?

EUGENE FAMA: There's been a ton of work done on asset pricing, risk, measurement of risk, and measurement of the relationship between expected return and risk, but it hasn't been all that satisfying. For example, if we knew more, the Fama-French three-factor model would not have had such a large impact, because it's a pure empirical asset pricing model.[10] We concocted that model to cover what we observed. It's used among academics; it's used everywhere. That's a comment on the fact that more formal theories developed to explain risk and return just haven't worked that well. An empirically generated theory such as the Fama-French model seems to do better than the theoretically constructed paradigms. Now when people do tests of risk and return, if they do as well as the Fama-French three-factor model, or even come close, they proclaim victory. I think that's the big challenge of the future: to find better ways to measure risk and the information that's coming out of the risk-return story.

■ ■ ■

An empirically generated theory such as the Fama-French model seems to do better than the theoretically constructed paradigms. Now when people do tests of risk and return, if they do as well as the Fama-French three-factor model, or even come close, they proclaim victory. I think that's the big challenge of the future: to find better ways to measure risk and the information that's coming out of the risk-return story.

MEIR STATMAN: Do you think that size, or market capitalization, and book-to-market ratio (i.e., growth versus value) indeed are measures of risk, or do you think they might possibly be matters of taste?

EUGENE FAMA: They might be matters of taste. It could just be that people like growth stocks and dislike value stocks. If it turns out that people just like growth stocks and dislike value stocks, then that's taste.

EDWARD BAKER: Do you think further work will be done with asset models? You've recently introduced your momentum factor. Do you think that's just the first of new factors that might be identified, or has that subject been exhausted?

EUGENE FAMA: That's again in the vein of something totally empirical. We have probably 20,000 finance researchers and academics out there, maybe more. They're all spinning the same two tapes, Center for Research in Security Prices (CRSP) and Compustat. They're going to come up with everything that's in the data, whether it's there by chance or whether it's a systematic risk story. My hope is that momentum turns out to be the one thing that looks robust at the time but in fact is a purely chance phenomenon. If you want to characterize past returns, adding a momentum factor will help you, because we know it was there in the past. Adding a momentum factor to your empirical description of the sources of return—calling it an asset pricing model is to glorify it—or to your return attribution model may be a better way to put it, will definitely help to enhance that model.

EDWARD BAKER: You think going forward that may not be the case? Is that what I hear you saying?

EUGENE FAMA: I'm hoping it isn't. I look to the Fama-French three-factor model. First you have the market—every asset pricing model says you need the market. Then you have the size factor—well, we can tell different stories about that one. Then you have the value/growth factor—and we can tell different stories about that. Then if you add the fourth factor—the momentum factor—you can tell really different stories about that, some rational and some irrational. The momentum factor gives me more difficulty because the population turns over too quickly. It discourages me to think that the risk characteristics of securities are changing so rapidly, because that makes things rather difficult empirically.

EDWARD BAKER: But if taste factors are driving these identifiable factors, couldn't you expect a certain amount of transfer?

EUGENE FAMA: I can tell a taste story for value versus growth. I may be able to tell a taste story for small cap versus large cap.

MEIR STATMAN: I remember that Merton Miller had very little patience with studying the behavior of individuals—and even professionals. He said just show me that in the prices. It sounds like your view may be a bit different?

EUGENE FAMA: Merton basically was saying what I said earlier. That is, maybe a lot of the behavior at the individual level is irrational, but it doesn't have any particular implications about whether prices are irrational. I think that's what he was trying to emphasize. You can't make that leap. Just because individual behavior is irrational, to jump from there to say that prices are irrational is a leap that must be documented with empirical support.

■ ■ ■

> There's a great deal of demand for anomalies. It's basically a way for the popular press and active managers to justify what they're doing. If people find anomalies in the market, they can make jumps to say therefore active management can work. People want to do that because there's big money to be made.

MEIR STATMAN: In my time in the profession, which is almost as long as yours, there was a point at which it seemed that we had solved everything. We had the capital asset pricing model (CAPM), we had market efficiency. Now it seems like everything is in tatters. Would you comment on that?

EUGENE FAMA: There was a topic on your list that asked why academics seem to be focusing on market inefficiencies, or the tatters as you called it. I think there's just increased demand for it. Academics, like everyone else, respond to demand. There's a great deal of demand for anomalies. It's basically a way for the popular press and active managers to justify what they're doing. If people find anomalies in the market, they can make jumps to say therefore active management can work. People want to do that because there's big money to be made.

MEIR STATMAN: It's not just anomalies. We had a beautiful model in the CAPM that started with individuals and rational choices and went to asset pricing. Now instead we have an empirical model, which you introduced, that does the job, but evidently even you don't find it beautiful. I think the same applies to, say, mean variance. Surely Harry Markowitz[11] would say that people don't follow his rules to form portfolios, and so on. It seems like there's a disconnect between reality and theory. Theory is, as you say very frankly, I don't know—too many questions and too few answers.

EUGENE FAMA: At the peak of euphoria in research on finance in the early 1970s, about the time the Fama and MacBeth (1973) paper was published, until then, and including that paper, the CAPM looked rather good, and market efficiency looked rather good. However, then things on the asset pricing side started to fall apart. In my view, people are spending inordinate amounts of time on consumption-based asset pricing, and it hasn't yielded anything. Some of the best brains in the business have spent their lives on that, and empirically it hasn't amounted to anything. The other theories? It turned out that the CAPM never really worked. We had just never looked at it carefully enough. So we have more uncertainty now about what it means to say something is risky and how you measure the relation between risk and expected return. In the process, however, we've learned a great deal about how prices actually behave. We're just much more uncertain about how to interpret it.

EDWARD BAKER: Moving to another topic if we could, the area of regulation in capital markets certainly has seen a huge shift toward excess in the face of some of the issues we've had. What are your thoughts about that?

EUGENE FAMA: That's a very difficult question. It's very difficult to say what is excessive, because a world in which there is no fraud is impossible. I know that people spend a lot of time trying to measure the costs and benefits of regulation, but I don't know how you answer that question in a convincing way. I think Sarbanes-Oxley probably went too far, but I don't know how to document that.

EDWARD BAKER: Do you think that's an area where academics should put some more effort?

EUGENE FAMA: Yes, definitely.

EDWARD BAKER: And why aren't they, do you think?

EUGENE FAMA: Because it's such a difficult topic. Measuring costs and benefits is just so difficult.

MEIR STATMAN: Some insight into that comes from a comparison of regulations among different countries and the effects of different cultures on financial markets. For example, a recent paper entitled "Trusting the Stock Market" (Guiso et al. 2008) found that places where people trust one another are also places where people are more likely to invest in the stock market. Do you see that as a promising avenue?

EUGENE FAMA: Indeed, I think that type of research is very promising. Explaining the kinds of situations—cultural, institutional, and so on—that give rise to more successful economic outcomes—what question could be more important than that? It's hard to think of one.

EDWARD BAKER: What about the area of international investing generally? How would you suggest people should think about that? Should they be thinking globally, or is it still appropriate to think of international as a separate part of their investment portfolio?

EUGENE FAMA: Your portfolio always has to be viewed as a whole. If we never had wars or conflicts, the answer would be simple. What do boundaries mean if everything is integrated economically? The only problem with international investing in the past has been that returns for local investors were different from returns for foreign investors, because of the intervention of major events such as wars. In a war, investors of the enemy automatically get expropriated. They never get their investments back, and nobody cares. If you look at international investing during wars, there have been major losses that don't show up in the data we typically use to measure the benefits of international investing, because that's all post-1973. The same is true for countries that experience financial distress. Those kinds of events never make it into the data. A government tells foreign investors that they can't repatriate their gains for who knows how long. That's a cost to foreigners not borne by locals. It gives rise to some amount of home bias in investing. It's not irrational to take into account the possibility of this kind of expropriation. And it's not as if it's unusual. In the past twenty years, many countries have imposed capital control—Spain, Great Britain, France—and that's without even getting into emerging markets, where it's a fairly frequent occurrence.

MEIR STATMAN: Home bias changes depending on the relative returns. I think home bias generally has declined during the past ten years, as foreign markets have performed better than the U.S. markets.

EUGENE FAMA: That's true. It's also that the frequency of major events, at least in Asian markets, has gone down. But even differential taxation can have an effect.

EDWARD BAKER: And that's a constantly changing playing field, so it's hard to hedge that.

EUGENE FAMA: Europeans probably never pay taxes on dividend income. They just don't file tax returns in most European countries. But if Europeans invest in the United States, they are subject to a withholding tax, while U.S. investors aren't. So differential taxation on foreign investment will have an effect.

MEIR STATMAN: Do you have one more moment to say something about fundamental indexes?

EUGENE FAMA: Fundamental indexing is a triumph of marketing over new ideas.

ROGER EDELEN: So marketing over economics is what you're saying?

EUGENE FAMA: No, there's just nothing new there.

MEIR STATMAN: But we in finance tend to underestimate marketing.

EUGENE FAMA: But I don't.

EDWARD BAKER: And most of the other practitioners don't either.

EDWARD BAKER: Unfortunately, Gene, I think we've used up our time with you. Is there any final comment you'd like to leave us with, or a word of inspiration?

EUGENE FAMA: Actually, I was waiting for you to ask me about my thoughts on portable alpha, because I had an answer prepared.

EDWARD BAKER: Okay, what are your thoughts on portable alpha?

EUGENE FAMA: It's very simple. Since alpha is equal to zero, it's very light, and that makes it portable.

■ ■ ■

ENDNOTES

1   Merton H. Miller (1923–2000), winner of the Nobel Memorial Prize in Economics in 1990 (with Harry M. Markowitz and William F. Sharpe) for "pioneering work in the theory of financial economics," served as Dr. Fama's doctoral advisor at the University of Chicago Graduate School of Business.

2   Harry V. Roberts (1923–2004) was a professor of statistics and quality management at the University of Chicago Graduate School of Business.

3   *The Journal of Business* (1965a), under the title "The Behavior of Stock Market Prices," published Dr. Fama's PhD thesis, which concluded that stock prices follow a random walk.

4   Statisticians often divide their data into in-sample portions, which they then use to develop a forecasting model, and holdout portions, which they then use to test the model's predictive ability.

5   The efficient market theory holds that it is impossible to "beat the market" because stock market efficiency causes existing share prices to incorporate and reflect all relevant information.

6   Irving Fisher (1867–1947) was one of the first to subject macroeconomic data to statistical analysis. The focus of Fisher's work was monetary economics, including the behavior of interest rates and inflation.

7   Benoît Mandelbrot (1924–2010), Sterling Professor of Mathematical Sciences Emeritus at Yale University, is known as the father of fractal geometry, one of the major developments in twentieth-century mathematics.

8   In a normal bell-shaped distribution of portfolio returns, the majority of returns can be found in the "bell," which centers around the weighted average return for the entire market. The ends, or tails, of the curve represent returns that are either extremely bad (left) or extremely good (right). Larger than normal tails are called "fat tails," indicating more data on the extremes than expected. Fat tails indicate that extreme market moves were more likely than would be predicted by normal distributions.

9   In addition to a percentage of assets under management, hedge funds typically charge a percentage of their profits. The standard fee arrangement is known as "2 and 20," i.e., a charge of 2 percent of assets under management plus 20 percent of profits above a predetermined benchmark, such as the London Interbank Offering Rate (LIBOR).

10 While the capital asset pricing model (CAPM) relies on a single factor—beta (risk)—to compare excess portfolio returns with excess returns of the market as a whole, Fama and French (1993) added two other factors to CAPM: market capitalization (size) and book-to-market ratio (value). The resultant three-factor model was based on their observations that small-cap stocks and those with high book-to-market ratios historically tended to perform better than the market as a whole.

11 Harry M. Markowitz (1927–), an economist at the Rady School of Management at the University of California, San Diego, is best known for his pioneering work in modern portfolio theory, studying the effects of asset risk, correlation, and diversification on expected investment portfolio returns. In 1990, he shared the Nobel Memorial Prize in Economic Sciences with Merton Miller and William Sharpe.

REFERENCES

Fama, Eugene F. 1965a. The Behavior of Stock Market Prices. *Journal of Business* 38, no. 1 (January): 34–105.

———. 1965b. Random Walks in Stock Market Prices. *Financial Analysts Journal* 21, no. 5 (September/October): 55–59.

———. 1970. Efficient Capital Markets: A Review of Theory and Empirical Work. *Journal of Finance* 25, no. 2 (May): 383–417 (Papers and Proceedings of the Twenty-Eighth Annual Meeting of the American Finance Association, New York, NY, December 28–30, 1969).

Fama, Eugene F. and Kenneth R. French. 1993. Common Risk Factors in the Returns on Stocks and Bonds. *Journal of Financial Economics* 33, no. 1: (February): 3–56.

———. 2007. Disagreements, Tastes, and Asset Pricing. *Journal of Financial Economics* 83, no. 3 (March): 667–689.

———. 2008. Mutual Fund Performance (June 30). Available at SSRN: http://ssrn.com/abstract=1153715.

———. Data available at www.dartmouth.edu/~kfrench.

Fama, Eugene F. and James D. MacBeth. 1973. Risk, Return, and Equilibrium: Empirical Tests. *Journal of Political Economy* 81, no. 3 (May/June): 607–636.

Fama, Eugene F. and Merton H. Miller. 1972. *The Theory of Finance.* New York: Holt, Rinehart & Winston.

———. 1976. *Foundations of Finance: Portfolio Decisions and Securities Prices.* New York: Basic Books.

French, Kenneth R. 2008. The Cost of Active Investing. Working paper. Available at http://ssrn.com/abstract=1105775.

Guiso, Luigi, Paola Sapienza, and Luigi Zingales. 2008. Trusting the Stock Market. *Journal of Finance* 63, no. 6 (December): 2,557–2,600.

Lintner, John. 1965. The Valuation of Risk Assets and the Selection of Risky Investments in Stock Portfolios and Capital Budgets. *Review of Economics and Statistics* 47, no. 1 (February): 13–37.

Mandelbrot, Benoît. 1963. The Variation of Certain Speculative Prices. *Journal of Business* 36, no. 4 (October): 394–419.

Sharpe, William F. 1964. Capital Asset Prices: A Theory of Market Equilibrium under Conditions of Risk. *Journal of Finance* 19, no. 3 (September): 425–442.

This interview was published in its entirety in *Journal of Investment Consulting* 9, no. 1, Fall 2008.

CHAPTER 4

DANIEL KAHNEMAN:
FATHER OF DECISION MAKING

DANIEL KAHNEMAN, PHD

Recipient of the 2002 Nobel Memorial Prize in Economic Sciences; Senior Scholar at the Woodrow Wilson School of Public and International Affairs, Professor of Psychology and Public Affairs Emeritus at Princeton University; author, *Thinking, Fast and Slow* and numerous articles in academic publications.

Daniel Kahneman's life experiences, from growing up Jewish in Nazi-occupied France to serving in the Israeli Defense Forces, taught him first-hand how people make decisions. In collaboration with Amos Tversky, Kahneman laid the foundation for behavioral finance by challenging the fundamental assumptions of the rational man. When we asked Kahneman to participate in our Masters series on finance and economics, he wanted to make sure we understood that he is a psychologist who studies judgment and decision making—not an economist or a finance professor. We invited him because we wanted to learn how his research might inform the prevailing wisdom of economic science and finance theory. Thanks to his book *Thinking, Fast and Slow*, we now have an accessible summary of his best research.

■ ■ ■

MARGARET TOWLE: First of all, Dr. Kahneman, thank you so much for agreeing to spend some time with us today. We're all well-acquainted with your exceptional background and contributions, and we hope to get a little more insight into the factors that helped to shape your career. Looking back over your experiences—from your childhood in Nazi-occupied France, your collaboration with Richard Thaler[1] in behavioral economics, through your recent work in intuition and the role that it plays in scientific investigation—what do you regard as the major factors that shaped your career and brought you to where you are today? Your accomplishments are too numerous to list, of course, but what do you consider your major achievements?

DANIEL KAHNEMAN: I think there's no question about the main determinant of my career, and that was the joint work with Amos Tversky.[2] As you know, most of my research has been collaborative. So having brilliant friends, I think, is the secret of any success I have achieved. In addition, there is a large element of being in the right place at the right time intellectually, that is, answering questions to which people are interested in hearing your answers. So, yes, I've been very fortunate. Clearly, if you want to understand what I've done, it's mostly collaborative.

■ ■ ■

As you know, most of my research has been collaborative. So having brilliant friends, I think, is the secret of any success I have achieved.

MARGARET TOWLE: What about on the other side, that is, what you would consider—I don't know if we want to call them mistakes—but your biggest disappointments in terms of events that happened throughout your career?

DANIEL KAHNEMAN: The worst thing that happened in my career was that, as I just mentioned, Amos Tversky and I collaborated for a long time, beginning in 1969, and then [in 1978] he went to Stanford University and I went to the University of British Columbia. We went on collaborating for a while after that, but it became very difficult for many reasons, mainly the physical separation. I think that together we were doing work that was better than either of us did separately. So the fact that we stopped working together was a major disappointment. I think I would have done better work if we had gone on working together, and probably so would he.

MEIR STATMAN: In your most recent book, *Thinking, Fast and Slow*, you talk about the organizing principles of System 1 and System 2.[3] I was speaking some months ago to a group of wealthy investors and business owners, noting the need to check intuition by the rules of science. One of the participants said that he still trusts his gut much more than scientific evidence. How can we persuade people to check their intuition? And should we persuade people to check their intuition?

DANIEL KAHNEMAN: I don't know that you can persuade everybody. The confidence that people have in their intuitions is a genuine feeling; it is not an opinion. You have the immediate feeling that your thinking is right, that your intuitions are valid, and it's like something you see, an illusion. People are very resistant to changing their minds about their cognitive illusions. We're much more willing to accept visual illusions, but people really resist when you tell them that their thinking in a certain way is an illusion. It's very difficult to convince them. On the whole, the ideas of System 1 and System 2 are penetrating, that is, there is more and more readiness to accept them. However, it's slow, and when they conflict with people's direct intuition, you'll find they quite frequently lose.

MEIR STATMAN: The people to whom I was speaking were members of families who had established very successful businesses. I was wondering whether their experience had involved one or two decisions that went spectacularly well, which persuaded them to believe in a version of the law of small numbers.[4]

DANIEL KAHNEMAN: Absolutely. It's very clear that it doesn't take very much for people to think that there is a pattern, and it doesn't take many successes for people to think that they are very, very smart, and it doesn't take many successes for others to think that a successful person has been very smart. People can be lucky, and that will feed into overconfidence. But even without luck, people are prone to overconfidence.

EDWARD BAKER: I have a slightly different question, but related to that. I picked up on one comment you made in your Nobel Prize autobiography, which I found to be just fascinating. In particular, you said that most highly cognitive performances are intuitive. I wondered, when it comes to identifying skill, does that make it harder or easier? Is there something about this characteristic that one can identify, or is it really just unique from instance to instance? Is there a pattern that one can see?

DANIEL KAHNEMAN: What we call intuitive thinking refers to the ideas that come to mind quickly and without reflection, quite often automatically. You're in a situation, and you know what to do or you know how to understand that situation. Most of the time, our intuitions are just fine. We mostly run on what I call System 1 intuitively and with high confidence and very successfully. That is true both in very simple matters—for example, recognizing a speaker's emotion on the telephone from hearing one word, this is something at which all of us are quite skilled. Intuition is often excellent in complex tasks as well. We have learned hundreds of skills that actually are at the level of a chess master, except we don't think of them that way. When we get highly practiced, we develop skills. The problem with intuition and with people who want to trust their gut is that intuitions come with high confidence. The confidence is justified when intuition is a product of skill, which people have acquired through numerous experiences with immediate feedback. However, some intuitions are products of heuristics of judgment and are quite often mistaken.[5] The problem is that even the mistaken intuitions come to mind with considerable confidence. It's very difficult to distinguish between intuitions that reflect real skill and intuitions that don't. It is not easy for an observer, and even harder for the individual who has the intuition. We don't know the boundary between skill and heuristic in our own thinking.

EDWARD BAKER: So that makes this type of behavior very difficult to distinguish, that is, when it's an example of skill and when it's not?

DANIEL KAHNEMAN: In *Thinking, Fast and Slow*, I described my collaborative work with Gary Klein[6] on determining whether you can trust intuitive thinking. The conclusion is that if you want to know whether you can trust intuition, your own or somebody else's, you shouldn't ask about subjective confidence, because that can be very misleading. Instead, you should ask about the probability that a person's intuitions arise from genuine skill. For that, you have to look at whether the world is sufficiently regular to support skill, which is true for chess masters and for recognizing the emotion in your wife's voice but probably isn't true in the stock market. Second, you have to ask whether the individual has had sufficient practice to acquire this skill. So confidence is not it. You've got to look from the outside. When a person makes a judgment, you have to ask what are the probabilities that this judgment is well-founded given the nature of the world in which that individual operates and the nature of the practice that the individual has had.

EDWARD BAKER: Interesting, but there certainly are contexts in which confidence plays a dominant role in success, for example, in a leadership setting.

DANIEL KAHNEMAN: Absolutely. We reward confident optimists. There is no question that, in the context of leadership, somebody with high confidence is more likely to inspire trust in others and is more likely to attract resources that are needed for success. Optimism also facilitates resiliency in the context of execution. However, we need to distinguish situations in which optimism and confidence are useful from situations in which they are not. Roughly speaking, confidence is very useful in the context of execution, that is, when you are already committed to a course of action, you need to believe that you can do it. That will make you more resilient if things go badly, and thereby improve the real chances of success. If I have a favorite football team, I would like those players to be optimistic when they are on the field. In the context of decision making, however, I have absolutely no interest in my financial advisor being an optimist. I would like him to be as well-calibrated as possible.

■ ■ ■

Optimism also facilitates resiliency in the context of execution. However, we need to distinguish situations in which optimism and confidence are useful from situations in which they are not.

MARK ANSON: I've had experience working with pension funds over the years, and it's interesting to observe the group psychology and herding that you see associated with large institutional investors. At least I've observed it from time to time with pension funds tending to move in the same direction at the same time. I noticed in your book that you talk about System 1 versus System 2 and the behavioral biases that can impact either of them. I was curious, from your point of view, do you find more behavioral bias embedded in a System 1 process versus a System 2? It seems like a System 2 process, which you refer to as a bit more analytical, might at times have the potential to be lazy and just accept what the rest of the herd is doing. Can you comment on that?

DANIEL KAHNEMAN: The way I analyze this in the book, most actions involve both systems. That is, System 1 quite often is the one that originates an idea or an impulse for an action. Then System 2 quite often endorses it, without checking sufficiently. That happens a great deal. In addition, System 2 quite often lacks the necessary knowledge. So you can slow yourself down, but mobilizing System 2 won't do anything for you if you don't have the tools to understand the situation. Slowing down is good when it allows you to deal with a situation more intelligently. Slowing down won't help when you are out of your depth.

MARK ANSON: When people slow down, doesn't that tend to mean that they fall back in with the pack again, in that herding behavior that many have written about?

DANIEL KAHNEMAN: I'm not at all sure of that. I would attribute herding to a System 1 tendency. In situations of very high ambiguity, and when you have lost your confidence in your own ability to understand the world, then the tendency to do just what other people are doing is extremely powerful. It's also reinforced by social norms and by groups. If you see other pension funds doing something and you don't do it, you will get severely punished if you lose for not following the herd. So following the herd has an element of safety in it, and it's bound with System 1. I don't think of it as primarily a System 2 process. Herding is not necessarily something one does as the result of analysis. It is what one does when one's confidence is impaired.

MEIR STATMAN: There are two areas that I hope you will not end this interview without addressing. One has to do with your work on well-being, and the other has to do with your work on fairness. Why do people with billions of dollars—hedge fund managers as one example—want even more money? I know what it does to their wealth, but what does it do to their well-being? Is it possible that a good part of what financial advisors do is increase investors' well-being while potentially diminishing their wealth?

DANIEL KAHNEMAN: Those are two very different questions, so I'll take them one at a time. We know from recent research that, beyond a certain income threshold, which is actually quite low—it's about $70,000 per household, emotional happiness doesn't seem to increase at all. Now, life satisfaction probably increases reasonably steadily with wealth. When people seek more wealth, although they will never spend what they already have, this is clearly because money is a proxy for something else. I mean, money is a proxy for ego satisfaction. So most of these people are in it because they need success, and money is just an index of success. That, I think, is the motivation for many people. Actually, I think the people who are strictly motivated by money rather than by success are mainly the poor and the very poor. For most of us professionals, money is a proxy for something else, and that is certainly true for hedge fund managers. So that's an answer to your first question.

Your second question is a very interesting one—what is the relationship between financial advising and the client's well-being? Actually, I've worked with that question before. In fact, with a well-respected investment advisory firm, Andrew Rosenfield[7] and I were involved in devising a program for advising very wealthy investors. There you're really more concerned with their well-being than with their wealth. Primarily you want to protect them from regret, you want to protect them from the emotions associated with very big losses. So you end up focusing more on their emotions than on their wealth.

MEIR STATMAN: Can you give an example of how you might have done this?

DANIEL KAHNEMAN: That relates to another question, that is, how does one identify risk tolerance? Our thinking on this was that the issue is not so much tolerance for risk as it is tolerance for losses. Tolerance for losses means that you have to know—the individual investor has to know and certainly the advisor has to try to know—how much loss the person will be able to tolerate before he changes his mind about what he is doing. Clearly, changing course by and large is not a good idea, and selling low and buying high is not a good idea. You have to anticipate regret and identify the individuals who are very prone to regret. They're not going to be very good clients for the financial advisor. If people are very prone to regret, then you have to help them devise a plan that will minimize their regret. For the very wealthy, emotion is clearly important in determining what policy is appropriate.

GEOFFREY GERBER: I remember hearing Amos Tversky present the findings of your collaborative research at a University of California, Berkeley, seminar on finance back in the early 1980s. He introduced the concept of loss aversion bias that you're talking about, which, as you say, is the tendency to fear losses more than we value gains. The question from an investment manager's perspective or an investor's perspective is does the implementation of stop-loss limits[8] help alleviate the loss aversion bias?

DANIEL KAHNEMAN: The main question that I have found useful to ask when someone is very wealthy is how much loss is the individual willing to tolerate? That is, what fraction of their wealth are they actually willing to lose? It turns out that fraction is usually not very large. That's a very important parameter. How much do they really want to protect as much as possible, and how much are they willing to consider losing? That varies a lot among individuals. By and large, the very wealthy mostly want to protect their wealth, and they're willing to play with a small fraction of it. That is the fraction they are prepared to lose, but it's not a large fraction. So they're loss averse, not risk averse as such.

GEOFFREY GERBER: So you're suggesting that setting a stop-loss higher or lower depends on your willingness to accept a loss? Is that a good approach?

DANIEL KAHNEMAN: For the individual who is very concerned about losses, I think this is certainly a good approach. That's the major question you want to ask the investor. How much are you willing to lose? Then you have to take steps so that they won't lose more than they are willing to lose. That's in effect stop-loss policy.

EDWARD BAKER: Could you in fact organize questions that involve costs of insurance to see how much they'd be willing to pay for insurance that would protect against losses?

DANIEL KAHNEMAN: That's interesting. I hadn't thought of it that way—in terms of insurance. Yes, that would be an interesting approach. Also, people have to become aware of the fact that by stopping their losses, they are giving up some potential upside. Looking at the trade-off between the upside and the downside gives you a sense of their attitude toward losses and what you should encourage them to do.

MEIR STATMAN: You mentioned that people are willing to play with or lose some portion of their money. I don't know if you have in mind that they keep two mental accounts: one is money that is not to be lost, and the other is money that can possibly be lost?

DANIEL KAHNEMAN: That is exactly what we have in mind. We actually had the individual construct two portfolios. One is a portfolio that is designed mainly for safety, and the other portfolio is designed to take advantage of opportunities. The relative size of the two portfolios represents one way of identifying loss aversion because with your riskier portfolio, that's an amount you can consider losing. It's not only two mental accounts. At least with some clients, we make this completely explicit, that is, clients receive information about two accounts, about their safe account and their riskier account. This is a very natural way for people to think.

MEIR STATMAN: If I might move on to the issue of fairness, where you've done a lot of work, perhaps I can frame my question in the context of the fees that are charged by advisors. I think that financial advisors have more difficulty than other professionals, say physicians, lawyers, or accountants, in setting fees and justifying their fees. Advisors seem to be forever trying to hide their fees in one form or another. Can you speak to this issue of fairness?

DANIEL KAHNEMAN: Actually, this is a topic I haven't thought about, so I don't have a clear sense. In part, the need to hide fees comes from the fact that many of the advisors are frequently conflicted to some extent because if they're associated with a firm that provides products, then there is a problem associated with fees. Advisors who are completely hands-off, that is, those who are not involved with the products they are selling, probably should have no difficulties explaining their fees and charging for their services. It's those who are in a more ambiguous position who are probably sensitive about their fees. I haven't seen much discussion of the fairness of fees because clearly this is a competitive market, and there is enough variability in the fees for individuals to make their own choices.

EDWARD BAKER: Moving on to a different area, I was interested in asking about your new work in adversarial collaboration.[9] I found that to be a fascinating turn of events in your life. What motivated that? Have you found some interesting opportunities to do new creative work? How can this be applied? It seems that if you could develop some systematic rules, it could be a major breakthrough in the way negotiations work. I'm thinking, of course, in the area of government.

DANIEL KAHNEMAN: I got into adversarial collaboration because there is a system in the scholarly literature where people critique other people's writings, and then there is a reply, and then there is a rejoinder. That's the routine in scientific publications. I was just very struck by how totally wasteful this is, because in all these exchanges nobody admits to having made an error. It is very striking, and quite frequently it becomes an exercise in sarcasm. It's just foul actually. So having been involved in some controversy, I became very interested in the possibility of trying to meet people who don't agree with me. All of us have a shared commitment to science, and we—at least in principle—also have a shared commitment to truth. That gives us some basis for working together to achieve truth. Now it turns out that even among scientists, the commitment to truth is—well, it's a real commitment—but emotion comes in. One of the striking things about adversarial collaboration—and I've had several—is that at the end of the collaboration, nobody feels that he has changed his mind much. That's very typical.

■ ■ ■

I was just very struck by how totally wasteful this is, because in all these exchanges nobody admits to having made an error. It is very striking, and quite frequently it becomes an exercise in sarcasm.

You asked whether adversarial collaboration could be implemented in politics. The question is whether there is enough of a shared commitment, a shared goal, for people to be interested in searching for compromise or in searching for joint action. This clearly exists among scientists, but it's much less likely to exist among true adversaries in the political domain, except possibly in a situation of crisis when it would become natural for adversaries to collaborate. I'm not very optimistic that adversarial collaboration can generally be extended to areas other than science. I've had luck with it. I've had good experiences with adversarial collaboration, I've avoided lifelong quarrels, and I have made friends. In sum, my experience has been a good one, but adversarial collaboration takes a lot of time and a lot of patience. It also sometimes takes quite a bit of self-control not to lose your temper with somebody who seems stuck on refusing to see the truth as you see it. So it's a mixed bag of experiences, and I'm not sure how far it can go beyond science.

Let me add that there are two practices that quite probably can advance or spread beyond science. One is, almost as a technique, to encourage adversaries to take each other's point of view and to make a speech that is, as it were, for the other side. That induces empathy, and it really helps you to understand what the other side is doing. That's a very worthwhile exercise if you're really interested in advancing cooperation. The other practice that seems really useful is socializing. I think one of the disasters in Washington is that apparently there is now very little socializing across political parties, whereas thirty or forty years ago, it was a rule that adversaries would drink and smoke together and go to football games together and so on. That is enormously important to mitigate adversarial relations, and we don't have that now.

MEIR STATMAN: In politics, persuasion is the thing. It's less a matter of finding the truth than getting people to vote for you. I think there is an equivalent of that in the financial services industry, exploiting cognitive errors rather than countering them. For example, we see advertising that magnifies people's overconfidence in their ability to beat the market, rather than tamp it down. Can you speak to that?

DANIEL KAHNEMAN: Obviously, there is a lot of pandering to System 1 in advertising. I don't know if you have in mind the ads that encourage you to trade so as to beat the market and become rich. Those ads are clearly directed at overconfident people, and are intended to enhance their overconfidence. Most of advertisement is addressed to System 1, not to System 2. There is very little information in advertising, and anybody who watches programs with loads of advertising, such as the Super Bowl for example, would be hard put to find any information about any product. It is very striking—there is none. It's all appealing to different types of emotions.

MEIR STATMAN: By one reliable estimate, U.S. investors would save more than $100 billion each year if they switched to low-cost index funds. Why aren't more investors using index funds? Why aren't they more sensitive to the fees involved?

DANIEL KAHNEMAN: I think that most people believe they are in the market to beat the market. If they are planning to beat the market, they are willing to pay some price. If, in your imagination, you're going to beat the market by a lot, then you become insensitive to fees. In order to become sensitive to fees, it's almost a precondition to accept that you're very unlikely to beat the market systematically, and that's a difficult realization for many investors. That relates to the other question of why aren't all investors in index funds. Clearly, there has been an increase in the amount of money invested in index funds, but I read the statistic of 25 percent of assets somewhere. Is that correct?

MEIR STATMAN: At most, I would say.

■ ■ ■

> There is very little information in advertising, and anybody who watches programs with loads of advertising, such as the Super Bowl for example, would be hard put to find any information about any product. It is very striking— there is none. It's all appealing to different types of emotions.

DANIEL KAHNEMAN: This is clearly overconfidence at work, and to some extent the people who are selling these services are themselves overconfident. I had a marvelous experience many years ago with a financial advisor, whom I actually left—well, I had already left him when we had this conversation. I had moved to a safer line of investments, and he called me and said: "Look, what you are doing is stupid. We could make a lot of money for you. You are limiting your gains to a fixed amount, and last year we had several funds that did so much better than that amount." Then I looked back at the letter he had written me a year earlier in which he recommended specific funds. None of the funds he had recommended was among those that actually made a lot of money a year later. But he didn't know it. He had no interest in lying to me, because I had already left him and he knew I wasn't coming back. He was fighting for his own overconfidence. I think there's much more sincere overconfidence than lying among the professionals who think they can beat the market, and so they convince investors, and investors think, "Here is a guy with a track record of five winning years," and off they go.

MEIR STATMAN: Obviously, cognitive errors get in the way, because the financial services industry is a great puzzle. In a world where people are smart—even if not rational—all would move on to index funds. The question I come back to is the question of well-being. Is it possible that we underestimate the joy that people derive from attempts to beat the market? Or that we underestimate the desire for the hope of getting rich through their investments?

DANIEL KAHNEMAN: I see the question you are raising, and it's a very interesting one. Clearly when people go to Las Vegas to gamble, most of them are not going to get rich, and they know that they are more likely to lose than to win, but they are going for the entertainment and the excitement and the thrill and the possibility of winning. Whether people who are investing think of it as going to Las Vegas, I personally doubt it very much. I don't think it's the same thing. They don't know that they're gambling—they think they're playing a game of skill.

EDWARD BAKER: However, there are examples such as Warren Buffett, and people see someone like that apparently making money consistently. Do they just misassess the probability of winning? Is that really what's going on?

DANIEL KAHNEMAN: I think so. Clearly from the examples you see or read about, there are successful people. If you went by the proportion of successful and unsuccessful people that you see in the media or that you hear talked about, then success overwhelms failure. Anybody who relies on what we call the availability heuristic[10] is going to find support for his overconfidence. That's overconfidence, not a search for well-being. The few who are in the market for the sheer excitement of it probably gamble small amounts, and know that they are in Las Vegas.

MEIR STATMAN: Perhaps, but if you ask people who drive a Lexus or Rolls Royce if they do it for status, they would surely deny it. They would say it's because of the car's high quality and so on. I wonder if investors lack introspection about their wants.

DANIEL KAHNEMAN: To some extent, I think you are right. There are two separate questions. First, do people know the odds? The best evidence suggests that they don't know the odds, but they are truly optimistic about the likelihood of their winning. Second, when they play, when they are in the market, do they by and large derive well-being from it? Well, that's a complicated question, because if somebody is more sensitive to losses than to gains, then they don't get much well-being from the winning and losing. They get some excitement, and they quite possibly are deluded about how much they are winning and losing. That is, people have selective memories for their successes and failures, and they may actually misremember their previous record and think that it is better than it really was.

MARGARET TOWLE: We've covered a wide range of topics so far today, Dr. Kahneman, but are there other areas of interest that you think are especially relevant when it comes to the investment industry as far as potential areas of research or areas that are unexplored now, given your conceptual framework?

DANIEL KAHNEMAN: Of course, there are many questions about the future, the future of research, and so on. I don't believe in long-run forecasting, and I don't believe that you can say the field is going in one direction or another. I have very little to say about where the field is going. Short-term, you can tell there is going to be more neuro-economics—that's fairly clear, because so many bright students are going into that field. The role of emotion in decision making is going to be discussed, and there's going to be more of it in the near future. Long-term, who knows?

MEIR STATMAN: One sentence in *Thinking, Fast and Slow* that struck and delighted me was one where you said that you cringe when you hear people say that Amos Tversky and you proved that people are irrational. Could you elaborate on that? What is your sense of rationality? What does irrationality mean to you? I know that I have been using the term "normal" to define the opposite of rational.

DANIEL KAHNEMAN: I'm delighted with that question, and I'm actually very pleased to talk about that. The word rational for me is a technical term. Rationality is defined in decision theory as logical coherence, and it's very easy to test. In fact, a significant amount of research—and the research done by Amos and me, specifically—was dedicated to showing that people are not rational by that definition. But to call people irrational makes me cringe because the meaning of irrationality is associated for most people with emotion, with impulsivity, with frothing at the mouth. Our research was concerned with cognitive biases; we did not deal with mistakes that people make that arise from emotional impulsivity. As I understand the word, what we studied was not irrationality. I see a lot of System 1 influence, and System 1 is the emotional one, but I don't see all that much irrationality.

■ ■ ■

> Rationality is defined in decision theory as logical coherence, and it's very easy to test. In fact, a significant amount of research—and the research done by Amos and me, specifically—was dedicated to showing that people are not rational by that definition.

EDWARD BAKER: On the other hand, you've resisted defining rationality, you said. If you were forced to come up with a definition, what would it be?

DANIEL KAHNEMAN: I think I just defined it. I accept the definition of rationality as a technical term. I don't use the word rationality except as that technical term. I don't say people are irrational. I speak of reasonableness, I follow Richard Thaler in talking about Econs[11] versus Humans, and I think Meir's use of normal is the same general idea. I just don't use the word much, except in its technical meaning. The so-called rational agent[12] hypothesis is outlandish and completely implausible. No finite mind could satisfy the requirement of rationality. The bottom line is that I don't need to define rationality, because it's defined as a technical term.

EDWARD BAKER: Is there some underlying condition, though, that leads to efficient markets?

DANIEL KAHNEMAN: I don't know enough economics to answer that question. I could quote second-hand or third-hand that it doesn't take many rational agents to have enough money to enforce market discipline and so on. But I don't really know enough.

MEIR STATMAN: Can you elaborate on what you said in your book about prospect theory?[13] You noted what prospect theory did to counter expected utility theory,[14] but you also pointed out the shortcomings of prospect theory in being true to reality. I'm not sure if I'm quoting it correctly, but I have this quote in my mind from Amos Tversky that "elegance is for tailors."

DANIEL KAHNEMAN: Amos attributed that quote to Albert Einstein. I don't know if he was right—I never checked.[15]

MEIR STATMAN: Any quote where we don't know the source, we attribute to either (John Maynard) Keynes[16] or Einstein. In any event, would you comment on the fascination we have with higher mathematics and formal models and the field's direction in terms of how it expresses itself? I know you don't forecast long-term, but perhaps short-term?

DANIEL KAHNEMAN: Clearly, people who know mathematics have an advantage over people who don't, because they speak a language that others don't understand, whereas psychologists, sociologists, and people in professions such as that—most of the social scientists—speak in a language that, even if they use a little jargon, everybody can understand. So mathematics is an exclusive club, and there is a certain pride in belonging to it. It creates a mystique, and those who belong probably get a little more respect than they deserve. On the other hand, I have seen examples where clear mathematical thinking really improves the quality of psychological theory. Amos Tversky was a master at it. He could use mathematics to think better. That's not true of all mathematical psychologists, but Amos really used mathematics to make himself think more clearly. There are other examples as well. In behavioral finance, for example, we have the demonstrations by Nicholas Barberis[17] of Yale University that one needs not only loss aversion but also narrow framing[18] in order to explain the behavior of individuals in the market. That was mathematical reasoning. It can be very fruitful when used in conjunction with good psychological intuition, so it is a very powerful tool.

MARGARET TOWLE: We're nearing the end of our time, Dr. Kahneman, so I'll ask you if there's anything we haven't covered that you'd like to discuss.

DANIEL KAHNEMAN: No, we have covered more than I know.

MARGARET TOWLE: Well, that's due to collective intelligence, I think, as far as the great questions that the group asked.

EDWARD BAKER: I have one final question as to whether you have any thoughts for the regulators. Could any of your more recent work in behavioral finance, in particular, be helpful in forming market regulation?

DANIEL KAHNEMAN: I think there is no question about that. There are direct implications of behavioral economics and of the idea of bounded rationality[19] for regulation. The idea of the rational agent model has two pernicious consequences. One is that you don't need to protect consumers from themselves because they are rational, and therefore can be trusted to make the choices that are best for them. So you can oppose Social Security on the dual assumptions that people are rational and that they should bear the consequences of their actions. However, I believe that regulation is essential to protect people from predictable mistakes. You have to do that without abridging freedom, of course, but that can be done. And then you need to protect consumers from actors in the market that would deliberately exploit people's ignorance and their intellectual sloth.

■ ■ ■

ENDNOTES

1   Richard H. Thaler (1945–) is an economist and professor of behavioral science and economics at the University of Chicago Booth School of Business. He is best known as a pioneering theorist in behavioral finance and for his collaboration with Daniel Kahneman and others in further defining the field of behavioral economics and finance.

2   Amos Tversky (1937–1996) was a cognitive and mathematical psychologist, a key figure in the discovery of systematic human cognitive bias and handling of risk, and a longtime collaborator of Daniel Kahneman.

3   Daniel Kahneman identified two styles of processing, System 1 and System 2. System 1 is rapid, intuitive, and emotional. System 2 is slower, more deliberate, and more logical.

4   The law of small numbers describes a judgmental bias that assumes that a small number of observations can predict outcome from a larger sample population.

5   Heuristics of judgment are principles or methods used to simplify assessments or judgments of probability.

6   Gary A. Klein (1944–) is a research psychologist noted for pioneering the field of naturalistic decision making, focusing on the ability of intuition to support human decision making in high-pressure circumstances, such as firefighting and medical emergencies.

7   Andrew Rosenfield is a managing partner of Guggenheim Partners, a financial services firm that provides wealth and investment management services to high-net-worth clients, foundations, and endowments.

8   Stop-loss limits are orders placed with a broker to sell a security when it reaches a certain price. A stop-loss order is designed to limit an investor's loss on a security position.

9   Daniel Kahneman describes adversarial collaboration as "a good-faith effort by unlike minds to conduct joint research, critiquing each other in the service of an ideal of truth to which both can contribute."

10 The availability heuristic is a mental shortcut that relies on immediate examples that come to mind, believing that if something comes to mind, it must be important.

11 Econs, a term coined by Richard Thaler, are the imaginary efficient individuals found only in economic theory who are able to weigh multiple options, forecast the consequences of each, and make logical choices, as opposed to actual humans, who are illogical, prone to generalize, biased in favor of the status quo, and more concerned with avoiding loss than making gains.

12 In economics and decision theory, a rational agent, which can include individuals, companies, or computer programs, has clear preferences, models uncertainty using expected values, and always chooses to perform the action that results in the optimal outcome for itself from among all feasible actions.

13 Prospect theory describes the ways in which individuals make choices among probabilistic alternatives that involve risk or uncertainty and evaluate potential losses and gains. Prospect theory, which attempts to model real-life choices rather than optimal decisions, holds that individuals make decisions based on the potential value of losses and gains (loss aversion) rather than the final outcome. The theory was developed by Daniel Kahneman and Amos Tversky in 1979 as a psychologically more accurate description of preferences versus expected utility theory.

14 In decision making, expected utility theory, which is based on elementary rules of rationality, addresses the analysis of choices among risky or uncertain prospects by measuring the value of various outcomes relative to respective probabilities, with the focus on the final outcome.

[15] "If you are out to describe the truth, leave elegance to the tailor." The phrase is attributed to both Albert Einstein (1879–1955) and Ludwig Boltzmann (1844–1906), an Austrian physicist.

[16] John Maynard Keynes (1883–1946) was a world-renowned British economist whose ideas, known as Keynesian economics, had a major impact on theories of modern economics and politics as well as on government fiscal policies.

[17] Nicholas C. Barberis (1971–) is a professor of finance at the Yale School of Management, where his research focuses on behavioral finance, specifically using cognitive psychology to understand the pricing of financial assets.

[18] Framing refers to the context in which a decision is made. An investor is said to use narrow framing when he makes an investment decision without considering the context of his total portfolio. Together, narrow framing and loss aversion may provide a method for understanding how individuals evaluate stock market risk by examining their evaluation of risk in experimental settings.

[19] In decision making, bounded rationality holds that the rationality of individuals is limited by the information they possess, their cognitive limitations, and the finite amount of time available to make a decision. Economic models typically assume that the average person is rational and will, in large enough numbers, act according to preferences. The concept of bounded rationality revises this assumption to account for the fact that perfectly rational decisions are, in practice, often unfeasible because of the finite computational resources available for making them. Daniel Kahneman has proposed bounded rationality as a model to overcome some of the limitations of the rational agent model in economic literature.

REFERENCES

Kahneman, Daniel. 2002. Autobiography. http://www.nobelprize.org/nobel_prizes/economics/laureates/2002/kahneman-autobio.html.

———. 2003. Maps of Bounded Rationality: Psychology for Behavioral Economics. *American Economic Review* 93, no. 5 (December): 1,449–1,475.

———. 2011. *Thinking, Fast and Slow*. New York: Farrar, Straus and Giroux.

Kahneman, Daniel, and Angus Deaton. 2010. High Income Improves Evaluation of Life but Not Emotional Well-Being. *Proceedings of the National Academy of Sciences* 107, no. 38 (September 21): 16,489–16,493.

Kahneman, Daniel, and Edwin E. Ghiselli. 1962. Validity and Nonlinear Heteroscedastic Models. *Personnel Psychology* 15, no. 1 (March): 1–11.

Kahneman, Daniel, and Gary Klein. 2009. Conditions for Intuitive Expertise: A Failure to Disagree. *American Psychologist* 64, no. 6 (September): 515–526.

Kahneman, Daniel, and Amos Tversky. 1979. Prospect Theory: An Analysis of Decision under Risk. *Econometrica* 47, no. 2 (March): 263–291.

Thaler, Richard H., Amos Tversky, Daniel Kahneman, and Alan Schwartz. 1997. The Effect of Myopia and Loss Aversion on Risk Taking: An Experimental Test. *Quarterly Journal of Economics* 112, no. 2 (May): 647–661.

Tversky, Amos, and Daniel Kahneman. 1971. Belief in the Law of Small Numbers. *Psychological Bulletin* 76, no. 2: 105–110.

———. 1974. Judgment under Uncertainty: Heuristics and Biases. *Science* 185, no. 4157 (September 27): 1,124–1,131.

This interview was published in its entirety in *Journal of Investment Consulting* 13, no. 1, 2012.

CHAPTER 5

DEAN LEBARON: INVESTMENT FUTURIST

DEAN LEBARON

Recipient of the 2001 Association for Investment Management and Research Award for Professional Excellence; founder and former chief executive officer of Batterymarch Financial Management; author of *Mao, Marx, & the Market* and *Book of Investment Quotations*.

Dean LeBaron, like many of our Masters, easily straddles the worlds of academia and applied finance. Following a successful academic experience at Harvard, he jumped into investment management. He is fond of proclaiming that being first is preferable to being best, yet he is often both. He was a visionary in using complexity science and computer models to manage equity portfolios when most portfolio managers still did everything on paper. He was an early adopter of contrarian investing, which holds that astute investors seek opportunities where others are not looking. This led him to add emerging markets to client portfolios long before his colleagues. LeBaron continues seeking to be first even in retirement, where he is exploring the creation of a virtual investment management process.

■ ■ ■

MARGARET TOWLE: We're really pleased to have you take part in our Masters series. As we've noted, you have some great information about your background on your website. However, we'd like to hear from you directly as to what you believe were the major factors that helped to shape your career and bring you to where you are today.

DEAN LEBARON: Well, let me start in terms of where I am today. Essentially, I have been out of active money management—meaning managing money for other people—for the past ten or fifteen years. I now manage money for myself, doing the same foolish things that I always did, running the odd markets and odd strategies, and trying to do different types of things. So I've continued down the path for uniqueness. However, since I'm unlikely to fire myself, I have a little bit more freedom than I used to—although that never made too much difference. I think I might start at the beginning and talk about why I went into investment management in the first place.

When I graduated from the Harvard Business School (in 1960), the appropriate thing to do was to be the man in the gray flannel suit who aspired to be an assistant plant manager for General Motors someplace. Only about two or three people in my graduating class were going into what was then referred to as "Wall Street." When I became an analyst, the sign on my door said that

I was in the statistical department. Ultimately, I decided on Wall Street because a professor of mine, Dick Vancil[1], looked at me and said: "Dean, most people in the investment business fail more than half the time. They do so publicly with large amounts of money, and they have to go back and start over again. Most people don't have a personality that will stand that type of assault, but I think you do, and you will succeed better than half the time." There was some merit to that, I thought, and the merit was that what he really was saying was you had to buck the crowd, and if you did that in the field of investment management, you could be recognized and given responsibility at a fairly young age. There was very little competition because very few people were going into that field. Most people were, as I said, going to General Motors and the like.

I then moved to the point of view that in investment management you should match the investment style to your own personal psyche. So if someone said to me, "You should be a momentum manager or get into super-hot stocks," I knew that was not for me. Although I was an expert on fiberglass boats at one time, believe it or not, I'm a bottom fisher, and psychologically that suits me in many things that I do. I look for the questions that are not being asked, not so much taking the opposite of questions that are asked and coming up with the negative, but what questions literally are not being asked. That really characterizes my investment style. I continue to do that today, looking for the things that are just not covered by other people. I look in the holes. I'm attracted to dirt and places where there's dirty data, not clean data. I'm attracted to the areas where other people fear to tread because of potential criticism. Those opportunities continue to exist—sometimes favorably, sometimes not.

■ ■ ■

> # I look for the questions that are not being asked, not so much taking the opposite of questions that are asked and coming up with the negative, but what questions literally are not being asked. That really characterizes my investment style.

MARGARET TOWLE: That certainly is consistent with how we understand your career. When we look at your career, we think of Batterymarch, and I think we all consider that a major achievement.[2] What do you regard as your major achievement?

DEAN LEBARON: My major achievement is surviving failures.

MARGARET TOWLE: That's a great way to put it.

DEAN LEBARON: For example, I thought at one time, probably twenty or thirty years ago, that farm assets would be a major institutional asset category. I started a farm management company and managed $100 million or something of that nature for pension funds, and the company was a failure. A failure not so much from a financial standpoint, because it made a few percent a year, but from the standpoint that it was a very localized business. It did not lend itself to institutionalization. I learned that if you sat at a table in a farm negotiation, and your adversary referred to someone else as "Bubba," get up, you're in the wrong place. The Bubba principle helped. So I was able to sell the farm management company for a tiny profit and move on. Farm assets are very popular now, but it's an extremely expensive business to manage. You can burn up 7 or 8 percent in fees every year, and the returns, attractive though they may be, don't support that sort of thing.

The other thing I tried very hard to do throughout my career was to sell investment managers on the idea of ethics as a good practice to follow. Ethics could be a disdain for soft dollars, which is heresy, of course. I never took soft dollars from clients to pay for services that were provided. I voted against directors of our own clients when they voted for shark repellents[3] and the like and proceeded to get fired in 20 to 25 percent of the cases. Matters that I considered to be ethical issues for investment managers, I don't think I was very successful at selling. It cost money. The dean of a business school recently asked me, "How much money did you make pursuing ethical strategies?" and I said, "It cost me about $50 million." I then went back and calculated the number, and I was underestimating. It was more than that.

A last failure was in tying investment thinking to a whole variety of other topics. Again, I'm a fan of bringing the hard sciences and the so-called soft sciences together. However, that didn't move as fast as I thought it should, and it's still going on—evolutionary finance, behavioral finance, whatever you want to call it. I think there's a big future there, and we may see that as it comes along. Let me just insert one other idea because it will relate to a number of things I say. I'm a secret fan of Kondratieff waves,[4] and I think we have been in a ten-year transition period, from one fifty-year period of investment management style to something else, and I don't know yet what the something else is. We probably won't know for another ten years as we go through this Kondratieff long-wave winter.[5] Our biggest exercise is, "What is that period in the future going to look like?" I have some guesses, but I don't have any very firm convictions.

GEOFFREY GERBER: High-frequency trading[6] and many of the statistical arbitrage strategies were developed from the perspective of engineering or practical science—what you have termed "hard science." Will the next set of academics entering the real world of investing come more from the social-media side, rather than the engineering side?

DEAN LEBARON: Yes, I believe so. That's my guess, and it's only a guess. I think high-frequency trading has more to do with scalping[7] than with engineering, frankly. With dark pools[8] and high-frequency trading, it looks like what we used to call it back in the old days—front-running more than anything else. I don't mean to be so cynical, but it's flashing lights, and it's one set of investors having a privilege of information over others. There are a couple of ways of dealing with that. The old-fashioned way would have been for a firm to sell its expertise or rent its expertise in high-frequency trading to a group of investors and do that as a point of greater return. In the present world, we don't do that. That would be perceived as being very stupid. The intelligent thing is to do it for your own account as a trading account and trade against your own clients in that way. I'm an old-fashioned guy. I would still do it according to the former technique rather than the latter.

EDWARD BAKER: Would you say then that the old ways of investing—the traditional styles of value investing and growth investing, if you will—are dead? Do you think those approaches now are just nonsensical?

DEAN LEBARON: Oh, I hope not, but you're quite right. You've pinned me to the wall. I think I'm skeptical about anything that has worked so well for fifty years that it becomes almost our hallmark. Then you go through a period of change, which is what we seem to be in at the moment. I mean, who would have guessed—maybe you would have, but I wouldn't—that governments would price the riskiest of assets at, in effect, zero return and completely throw what we thought of as the purpose of markets—being defined as the relationship between risk and return across the risk spectrum—throw that completely in a top hat and go on and have "administrative" markets. We can't seem to get out of it—and may not be able to get out of it. So, yes, I think you're quite right. You have to be suspicious of anything that becomes almost part of our daily lexicon and is used so much, and I'm suspicious of something like value investing, although certainly that's the kind of ratio analysis that Batterymarch did. It was essentially value investing in terms of simple things like book value, yield, and all the usual stuff. Yes, I'm a cynic about a future for that.

■ ■ ■

> You have to be suspicious of anything that becomes
> almost part of our daily lexicon and is used so much, and I'm
> suspicious of something like value investing, although certainly
> that's the kind of ratio analysis that Batterymarch did.

GEOFFREY GERBER: The Internet obviously has changed how investment work is performed and how it's conducted. As you've pointed out, it even makes location irrelevant, and it's enabled investors to become much more global without having to travel. Following up on Ed's question about value investing, will the old models of analysts who actually visit companies and talk to management in person go away completely?

DEAN LEBARON: It definitely won't, because some analysts will be good at reading body language—which you can't get on the computer—and making confirmed judgments about that. But, yes, the Internet has made the investment world flat. I thought it would make the investment world efficient. Jack Bogle[9] and I used to run around saying that there are going to be substantially fewer investment people in the world because of the use of machines. We've been wrong, and people have been very kind in not remembering our earlier forecast. I continue to make the same forecast, but that's because machines have been used more as a leveling device—that is, bringing more people into the market using machines—and because machines are being used as a sales tool rather than as they were first used, in effect, to replace the kind of analytical drudge work that people previously did with green eyeshades and John Magee paper.[10]

MEIR STATMAN: That brings us to a real puzzle as to the investment management industry. That is—knowing that the average alpha is, of course, zero and that costs are involved—how is it that we have such a large industry? What service does it provide?

DEAN LEBARON: It's very hard for any of us to phrase that question, because the answers are not very comforting. Several things happened in our industry that I think are particularly important. One is that the people who are receiving a service usually are not the ones who are paying for it, or at least paying directly. There are some exceptions in terms of individual investors and the like. However, since we're servicing institutional investors, the person who's receiving the service often is the ultimate beneficiary of an institutional account, and there may be several layers of agents in between. Your consultants are certainly among those. One of the jobs of a consultant—and I think most of them would agree, at least privately—is to provide employment insurance to people on trust committees and the like, because the trustees can then say, "I wasn't the one making that decision—it was XYZ consultant who did," and it's laying off blame and adding support to all consultants. That doesn't apply just to investment management. It's well understood that the function of any consultant is to give job security cover to the people who hire them.

The other thing that happens when you separate the receipt of the service from the payment is that costs tend to skyrocket. That happens in medical services, where the costs are paid for by insurance or by the government and the person receiving the service is the patient. Even the CFA [Chartered Financial Analysts] organization, of which many of us are part and enthusiasts, now has 130,000 members paying $500 a year in membership fees. But very few of those 130,000 actually pay the $500 themselves. Their firms pay it. None of us would have originally forecast that the organization would have achieved that particular size, or there certainly would have been pressure brought to reduce the fee rather than experiencing the pressure if they can't find enough services to spend the money. I don't think I'm telling any secrets.

EDWARD BAKER: Government and central bank policy and actions have dominated the markets in the past few years. One could almost think that we've shifted into a more top-down world than we used to have, when managers were so bottom-up in their approach. Do you think that's going to continue? Does that mark some kind of a seismic shift in the way the markets work?

DEAN LEBARON: I don't know. I'm not sure that I think that the markets have been so dominated by regulation and the like. There's been the appearance of that. I chaired an SEC [Securities and Exchange Commission] committee on corporate governance some thirty years ago, and I proposed at that time that you wanted to have as much trading as possible, including insider trading. That was because you wanted to have good price discovery, and you couldn't get good price discovery as long as you had some of the best-informed market participants being excluded from the market. That was like saying you could be a clunk and not well-informed, and that would still produce a good price. That was stupid in my opinion, but the idea that you would encourage insiders to trade by some means was offensive to many people. I'm a great fan of libertarianism,[11] but with disclosure, and I think sometimes we lock up the disclosure. For example, as we all know, there's a fair amount of lobbying going on in the United States. It's a big industry, and it's highly profitable. Some people would call that bribery, but it's a subtler form of bribery, and basically you don't see very much information about it. Take, for example, the story on national security leaks. That involved an employee of a private contractor, a defense-oriented firm with many government connections. That's an insider situation, and nobody asked the question about how much the NSA [National Security Agency] spends and whether it was included under the sequester program—which, of course, it was not. What I'm saying is that there's not as much disclosure as there should be in a fully regulated market. It's an administrative market, I agree, but much of the administration is just sort of an aside, just lip service. We're all familiar with the huge prospectuses that are written in the United States. Most of us tend not to read them and don't rely on them for investment information.

MARGARET TOWLE: It seems like what you're really talking about is accountability on the part of the advisor and the investment manager. To go back to an earlier comment that you made regarding trust committees relying on advisors, it's like the principal-agent problem. What do you think about recent trends in the industry toward fully discretionary accounts—what you might call the outsourced chief investment officer—where the advisor is a consultant who's actually assuming accountability as a co-fiduciary with institutional clients? It's great to have full disclosure, but if you don't have accountability, it's really not going to do much.

DEAN LEBARON: As nearly as I can tell, most of the people who have accountability also have directors' and officers' insurance to make sure that if they get stuck, they're not the ones who pay for it. If you have accountability where it's actually got some teeth in it, I think that's fine. I'm just not aware that it's taking place.

MICHAEL DIESCHBOURG: The issue of whether the market is a puzzle, or a mystery, really comes up in your complexity series and your thoughts along those lines. With the increased complexity and volatility surrounding our global markets and, as we've talked about, the changes going forward, do you see a wave of innovation to navigate through the financial markets' booms, busts, and bubbles by using a multi-lens framework? We've talked about the death of value and growth investing and the bottom-up approach. Do we need to be moving to our multi-lens framework that includes micro and macroeconomics, finance, physics, behavioral finance, the political aspect that we've talked about, even biological disciplines, to navigate these markets? Is that where you see the market going? Is it really more of a dynamic in action?

DEAN LEBARON: When I look at the divisions in some market portfolios, I'm amazed as to who's doing what. I mean, there are tiny little increments of great specialists and specialties. I like to stand a bit back from that, as I mentioned earlier in somewhat parenthetical expressions. I'd prefer, if I can, to find the questions that nobody's asking. I recently thought of an old letter that was written by our friend, the late Fischer Black,[12] who reputedly—and I think it's true—suggested that he would start an investment service. People would pay $5,000 a year for his service, and he was offering his first newsletter for free. His first issue said something along the lines of: "Since the markets are efficient, whatever portfolio you're holding is the right portfolio. Do not incur any transaction costs to make any changes whatsoever. Hold this portfolio forever. Please send $5,000 for a continued subscription if you would like me to repeat this advice to you every month." Needless to say, Fischer didn't get very many subscribers.

However, I think his advice is probably true in the sense that today, it's not so important what you own, but it's all in how you own it. Almost everyone who has a security of any form has it in the name of a custodian or trustee or in some name other than his or her own. Those of us who know or remember people who were around during the Depression know that people then didn't trust banks or the like; they didn't trust other people. They put their assets in their own mattresses or in gold bars in a Midas room, or whatever the case was. In any event, they held them in their own names. So it strikes me that one of the investment imperatives that we may run into as we come out of a Kondratieff wave is: "Who owns the assets? Do you own the assets, or is it an intermediary, such as a large financial services company (and what you really own is an unsecured obligation payable by that broker or bank)? Do you really want that type of company to be the holder of your assets, adding that to your other risks of investing?" Probably not. So I don't know. I've used that as an example of an investment strategy that, to me, is more meaningful than owning small-cap Asian stocks ex-Japan, or whatever the case may be. I mean, there are all these little small increments of specialty. On the other hand, I do agree with the implication of the question in the work being done on behavioral finance, bringing psychology into investment management. It's just going much slower than I expected.

■ ■ ■

> It's not so important what you own, but it's all in how you own it. Almost everyone who has a security of any form has it in the name of a custodian or trustee or in some name other than his or her own.

I will admit to one other of my many mistakes, and that is that I've always been interested in prediction markets.[13] The idea is that people can bet on an outcome, and they reveal their biases by placing their bets on certain outcomes. Most individuals have a higher degree of conviction about their anticipated outcomes than is warranted, except there's probably an insider somewhere who has the judgment or knowledge and who will reveal their convictions with money and make money out of prediction markets. That was fine, except the leading prediction market company turned out to have problems, and that didn't help. It's still alive, but it's sputtering. The idea is a good one.

MICHAEL DIESCHBOURG: So the follow-up for that would be, if you like complex theories—and you talked about that, the information that is in prediction markets—it seems that to be successful going forward, the next generation of wealth management from an advisor, consultant, or the investment management side needs to be almost a master of complexity in order to look at all of the different disciplines and be successful in navigating through. Is that what you're saying?

DEAN LEBARON: Right, a master of complexity—and ideally more holistic than a separate specialist. Now the world shouldn't have too many holistic managers. You can't have too many. However, if that approach happens to fit your psyche—and this goes back to my observation at the beginning of finding an investment strategy that fits you—you're more likely to succeed. If a market phase is not one that suits your own particular psyche, you're just out of luck. Don't try to adjust to it; go do something else.

MARGARET TOWLE: It seems like that's good advice for anyone, not just advisors.

DEAN LEBARON: Yes, I think that's probably true.

LUDWIG CHINCARINI: One of the complications right now for many people is what to do with their money. Gold seems to be going down. Inflation, not yet. Treasuries seem to be going up—I mean, yields are going up and Treasury prices are going down. China may be overvalued. What does one do at this point?

DEAN LEBARON: You're right that there's no place to hide. In the first place, you have to start out by saying, "My investment goal is to lose as little money as possible, not to make money." That's a tough resolution to make, and this does not win you clients. Secondly, you more or less have to ignore some of the current market. The advantage of gold is not so much that the Chinese and the Indians and so forth like it, but that you can own it conveniently in your own name. Banks have underground bins with your name on them that hold your gold. It's rather funny. I'm not sure what it means when Germany asks for its gold back from the United States, and the United States tells Germany that it will take seven years to deliver.[14] Somehow, the gold market is weird. I don't understand it. I think that some strange things are going on there, which would seem odd even to an experienced gold trader. The difference between physical gold prices and GLD—paper gold—also just makes me suspicious. In any event, I am not a gold bug, but I'm attracted to gold because it is an asset that you can hold conveniently in your own name. Similarly, unencumbered land would offer the same advantage.

■ ■ ■

In any event, I am not a gold bug, but I'm attracted to gold because it is an asset that you can hold conveniently in your own name. Similarly, unencumbered land would offer the same advantage.

A year or so ago, a company that prints currency came to my attention. It had no debt, and I thought, "My goodness, that, in my mind, is the ideal company investment." It seemed attractive, and it had never occurred to me as an asset niche. Needless to say, it doesn't account for much money as a category. But you're quite right. There are very few obvious places to hide. I am a fan of China, only because I think China is conceivably the country that is proving to the United States that we're not number one. I've been a fan of China ever since I was there twenty-five years ago, and it's the only country in which I own stock. Its government has the discipline. When they say they're going to shut down the economy in order to dampen inflation, they will shut down the economy. I don't believe the United States would do it, or could do it.

EDWARD BAKER: And should one hold government bonds now? For example, if you're an investment advisor and your client has a large allocation to U.S. Treasury bonds, what advice are you going to give them at this point? Are you going to sit there and let them passively watch interest rates rise?

DEAN LEBARON: I don't know. I am an investor, and the U.S. currency that I own, which is not much, is in the form of TIPS [Treasury inflation-protected securities]. So presumably, some of that's taken care of. Obviously, TIPS are doing well. Normally I would not own that, in the sense that the U.S. government market has been administered, and it hasn't been a free market for more than two years. I will admit also that I own some Brazilian real. In the case of the United States, we're benefiting from being, as somebody said, "the best-looking horse in the glue factory."[15]

MARGARET TOWLE: Just to shift gears slightly away from current strategy and outlook, let's go back to an earlier point you made about ethics and talk about what you said prior to the 2008 financial meltdown. Back then you really implicated financial analysts and independent directors, and you touched on that somewhat again today. I was wondering, now that we've been through a number of fiscal mismanagement and corporate scandals, do you still believe these two groups are the primary drivers in this conduct, or are there other influences?

DEAN LEBARON: I now think that financial analysts and independent directors are off the hook. It comes back to shareholders, and the first part, of course, is that institutional shareholders aren't real shareholders. I mean, they don't exercise their governance role at all, so they're not really very good shareholders. Individual shareholders are not sufficiently well-informed, so the corporations really function as unrestrained sources of power, and they're getting away with it. It's obvious when chief executives on the team are paid multiples—I forgot what the current multiple is, 100 to 200 times the average salary of an employee in that corporation[16]—that something is terribly, terribly amiss. I live in Switzerland a fair amount of time, and the Swiss blame all of this on the United States. They call it the American disease—corporations operating without any accountability. The Swiss banks, of course, also are completely guilty of the same thing. They're throwing stones at Americans when they shouldn't. But certainly Americans were the leaders in unbridled executive salaries, in unrestrained salaries for corporate leaders, which is probably the best illustration of this.

GEOFFREY GERBER: Looking ahead, you've always argued that being first is often best, sometimes even better than being lucky, but being first is best. Obviously, you were one of the early institutional investors in emerging markets. I know you've mentioned China already, sitting here today, in what area would you look for the next first?

DEAN LEBARON: You're absolutely right. First is best, and it's more fun. If you're wrong, people don't remember it because nobody else picked it up. If you're right, people will remember it and give you great applause and satisfaction. So I'm still of that same vein, and I've offered my best choice for that: It's not what assets you own, but how you own them that may be the best consideration today. In terms of location, I'm not sure it makes any difference. I'm a subscriber to the view that you should go where the Chinese are going. The Chinese have got the money. At the moment, the Chinese are investing large amounts of money in Middle Africa (Nigeria, Ghana, Kenya, and so forth), and that's probably not a bad thing to do. You can't invest much money that way. As an individual, you can, but as a large institution, you can't. Also, the Chinese are not investing in the United States, but they are investing in Canada and Mexico. That's probably very good. So, looking at North America as a whole, I would have Canadian and Mexican portfolios, and I probably wouldn't have very much in the United States. I think that's probably it. In addition, as I said, unencumbered land—a couple of large land-holding companies look really interesting. However, in general, this is probably not a time to be terribly cute with investments; it's a good time to be fairly sleepy. Maybe it's an excuse.

■ ■ ■

You're absolutely right. First is best, and it's more fun. If you're wrong, people don't remember it because nobody else picked it up. If you're right, people will remember it and give you great applause and satisfaction.

EDWARD BAKER: Do you think there's a role for hedge-fund-type investing? It seems like most of what you've alluded to has been long-only. But what about strategies that try to go on both sides of markets?

DEAN LEBARON: I always think that's terrific. I like it, and I've done it. It's hard to do psychologically— it doesn't make any sense. On the short side, there's unlimited loss, of course. Not so on the long side. However, most of the hedge funds I know don't run long/short portfolios. It's just a cover for how they treat the income. But, yes, if you've got the propensity and you can stand the heat of being short in a rising market, good, go to it. I must admit I've done it a few times, and I find it's not very good for my stomach.

EDWARD BAKER: But if you can trade multiple asset classes, obviously, you can effectively introduce hedging strategies.

DEAN LEBARON: Yes, you can, and it's a good idea if you've got the stomach for it. Most people don't, which is why it's not done except on a trading basis. However, on an investment basis—I'm trying to think of an investment example. I know a few people who have done and are continuously doing what you call investment shorts, by which I mean an indefinite time horizon on which they plan to be short on some asset. It's rare, but yes, it's probably a fairly good return. The fact that it's done mostly inside firms suggests that it's the kind of strategy that would produce a return of a couple hundred percent a year.

MICHAEL DIESCHBOURG: With all of your background in the different hard and soft sciences, what tools do you think we need today to capture the complexities of the marketplace? You did a great job on the client side. What tools do you think we need to build today to be successful going forward in the future as investors?

DEAN LEBARON: I would encourage people who are in investments to spend some time in another field for ten or fifteen years and then come back to investments, and vice versa. I've been amazed at the intensive specialization that we've gone through, and there tends to be more demand for specialization as we report in lines to other people. I'm holistic in approach, and I don't quite know how to put that into place. However, I remember looking for people who didn't have the traditional Harvard business school track, although that was the track that I had done. I look for people who are musicians or philosophers or otherwise. I think more of that would be better.

MEIR STATMAN: Can you say something about the current state of academic finance as you see it? You've been part of it, and surely you have been working alongside it. When you look at what has happened in the past decade in this area, what do you see, and where do you think we should go?

DEAN LEBARON: I'm not close enough to really comment on that very well. I'm asked to speak in an academic setting every once in a while, and I do. I'm always so impressed with the bright people around—and the bright questions—particularly the individuals who are continuing to be attracted to the United States from other countries. I keep saying that I think it's going to reverse and that there will be a flow from this country.

MEIR STATMAN: I'm actually not asking about academia generally or American universities, but rather the state of our knowledge of finance and the role of academics in finance in generating that knowledge.

DEAN LEBARON: It should be better. We should know more about finance and the markets than we really do. I'm amazed, and I have always been amazed, at how little we know. However, there's good research going on. Back in 1980, as a way of showing my appreciation to the academic world that helped shape Batterymarch's approach to investment management, we established a fellowship program to promote academic research in the fields of finance and investment. In fact, Meir Statman was a Batterymarch Fellow way back when. He did good work, and I'm a fan of promoting it. I think our research into finance is coming along fine, but I can't say how I would change it.

■ ■ ■

ENDNOTES

[1] Richard (Dick) F. Vancil (1931–1996), whose teaching career at the Harvard Business School spanned thirty-eight years, was a nationally recognized expert on accounting and considered an authority in the area of chief executive succession.

[2] Headquartered in Boston, Batterymarch Financial Management, Inc., was founded by Dean LeBaron in 1969. Since 1995, Batterymarch has been a wholly owned, independently managed subsidiary of Legg Mason, Inc., one of the world's largest investment management companies.

[3] Shark repellents are any measures undertaken by a corporation to discourage unwanted or hostile takeover attempts.

[4] The Soviet economist Nikolai Kondratieff (also Kondratiev) (1892–1938) was the first to suggest that industrial economies followed a cycle of change in prices and production. Kondratieff waves—also called super cycles, great surges, long waves, K-waves, or the long economic cycle—are described as regular, sinusoidal-like cycles in modern capitalist economies. Averaging approximately fifty years in length, the cycles consist of alternating periods of high sectoral growth and relatively slow growth.

[5] A "Kondratieff long-wave winter" is a reference to the four-season Kondratieff model favored by investment theorist Ian Gordon, in which spring represents moderate growth from a stock market and inflationary bottom, summer is characterized by accelerating growth and high inflation, autumn is typified by declining inflation and asset bubbles, and winter involves the collapse of asset bubbles.

[6] High-frequency trading (HFT) is the use of sophisticated technological tools and computer algorithms to trade securities in a rapid manner. HFT uses proprietary trading strategies carried out by computers to move in and out of positions in fractions of a second.

[7] Scalping, also often known as "front running," is the practice of purchasing a security for one's own account shortly before recommending that security for long-term investment and then selling the security at a profit upon the rise in the market price following the recommendation. The U.S. Supreme Court has ruled that scalping by an investment advisor is a fraud upon clients or prospects and is a violation of the Investment Advisers Act of 1940.

[8] Dark pools are trading platforms that allow traders to buy or sell large blocks of shares without the prices being revealed publicly until after trades are completed. Dark pools have been criticized for their lack of transparency and the potential for less-efficient pricing in traditional open stock exchanges.

[9] Jack Bogle (1929–) is the founder and former chief executive officer of The Vanguard Group. In 1975, Bogle established the Vanguard 500 Index Fund, the first index mutual fund available to individual investors.

[10] "John Magee paper" is so called in reference to John Magee (1901–1987), a stock market analyst and leading authority on technical analysis and classical charting. In 1948, Magee and Robert D. Edwards published *Technical Analysis of Stock Trends*, widely considered to be one of the seminal works on trend analysis and chart patterns.

[11] In general, libertarianism is a set of related political philosophies that uphold liberty as the highest political end. This includes an emphasis on individual liberty, political freedom, and freedom of association. The principal-agent problem, or agency dilemma, concerns the difficulties in motivating one party (the agent) to act in the best interests of another (the principal) rather than in the agent's own interests. A common example of this relationship is corporate management (agent) and shareholders (principal).

[12] Fischer Black (1938–1995) was an American economist associated with the University of Chicago, MIT Sloan School of Management, and Goldman Sachs. In 1973, Black and Myron Scholes (1941–) published their option-pricing formula, which became known as the Black-Scholes model. This model, which represented a major contribution to the efficiency of the options and stock markets, remains a widely used financial tool.

[13] Prediction markets (also known as predictive markets, information markets, decision markets, idea futures, event derivatives, or virtual markets) are speculative markets created for the purpose of making predictions. Current market prices can then be interpreted as predictions of the probability of the event or the expected value of the parameter.

[14] In January 2013, the Bundesbank, Germany's central bank, announced it would move 647 tons of gold—or 54,000 gold bars worth about $36 billion—to Frankfurt from central-bank vaults in the United States and France. This would bring the Bundesbank's holdings in its Frankfurt storehouse to 50 percent of its total gold assets, up from the current 31 percent. The Bundesbank, the second-largest gold holder in the world, said that part of its goal in the move was "to build trust and confidence domestically." According to the plan, Germany's gold repatriation will be completed by 2020. Questions have been raised as to why the transfer will take seven years to complete.

[15] "Best-looking horse in the glue factory" has been attributed to Erskine Bowles, the former co-chair of the National Commission on Fiscal Responsibility and Reform (2010).

[16] According to a Bloomberg report in April 2013, the average multiple of chief executive officer (CEO) compensation relative to the pay of rank-and-file workers across the companies in the Standard & Poor's 500 Index is 204, up 20 percent since 2009. This multiple was based on CEO pay for fiscal years ending in 2011 or 2012, as disclosed in the companies' most-recent filings, and U.S. government data on worker compensation by industry.

REFERENCES

Edwards, Robert D., and John Magee. 1948. *Technical Analysis of Stock Trends*. Springfield, MA: Stock Trend Service.

LeBaron, Dean. 2001. *Mao, Marx, and the Market: Capitalist Adventures in Russia and China*. Hoboken, NJ: John Wiley and Sons, Inc.

———. 2005. Our Role in Corporate Malfeasance. *Financial Analysts Journal* 61, no. 1 (January/February): 25–26.

———. 2010. *Why I'm Investing in China* (New Word City). http://www.newwordcity.com/books/investment/why-im-investing-in-china/.

LeBaron, Dean, and Romesh Vaitilingam. 2001. *Treasury of Investment Wisdom: 30 Great Investing Minds*. Hoboken, NJ: John Wiley and Sons, Inc.

LeBaron, Dean, Romesh Vaitilingam, and Marilyn Pitchford. 2002. *Book of Investment Quotations*. Hoboken, NJ: John Wiley and Sons, Inc.

Treynor, Jack L., and Dean LeBaron. 2004. Insider Trading: Two Comments. *Financial Analysts Journal* 60, no. 3 (May/June): 10–12.

This interview was published in its entirety in *Journal of Investment Consulting* 14, no. 2, 2013.

CHAPTER 6

MARTY LEIBOWITZ: WALL STREET'S BOND GURU

MARTIN L. LEIBOWITZ, PHD

Managing Director, Morgan Stanley; Vice Chairman and Chief Investment Officer, TIAA–CREF; Managing Director, Salomon Brothers; co-author, *Inside the Yield Book*, and more than 200 articles on financial and investment analysis topics.

Marty Leibowitz has a background in pure mathematics that is tempered by a practical point of view. Throughout his career, he has epitomized the perfect balance between the theoretical and the applied. He describes his position at Salomon Brothers—the firm Michael Lewis made famous in the book *Liar's Poker*—as that of the "house mathematician," and it was in that role that Leibowitz transformed Wall Street's understanding of the bond market. During 26 years at Salomon, he helped pioneer key market innovations such as zero coupon bonds, immunization, mortgage-backed securities, and dedicated portfolio theory. His book *Inside the Yield Book*, which he co-authored with Sidney Homer, has gone through twenty-one reprintings and remains a standard in the field.

■ ■ ■

MARGARET TOWLE: First of all, Dr. Leibowitz, we are pleased to have you as part of our Masters interview series. Our approach to this issue of the *Journal of Investment Consulting* differs slightly from our usual approach in that it focuses directly on a single topic—the pension crisis—and we know your expertise in the area of pension management will be very valuable. We admire your background and experience, which represent significant contributions to the industry. Perhaps you could tell us about the major factors that helped to shape your career. It would also be interesting to hear what you regard as your major achievement. In addition, we'd like to hear about your biggest learning opportunity or how you might have done things differently if you were able to go back and do them over.

MARTIN LEIBOWITZ: I had so many breaks, as I would call them, so many learning experiences. In fact, one thing that I really do believe—this is not just some kind of humble pie—but I think in some ways I've been in a continuing, maybe continuous, learning experience, and that goes way back. In the years at Salomon Brothers, I learned greatly from talking to clients. Clients have problems, and if you listen carefully—even if in some ways their problems are misstated, so to say—you can still learn something by paying attention to where they're coming from. I found that to be very useful. I discovered that if you could find ways of addressing the issues they had, it could be productive for them and for my work for Salomon. As I look back over the work we did, I can see that it was driven by either listening to what were the issues of the day or listening to clients' ideas. Actually, the whole issue of immunization was sparked by a client who realized that the corporate environment at the time—way back then—just begged for a solution that immunization could provide. By working with several corporate pension funds, that client had put together a few issues that were not totally obvious in context to anyone else: One, interest rates obviously were very high—this was back in the 1970s and early 1980s; two, corporations were at that point very much hurting for earnings, and their pension funds were a great drag; and three, accounting for pension liabilities was based on a rigid, super-conservative discount rate of typically 4 percent, a situation that was, one could argue, a little bit the opposite of what we have today. The only way to convince an actuary that a 4-percent discount rate was totally absurd was to actually do an immunization and show that pension liabilities, as stated by the actuaries, could be immunized on a cash-flow basis at a significantly lower asset value than the pro forma based upon their calculations. That was a win-win-win situation. The beneficiaries won because their pensions were more secure, the corporations won because they reaped the reward of knowing the reality of their pension liabilities rather than the much higher fiction, and—needless to say—the firm I worked for got some rewards as well. That was very gratifying and, I have to say, a particularly happy example of how these things happen. It was a solution that was actually brought to me because of some of the work we had done in bonds and bond duration, and it was thought that we could help make this process happen.

■ ■ ■

> Actually, the whole issue of immunization was sparked by a client who realized that the corporate environment at the time—way back then—just begged for a solution that immunization could provide.

MARGARET TOWLE: I think that's a great lesson for everyone in terms of looking at the needs of the client from a solution perspective, rather than just from the standpoint of the product that one is presenting.

MEIR STATMAN: That was a wonderful description of a win-win-win situation, but very often there is a win-lose relationship between Wall Street firms and pension funds. We know this from the scandals in Orange County, California,[1] where what was good for the providers of financial services did not serve the citizens well. More recently, there was the Bank of New York story,[2] where it seems that fees that were good for the bank's traders in currency were not good for pension funds. My own sense is that Wall Street companies flatter the staff of pension funds, making them feel more sophisticated than they really are, and then take advantage of them and the beneficiaries. I hope that's not too harsh. Could you comment on that?

■ ■ ■

That was a wonderful description of a win-win-win situation, but very often there is a win-lose relationship between Wall Street firms and pension funds.

MARTIN LEIBOWITZ: Let me make a couple of points. Certainly these days I think the larger pension funds are every bit as sophisticated as corporate plans. In fact, not only are they sophisticated, but they have so many more tools available to level the playing field, the buy side and the sell side. Now, having said that, what you describe actually does happen, no question about it. There's no defending it, and it's totally wrong. However, I think the broader issue is that any service provider—Wall Street or otherwise—that does not find a middle point where both the provider and the receiver get a reasonable degree of benefit—and frankly the receiver should get the most benefit out of any sort of interaction—is doomed to not remain in business for very long or to pay a very hefty price in reputation and otherwise. So I think there is a natural check, and that over the years, on balance, most of the successful firms have found that middle point—not that there aren't incidents along the line such as you just described. They are sad and tragic and just should not happen.

MARK ANSON: My own perspective from having managed pension funds[3] is that while the situation Meir described might have been the case a decade ago, as you know and are well aware, the large investment banks and brokerage firms now have pension consulting services in-house because they recognize that, yes, there can be a short-term gain from taking advantage of a pension fund, but it's not in the long-term interest of the business. So there's been greater education as a result, and the consultants have helped too. They're far more sophisticated today than they were ten years ago, when a consultant didn't really have the same level of understanding or expertise as an outside brokerage firm or investment bank. So I do think the playing field has been leveled.

I'd like to suggest that we take a step back before we get to the more detailed questions and talk a little more about your background, Dr. Leibowitz. Ed brought up a question that I'd like to pose to you because it talks about your background and then brings it forward as it relates to pension funds. As Margaret mentioned earlier, this issue is dedicated to pension funds, not only in the United States but also globally, in emerging as well as developed markets. Ed noted that you were extremely well-known in the fixed income industry at Salomon Brothers. That's where you built your early career, and it was one of the huge stepping stones for you. At the time you were at Salomon managing the fixed income floor, did you have any sense that the world of fixed income would become as complex as it is today? Furthermore, how has the world of fixed income changed for pension funds since those early days?

MARTIN LEIBOWITZ: Let's take the first part first. Simply put, the question is did I have any idea where we were going with the complexity of fixed income? The simple answer is no. No one could have imagined that. In fact, I remember fairly vividly when we first started getting into mortgage securities. It seemed very, very complex. Forget about things like collateralized waterfalls[4]—I mean just straight, simple Ginnie Maes.[5] There was great discussion as to what we should use as the average life. The position then, if I recall, was using a yield to a twelve-year average life, as if everything would be paid off at that point. It seemed complex to try to work out those expected prepayment schedules, which were a long way from doing prepayments by zip code and the whole bit with rating the securities and the waterfalls and the various zeros and PO (principal-only) and IO (interest-only) securities. Everything was a step-by-step process, and we went from one thing into the next into the next. In the early days before we had started moving in that direction, it was very far from anyone's thoughts. I think even the people who developed these instruments—the Lew Ranieris[6] and Larry Finks[7] of the world—I think they too were in a step-by-step process as they went up this ladder of ever greater complexity. So that's the simple answer to question number one.

Let's turn to question number two: What is the role of fixed income in pension funds today? In some ways, things have come relatively full circle. Well, it depends on how far back you go. In the very old days, there were many state funds that had charter limits that allowed only fixed income, and high-grade fixed income, as their asset investment. Basically these were investments where you were trying to earn a return, earn a yield in a very safe way. Durations were typically reflective of the intermediate duration that was the market average at the time, although that could be all over the place. Fixed income was basically used as the ultimate in safety. As we started to progress into stock and bond portfolios, the bonds were the safety part of the portfolio, the liquid part of the portfolio, and the secure yielding and cash throw-off part. However, the bonds weren't necessarily scheduled to specific liabilities. Then, as we moved into the immunization era that we just talked about, that's when bonds started taking on, at least to some degree in some funds, that special role of directly servicing the liabilities. Of course, ideally the whole pension fund services the liabilities in an indirect fashion. However, here we're talking about directly servicing the liabilities, either in terms of throwing off the cash necessary to pay the liabilities or of having a duration management strategy that would be some form of immunization that enables that particular immunizing component of the fixed income allocation to provide a flow of money as needed and still come out whole. What's transpired over the years is that fixed income has played multiple roles. Of course, it's moved in some cases to more complex investments with— let's hope—higher yields or better return-risk relationships, although as you pointed out earlier, it doesn't always prove to be the case. In some instances, matters were overdone on the risk side. However, you still have immunization coming back into the fore as the defeasance for different sets of reasons now. In some ways, aside from the nature of the instruments, which certainly comprise a much wider keyboard these days, we are servicing the same basic functions: one, certain types of defeasance functions, two—maybe simultaneously—certain types of volatility-reducing functions, and three, provision of a relatively secure source of return. And one other thing: Fixed income is sometimes viewed as a hedge against disastrous equity markets.

■ ■ ■

In some ways, aside from the nature of the instruments, which certainly comprise a much wider keyboard these days, we are servicing the same basic functions: one, certain types of defeasance functions, two—maybe simultaneously— certain types of volatility-reducing functions, and three, provision of a relatively secure source of return.

MARK ANSON: I know you've done some great analysis, including that for CalPERS (California Public Employees' Retirement System), that showed up to 90 percent of the risk exposure of an average institutional pension fund can come from equity beta. The first part of my question is whether a pension fund should maintain or reduce its equity beta exposure. At the same time, most of the public plans in the United States are significantly underfunded so, as a secondary question, do you think that pension funds should turn to a more aggressive asset allocation to try to "earn their way out" of their underfunded status?

MARTIN LEIBOWITZ: That is a real conundrum, and you can argue both sides of it. One of my favorite charts shows that when you're in the middling range of funding ratios and assuming you have sufficiently strong sponsorship, as your funding ratio goes up, you're in a position to be able to take more risk and—if you think the returns can be there—you perhaps should take some more risk up to a certain point, at which it caps out. If things get good enough, then you might want to say: "Well, look, why should I take any more risk? I might as well just defease the whole thing, put it to bed, not worry, and go on to other things." You can reach a point at which you peak off and flatten out your risk or, if you're in sufficiently good shape, you may actually choose to take your risk totally down and say that you are out of the game. You see this with individuals. There are individuals who reach a certain point where they feel they don't have to take any more risk, and they'd rather have their focus on other things. So they just buy an annuity with their basic financial resources. This sometimes comes out of largesse, aside from all of the other reasons an annuity purchase makes sense for individuals. Going in the other direction, when you find yourself in a deficit situation, there is certainly a logic that would say, "Hey, look, when we get down to a seriously low deficit position, we can't afford to take risks, and that's when we should derisk the portfolio the best way we can." Of course, one could argue what derisk means. On the other hand, you can take the position that you're in the soup, and you should really do your best to, as you say, try to earn your way out of it.

You see all forms of this behavior. I like to put it in the context of an individual approaching retirement. What should you do if you find yourself in a position where you're close to retirement or you're in retirement, and your assets get below the level you really need to survive on? You probably should not take any more risk at that point—unless that isn't the whole story. Suppose you had an uncle or a parent or a trust fund that you knew you could call upon to supplement your assets, if that became necessary. In which case, that is not the whole story, and you really do have more resources available. As you know, there are huge arguments that flare back and forth about taking any kind of equity risk in a pension fund environment. For the purists among us, including some of my co-authors and friends and people whom I respect greatly, they would say that there is no reason—certainly for corporate pension funds—to take any kind of equity risk whatsoever. To my mind, that's far too extreme, but I think there are certainly situations that call for basically putting yourself in a derisked position.

MARK ANSON: As we talked about earlier, you were a pioneer in immunization, or rather in what was then called immunization and today is called liability-driven investing. Different nomenclature, same idea. If you go back a decade or so to the late 1990s, when I was coming on board at CalPERS, the funding ratio for most public plans and certainly for corporate plans was quite high. In fact, it was close to 100 percent. Did we miss an opportunity to immunize at that point? Did we end up squandering that funding ratio and, if so, what is our path moving forward, for both corporate and public plans?

MARTIN LEIBOWITZ: Let's recognize, and you can check me on this, but it seems to me that if you freeze your plan and you're still in a live plan, you may find yourself not earning at the level of interest that you need for the emerging liabilities that are coming down the pike. You could find yourselves drifting down, even if you froze the plan at 100 percent, because new liabilities are always coming up. If it turns out that interest rates and earning rates decline in terms of any new investments of new contributions, the 100 percent could come unwound to some extent.

EDWARD BAKER: I wonder also, in this world, where credit risk is beginning to have a different look and feel to it, as we're seeing in Europe and even in the United States, if that doesn't raise some eyebrows at the use of bonds for these immunization strategies. It certainly introduces some new uncertainty about outcomes.

MARTIN LEIBOWITZ: That's a fair point. In fact, I think some of the situations that were cited earlier really had to do with deteriorating credits that were being used for pro forma defeasance. That's actually substituting one kind of risk for another and not fully derisking. The issue is having a sufficient level of quality to be able to have high assurance, in a portfolio context, of servicing those liabilities. If it turns out that one or two credits deteriorate as part of a portfolio, it's not the end of the world, but as we saw there can be instances and environments where entire swaths of credit securities undergo serious spread widening and come into question in terms of their viability—and entire governments, too.

EDWARD BAKER: It's certainly a brave new world.

MEIR STATMAN: You started our discussion with a great story about clients who ask questions that lead to creative answers. I know you've been working mainly with institutional investors. Some of the readers of this interview are advisors to institutional clients, and others advise individual investors. Can you comment on the frustrations that come when people like you try to educate clients, whether individual or institutional?

MARTIN LEIBOWITZ: I have a couple of things to say about that, but I don't claim to have any special expertise in this area. I find it very helpful when considering problems to use a way of thinking that I alluded to earlier, and that is to deinstitutionalize the framework. What would it be like for an individual facing this situation? What would be his or her parameters of actions? I find that brings it down from the airy institutional heights to a more concrete way of thinking. That's just a kind of mental framework for me. In terms of actually trying to advise individuals, let me just say that I think advising individuals is much more complex than advising institutions. This is due to the fact that the very specific situations that pertain to individual circumstances are far more complex. They involve other types of ingredients such as life events, contingency events, taxes, estate taxes, and so forth. There are also many more complicating factors, not the least of which is that you're dealing with not single but multiple objectives almost all of the time, and you're dealing with objectives that shift in priority with asset level. It's a very complex model to develop the right kind of way to look at an individual's overall asset allocation.

MARK ANSON: You wrote a great paper about alpha hunters and beta grazers, in which you talked about the pure alpha hunters and how hedge funds are a demonstration of that. However, I think the market has come to understand that hedge funds are some combination of beta grazer and alpha hunter. Do you see a role for hedge funds within a pension fund portfolio allocation, and how would you view that role right now if you were looking at an underfunded pension plan?

MARTIN LEIBOWITZ: Let me take the first part of your question. Hedge funds have, in aggregate and certainly in some segments, done very well in terms of producing viable alphas, not just beta rides, but alphas of some significance. They can do this also with relatively modest betas. What I think is important and all too often not well done is that people distinguish the returns that hedge funds generate between what they could have gotten from just riding a beta wave and that which is really the alpha, above and beyond that. People should make this distinction for the obvious reason, namely, that it can be much cheaper to ride a beta wave, and you shouldn't have to pay the fees for the benefits that come out of that, the kinds of fees that hedge funds typically charge. You're in there for the alpha. We've all seen that the hedge funds, as the ultimate in flexible investing entities, have managed, for various reasons and in various ways, to carve out some real alphas if you do the right kind of analysis. That answer says yes, this can be a way of getting alphas that are valuable, and they can be particularly valuable if one is trying to get a reduced beta and at the same time have the opportunity to generate some alphas. Having said that, you know that the alphas are not automatic, not every hedge fund produces them, and occasionally some hedge funds have had really horrendous blowups. Also, there are many more hedge funds chasing after the pie of opportunities that exist, although that pie itself may be expanding somewhat. This is not just like shooting fish in a barrel. One has to be careful in terms of both selection and monitoring.

MEIR STATMAN: One of the articles planned for this pension issue of the *Journal* is from Estonia, where they have a mandatory defined contribution plan to which both employees and employers must contribute. This is part of their "three pillar" system. One pillar is the equivalent of our Social Security system, another is a mandatory equivalent to our voluntary 401(k) system, and the third is personal savings. Would you comment on that? Does that seem like a good policy that we might adopt?

MARTIN LEIBOWITZ: It certainly is a policy worth thinking about, especially if it has a sufficiently high contribution rate. The defined contribution plan has its virtues, although I think there are ways of tweaking it so it can be improved. The key factor in just about any defined contribution plan is to get the contributions high enough and create an environment or system such that the contributions can go on long enough. I'm not familiar with the Estonian plan, of course, but it sounds like it has at least two of those ingredients. The three-pillar system goes back to a 1994 report written by Estelle James, an economist at the World Bank. Part of her analysis played off the Chilean system, which I think had just recently been instituted at that time. While that system had its problems, it had some of those characteristics as well.

MEIR STATMAN: I think that the difference is that the first pillar in the Estonian system is the equivalent of our Social Security so that you cannot take your Social Security money and put it into risky assets. I believe the Chilean system allows more risk-taking, and some people who are given a chance to risk their money manage to lose it.

MARTIN LEIBOWITZ: I also think the fees in the Chilean plan were rather excessive in the early years. My understanding is that they have resolved a lot of those issues. I believe Australia also has superannuation trusts based on the three-pillar approach. I was surprised to see a recent Towers Watson report (2011) that said about 40 percent of all pension liabilities worldwide have some defined contribution characteristic. That's growing very rapidly. By the way, do you have any idea of the magnitude of defined contribution plans in the United States at this point? Let's say that defined benefit plans are roughly $3 trillion and that corporate plans are about $2.5 trillion. So that's $5.5 trillion in defined benefit plans. How about $8.5 trillion in defined contribution plans?

MARK ANSON: That's certainly more than I would have guessed.

MARTIN LEIBOWITZ: Yes, it's more than I would have guessed too, and it's more than you'll see in the usual statistics for the following reason: The usual statistics give you the 401(k) plans and the analogs of defined contribution plans, but they don't give you the IRAs (individual retirement accounts), and the IRAs are the fastest growing area of defined contribution, not because of individual contributions, but because of rollovers from former corporate plans. That number is just mind-boggling, and it has all kinds of interesting implications for what is a massive coherent pile of assets in terms of their market behavior. For example, extrapolating from what we saw at TIAA–CREF, we know that institutional investors rebalance their plans fairly routinely in one way or another, either by having outside limits or on a periodic basis or some combination of the two. Individuals, for the most part, don't rebalance over short-term periods. They basically take the allocation that the market gives them. Over the long term, they will rebalance and—amazingly—seem to come back into the 60-percent equity/40-percent bond alignment, as if it's an act of nature in some strange way. However, over near and intermediate terms, they don't rebalance. In addition, they tend to rebalance with their cash flows rather than with an asset revision decision. At TIAA–CREF, participants could change their fixed income/equity allocations daily on existing assets in their 403(b) plans, but they didn't. Instead, if the market pushed equities down, participants would basically do nothing with their actual allocation, but they would change the allocation on their new flows and put more into equities, not immediately but over the course of time, and eventually bring it back up to the 60/40 level. So there's very different behavior between defined benefit and defined contribution plans, and the defined contribution plans are getting so large that it's worth taking note of the implications of that.

■ ■ ■

The usual statistics give you the 401(k) plans and the analogs of defined contribution plans, but they don't give you the IRAs (individual retirement accounts), and the IRAs are the fastest growing area of defined contribution, not because of individual contributions, but because of rollovers from former corporate plans.

EDWARD BAKER: What about the endowments and foundations? Are you observing any changes in behavior there, given the recent past?

MARTIN LEIBOWITZ: Well, yes, those plans have certainly paid a lot more attention to liquidity and contingency planning for liquidity. They have been much more careful in their commitment strategies for illiquid private equity investments. It's not as if they're not investing; they're just trying to be much more careful about the risks of overshooting their target allocations in a bad market.

EDWARD BAKER: But you think the allocation toward those sorts of assets is still high and should still be high?

MARTIN LEIBOWITZ: It depends. There's a big difference between the larger funds and the smaller ones. There's more of a focus on maintaining liquidity, not just for servicing those liabilities, but also for being able to take advantage of what may be dislocations in the market. It was frustrating in the depths of 2008 and early 2009 to know that there were some wonderful opportunities around, but you just didn't have the liquidity to even begin thinking about it. I think there's a general feeling that well-chosen private equity investments will provide a premium over time that can justify their illiquidity. Of course, if you can't afford the illiquidity, there's no premium that's worthwhile, but if you can, if you can earn a significant extra premium by the greater degrees of freedom that a private equity fund can give you, it's worth pursuing. Again, all of these things change over time. One has to be cautious not just about how individual managers change in terms of their business models as they become larger and larger, but about how the overall market changes. To answer your question, I think there's been relatively little change in the allocation assigned to illiquid investments. Maybe the advancing of it has slowed down a bit, but I think very few people have pared down that allocation significantly.

MARK ANSON: I'd like to ask you a question about the debate over the appropriate rate at which to discount liabilities in a pension plan. In corporate plans, they use a AA discount rate, but for public pension plans, there's a huge debate over using everything ranging from the yield on a long-term Treasury bond to a taxable municipal bond rate to the actuarial rate that pension funds currently use. It would be interesting to get your views for a public pension plan, keeping in mind that if we were using ten-year or thirty-year Treasury bonds right now with yields at 2–3 percent, that's a very low discount rate on liabilities.

MARTIN LEIBOWITZ: As you know, this argument has had people swaying back and forth in a theoretical sense and obviously in a very politicized sense. One of the things that concerns me is what do you use your liability calculation for? What does it really mean? What it's intended to mean is that this is the amount of money you have to set aside to fully fund at least those specified existing liabilities or future liabilities that are specified, given an investment in the corresponding instrument that gives you that yield. Essentially it's a kind of a notional defeasance. That's pretty harsh. That means you're taking all of the risk out of the game except for the inflation risk, which is what the beneficiaries suffer. By the way, it's worth noting that the United States is perhaps the only country, or certainly one of the very few, where most liabilities are denominated in nominal terms for the most part. I know there are certain COLAs (cost of living adjustments) in the public area, but relatively few in the private area. It seems to me that people think of the liability calculation as a notional construct of the amount needed to put the plan to bed. As we were talking earlier, would anyone put the plan to bed in a 2-percent interest-rate environment? I guess if you had a gun to your head, you might have to. There was a circumstance in the United Kingdom in late 2005 and early 2006 where British corporate pension funds were under pressure to derisk because their liabilities were real liabilities—that is, inflation-adjusted liabilities—and to do so by buying U.K. linkers.[8] These were fifty-year, inflation-adjusted bonds, and the forced buying by some funds drove the real yield on those bonds down to virtually zero, creating distortions in the British government bond market. It was clearly a very artificially sudden move, which then reversed soon after the plans did what they felt was the forced buying.

MARK ANSON: I had been in the United Kingdom a month at the time that happened, and it was a feeding frenzy. The more you pushed the rate down, the more inflated your liabilities became, and the more you needed to buy those bonds. It was a vicious circle, a vicious spiral downward.

MARTIN LEIBOWITZ: And something that made no sense at all. It was really counter-productive. That was an example of a lose-lose-lose situation. So the question we're trying to answer here is what is the appropriate rate to use to discount pension liabilities? My inclination would be to say that it certainly should be some kind of market rate, because we've seen what actuarial rates can do. What you want to do is use this rate to get a sense of reality, but don't take it as necessarily the ultimate call to action, because it's not necessarily what you're going to do. To the extent that a fund has liabilities that stretch out over a span of time and are not absolutely immediate, the fund is in a position to be able to take some degree of risk. To the extent that the fund has a sponsor with a willingness, let's say the extremis, to back up the plan, assuming that the prospect of returns can also benefit that sponsor so that there is a kind of return-risk sharing, that is, both return sharing and risk sharing, then the plan may be able to take some greater degree of risk. What you're really looking for is a gauge of the level of liabilities. You don't want to take it as gospel that automatically dictates what the asset structure should be. Unfortunately, that's where a lot of the disconnect seems to take place. You shouldn't use Treasury rates, not when they're at 2 percent, that's for sure. You certainly should use a market rate, but you shouldn't use a rate that is highly vulnerable to credit risk. The corporate construct may be a reasonable kind of compromise.

MARK ANSON: I have one final question that I think it's important to ask. There's this phrase: "the new normal." PIMCO (Pacific Investment Management Company) has been great at marketing that they created that phrase and that they know how to manage to it. The "new normal" essentially means that we're in for a prolonged period of slower economic growth rates, real GDP (gross domestic product) growth, not only in the United States, but globally; that we're in for a prolonged period of low interest rates; and that double-digit equity market returns should no longer be expected, that we're instead more in the area of maybe 8–10 percent total returns. With that in mind, what key suggestions would you have for the chief investment officer of a pension plan or for individuals managing their own portfolios? Do you in fact agree with the new normal? I guess that comes back to a broader question: What trends do you see in the market right now?

■ ■ ■

> So I think we are indeed going into a new world with different kinds of deflationary pressures in terms of sourcing cheaper labor abroad, but also more inflationary pressures in terms of demand for what may become scarce resources in this new evolution.

MARTIN LEIBOWITZ: I think that the phrase "the new normal" is a very useful way of clarifying that the world going forward may well be significantly different from the experiences and the return patterns we've had in the past. That's clear on a lot of fronts. Emerging countries are growing in a way that is going to transform the globe—there's no two ways about that. In many ways, that's very positive. First, in humanitarian terms, that's unbelievably beneficial; the welfare of the world has increased enormously. Second, on an economic basis, we're creating huge new markets for all kinds of products and services, many of which will be serviced by the emerging markets themselves, which is as it should be. However, it also creates opportunities for developed countries to grow new markets for new products as well. So I think we are indeed going into a new world with different kinds of deflationary pressures in terms of sourcing cheaper labor abroad, but also more inflationary pressures in terms of demand for what may become scarce resources in this new evolution.

So, yes, I think "the new normal" phrase is a good one, the game is changed, and to quote Rogoff and Reinhart (2009)—although this is a dangerous phrase—this time is different, that is for real, and things will be different going forward. Having said that, Rogoff and Reinhart's particular version of the new normal is a fairly dismal view of the future. For better or worse, I think the future is a lot more complex and unknowable than the view that we are going into a dismal decade or two in this country. I'd like to be more hopeful than that. Economies and countries and people tend to have a lot more resilience than you can almost intellectualize. I forget who said it, but I think there is great wisdom in the phrase: It's easy to think of all the things that can go wrong and put yourself into a depressed state on that basis, but the fact of the matter is that many of the things that go right are not so easily envisioned. They come out of some surprise or some subterranean or subliminal process. There's another great anecdote that I'll cite: A French count of the last century said that an individual who, as he contemplates a course of action, thinks what may be the outcome of each of the scenarios that could develop in response to his actions and then thinks for each such outcome what would be the subsequent actions he might take and what those outcomes might be—well, such an individual will make very few mistakes. But then the count goes on to add—and I'm sure it sounds even better in French—"But he will accomplish very little."

MEIR STATMAN: That's a good point. As far as resilience, I think people underestimate their own resilience, let alone the resilience of the system altogether.

MARTIN LEIBOWITZ: And I think that time is a healer in many ways. Just consider the statistic I saw that says the average car in the United States has about 120,000 miles on it, some big number.[9] I just can't believe that residual demand builds up over time and with family formation and so on. There is that kind of healing process from time alone as we consume some of the items we have, and the less elastic demand becomes in various areas. So I do believe in the new normal, but I don't believe we should be too convinced that we know what form it's going to take.

MARK ANSON: I wish we could predict it. Unfortunately, my crystal ball doesn't come in high definition.

MARGARET TOWLE: This has been a most useful discussion. Just one last question: Is there any area that we didn't cover or any trend or development that you think is especially significant that you'd like to comment on?

MARTIN LEIBOWITZ: I think you touched on virtually all of the areas that are on peoples' minds today. There is one issue that I think that deserves more discussion than it gets, and that is the whole issue of inflation in retirement. We mentioned that briefly. Just one quick comment: Even a low level of inflation, even a new normal level of inflation, over the span of the twenty to thirty years that people today can have a reasonable expectation of spending in retirement, can be devastating for what looked like an otherwise nominally comfortable level of payoff. I think that issue is not very well reflected in financial discussions in this country.

■ ■ ■

Even a low level of inflation, even a new normal level of inflation, over the span of the twenty to thirty years that people today can have a reasonable expectation of spending in retirement, can be devastating for what looked like an otherwise nominally comfortable level of payoff. I think that issue is not very well reflected in financial discussions in this country.

MARGARET TOWLE: I would agree completely. It's an area that needs to be addressed explicitly. I think we have been lulled into a sense of comfort because of the most recent experience in terms of inflation.

MARTIN LEIBOWITZ: That's right. Do you know the one retirement instrument that has been generally reasonably attuned to inflation in the past? It's Social Security. I'm not going to get into where that's going to go in the future, but it's been really beneficial for a lot of people in many regards, not the least of which is keeping up with inflation. Do you want to have fun? Try calculating, again assuming that all goes well, the value of that stream of payments in present value terms for a typical individual. That's a liability for the government, but it's a huge asset for individuals. Anyway, I'd just like to close by saying that it's been a pleasure to talk to you all.

■ ■ ■

ENDNOTES

[1]   In December 1994, Orange County, California, became the largest U.S. municipal entity to declare bankruptcy when the county lost approximately $1.7 billion in one of its principal investment portfolios. (This record stood until November 2011, when Jefferson County, Alabama, declared bankruptcy on $4 billion of debt.) Orange County's portfolio, which was intended to be conservatively invested in short-term vehicles as a way to manage the county's cash flows, had been invested in riskier securities such as reverse purchase agreements, collateralized mortgage obligations, and derivatives linked to the interest-rate yield curve. As the Federal Reserve began a series of interest rate increases in early 1994, the portfolio's valuation declined sharply, leading to the need to file for bankruptcy. In 1998, Orange County reached a settlement agreement with Merrill Lynch, the firm it held most responsible for steering the portfolio to riskier investments, as well as with other brokerage, law, and accountant firms.

[2]   In October 2011, the U.S. Department of Justice and the New York State attorney general filed civil lawsuits against the Bank of New York Mellon alleging foreign currency fraud over the past decade. The suits hold that the bank allegedly manipulated prices on foreign currency transactions on behalf of pension fund clients to the benefit of the bank. The Bank of New York has defended itself against the charges, maintaining that the fraud charges are false and that the accusations were based on flawed analysis of its role as a principal in the foreign exchange market. New York's action followed similar investigations by authorities in California, Florida, Massachusetts, North Carolina, Ohio, and Virginia, which are examining the bank's foreign exchange practices that may have affected their pension and other investment funds.

[3]   Mark Anson joined the California Public Employees' Retirement System (CalPERS) as senior investment officer in 1999 and served as chief investment officer from 2001 to 2005. He also was chief executive officer of Hermes Pensions Management and the BT (British Telecom) pension scheme from 2005 to 2007.

4   A "waterfall" refers to the sequential structure of monthly payments on a pool of mortgage-backed securities. On a monthly basis, the principal and interest received from all of the pooled loans is paid to the holders of bonds issued by the trust that maintains the pooled mortgage-backed securities, starting with those investors holding the most highly rated bonds. Then payments are made to the holders of the next highest rated bonds, and so forth.

5   Ginnie Maes (GNMA, or Government National Mortgage Association) are mortgage-backed securities issued by government-approved issuers that participate in the Ginnie Mae program. These securities are guaranteed by the Government National Mortgage Association, a wholly owned government corporation within the U.S. Department of Housing and Urban Development.

6   Lewis S. Ranieri (1947–) helped to pioneer the areas of securitization and mortgage-backed securities while working on the mortgage trading desk at Salomon Brothers in the late 1970s. Ranieri also worked to develop the capital markets as a source of funds for housing and commercial real estate and led efforts to enact federal legislation.

7   Laurence D. Fink (1952–), currently the chairman and chief executive officer of BlackRock, was instrumental in the creation and development of the U.S. mortgage-backed securities market while working at First Boston in the 1970s.

8   Inflation-indexed bonds, also known as inflation-linked bonds or linkers, are securities in which the principal is indexed to inflation, with the goal of minimizing the inflation risk of the credits.

9   According to a report from the U.S. Department of Transportation, the average life span of a vehicle in the United States is twelve years, or about 128,500 miles (MSN Money, March 22, 2010).

REFERENCES

Homer, Sidney, and Martin L. Leibowitz. 1972. *Inside the Yield Book: New Tools for Bond Market Strategy*. Englewood Cliffs, NJ: Prentice Hall.

Leibowitz, Martin L. 1992. *Investing*. Chicago: Probus Publishing Company.

———. 2004. *Franchise Value: A Modern Approach to Security Analysis*. Hoboken, NJ: John Wiley & Sons, Inc.

———. 2005. Alpha Hunters and Beta Grazers. *Financial Analysts Journal* 61, no. 5 (September/October): 32–39.

Leibowitz, Martin L., Stanley Kogelman, and Lawrence N. Bader. 1996. *Return Targets and Shortfall Risks: Studies in Asset Allocation*. Chicago, IL: Irwin Professional Publishing.

Leibowitz, Martin L., Simon Emrich, and Anthony Bova. 2008. *Modern Portfolio Management*. Hoboken, NJ: John Wiley & Sons, Inc.

Leibowitz, Martin L., Anthony Bova, and P. Brett Hammond. 2010. *The Endowment Model of Investing: Return, Risk, and Diversification*. Hoboken, NJ: John Wiley & Sons, Inc.

Reinhart, Carmen M., and Kenneth S. Rogoff. 2009. *This Time Is Different: Eight Centuries of Financial Folly*. Princeton, NJ: Princeton University Press.

Towers Watson. 2011. *Global Pension Asset Study* (February). http://www.towerswatson.com/assets/pdf/3761/Global-Pensions-Asset-Study-2011.pdf.

World Bank. 1994. *Averting the Old Age Crisis: Policies to Protect the Old and Promote Growth. A World Bank Policy Research Report*. Washington DC: Oxford University Press.

This interview was published in its entirety in *Journal of Investment Consulting* 12, no. 2, 2011.

CHAPTER 7

BOB LITTERMAN: STELLAR QUANT

ROBERT B. LITTERMAN, PHD

Robert Litterman spent most of his career at Goldman Sachs in investment, risk management, and thought leadership roles. During his tenure at Goldman, Dr. Litterman researched and published a number of groundbreaking papers in asset allocation and risk management. He is the co-developer of the Black-Litterman Global Asset Allocation Model, a key tool in the investment management division, and has co-authored books including *The Practice of Risk Management* (1998) and *Modern Investment Management: An Equilibrium Approach (*2003). Today, Dr. Litterman serves as senior partner and chairman of the risk committee at Kepos Capital LP, a global macro investment management firm based in New York.

Bob Litterman possesses a diverse academic and practical background: He earned a bachelor's degree in human biology from Stanford University and a doctorate in economics from the University of Minnesota, and he worked for a short stint as a journalist. He created an exceptionally successful career at Goldman Sachs and is currently a partner at the innovative New York-based hedge fund Kepos. Among his many accomplishments at Goldman, Litterman collaborated with Fischer Black to develop the Black-Litterman global asset allocation model, a reformulation of the standard asset allocation model, which allows investors to adjust equilibrium market returns by incorporating their own views on returns. Using an investor's return input, the model then generates an optimal portfolio adjusted for the investor's risk tolerance.

■ ■ ■

MARGARET TOWLE: Before we delve into your professional career, please share with us a bit of personal history, such as where you grew up and individuals you encountered early in your life who had a profound influence on you. We'd like to gain an understanding of the origins of your career.

ROBERT LITTERMAN: I grew up in Arizona. My undergraduate school was Stanford University, where I was a human biology major. My first job was as a journalist, and I decided that I wanted to specialize in economics. I earned my PhD in economics from the University of Minnesota. Then I taught for two years as an assistant professor of economics at the Massachusetts Institute of Technology (MIT) before I decided to go back to Minneapolis, to the Federal Reserve Bank there, where I worked for five years. It was during that time that I also became involved in a software venture, VAR Econometrics. We had one product, a regression program called RATS, or regression analysis of time series.

In 1986, I received a call from Goldman Sachs inviting me to come to Wall Street. I spent the next 23 years at Goldman, initially in fixed income research, then risk management. I became a partner and the head of risk management for Goldman from 1994 to 1998. In 1998, the firm asked me to take over the quantitative group in the asset management division that had been headed by Cliff Asness before he decided to start his own firm, AQR. Goldman asked me to take over that business, which I ran until 2009 when I retired. Then I joined some of the folks that used to work for me at Goldman—Mark Carhart, Giorgio De Santis, and others—at Kepos Capital. We just celebrated our third year managing money.

MARGARET TOWLE: That's a very diverse background with some interesting origins, especially journalism and human biology. If you look back on that background and all that you've accomplished, what were the major factors that helped to shape your career? You have a great combination of very theoretical experience in terms of your study at Stanford and Minnesota and your academic experience as well as applied experience with the Federal Reserve and Goldman Sachs.

ROBERT LITTERMAN: In terms of major factors, I would have to start with earning my PhD at the University of Minnesota in the late 1970s. As you probably know, that was a center of research in rational expectations.[1] My advisors were Tom Sargent and Chris Sims,[2] who shared the Nobel Memorial Prize in Economic Sciences in 2011. One of the other students there, who was a year ahead of me and also a Sargent and Sims student, was Lars Hansen.[3] He received the Nobel Memorial Prize in Economic Sciences in 2013. So it was an incredibly special place to be at that time. That had a big influence on me, and it led to my getting a job at MIT, which also was a great place to meet a lot of very smart and interesting people. That includes Fischer Black.[4] Actually, I guess I first met Fischer when he stopped by and gave a talk at Minnesota, and then he was a colleague at MIT and later at Goldman Sachs.

As to other important factors, I like to note that, when I was growing up in Arizona, there were no computers in the whole state. I was in high school before the first computer arrived, and I had this naïve but powerful dream that I would someday have access to computers and figure out how to use them to solve problems. I've had many opportunities to do that throughout the years, both in academia and at the Federal Reserve Bank. My PhD dissertation was on economic forecasting. Then I actually had the opportunity in quantitative asset management to use computers in even more powerful ways. So that was another major factor. I also was very lucky in terms of being hired by Goldman Sachs back in 1986, when I think investment banks were first really realizing that quantitative techniques could be very important, useful, and powerful on Wall Street. Right from the beginning at Goldman, I was asked to focus on risk management. In 1986, it really wasn't practical to understand, quantify, and aggregate all of the positions at the firm because we just didn't have the networks or computer power, but that was certainly something that Goldman was interested in and that I was able to work on. Then, in the early 1990s, the technology caught up with the desire to create a global, firmwide, real-time measure of risk, so that took my career in a different direction, in a very interesting direction. All of these things just came together.

MARGARET TOWLE: One of the questions that we like to ask our Masters is what they view as their major achievements. Often the answers are obvious, but occasionally we're surprised at what we learn. For example, the Black-Litterman model[5] is something that everyone connects with you and Fisher Black. What do you see as your greatest or major achievement and what is the biggest challenge that you've faced in your career?

ROBERT LITTERMAN: Well, I would have to say the development of the Black-Litterman model was probably the biggest achievement of my career, although I wouldn't want to take too much credit for that. I was in the right place at the right time, and Goldman needed someone to build an asset allocation model. I was given the assignment, and I had the opportunity to work with Fischer Black. Really it was Fischer who suggested to me the idea of incorporating a global equilibrium into the problem. I remember at the time thinking that was a very academic type of suggestion, but I was happy to try to run with that idea. It turned out, in retrospect, to be a brilliant suggestion. I also just happened to have the Bayesian[6] tools from my work on macroeconomic forecasting to implement the original version of the Black-Litterman model, which was really a rather simple idea. I would call it a reformulation of the standard asset allocation model. Instead of having to forecast returns for all assets, the equilibrium allowed the user to focus just on a discrete set of views that he or she really wanted to incorporate in the portfolio. The Bayesian context, I think, turned out to be a more realistic and flexible way and probabilistic context to address the asset allocation problem. It turned out to be one of those things that you can never predict, but which ended up working very successfully. So I think that was my major achievement. In terms of the biggest challenge, I'm currently working very hard to get carbon emissions priced globally, and that remains a huge challenge.

GEOFFREY GERBER: To follow up on the work on the Black-Litterman model for asset allocation, the real crux was the idea of global equilibrium. As you know, many practitioners today are suggesting a risk-parity approach, in which they allocate assets to balance risk. I was wondering what your thoughts are on risk parity as an asset allocation model and comparisons between that and the Black-Litterman model?

ROBERT LITTERMAN: Risk parity is a particular allocation, and there are various versions of it. Perhaps I should disclose that at the firm where I work now, we have what we call an exotic beta portfolio, which is our own particular version of allocating to risk premia. I think the various versions of risk parity are best thought of as expressing a particular view. The simplest version is probably the one where you put together several different asset classes so that each has equal volatility. If you had all uncorrelated asset classes, where you thought the expected returns or the risk premia were proportional to volatility rather than covariance to the market or anything else, then the optimal portfolio would be the risk-parity portfolio. So that's a particular set of views, it seems to me, about expected returns. I would contrast that with the Black-Litterman model, which is a framework for combining views with equilibrium. At Kepos, for example, we think more about risk factors, we recognize that those factors are correlated, and we put in views about the expected returns of those factors. Then we use the Black-Litterman model to optimize the portfolio.

So Black-Litterman is a tool. It can be used to structure a portfolio, but it doesn't tell you anything about the views themselves, and there are various sources of views. I think that's the best way to think about risk parity or investing in general, that is, it represents a set of views. The positive aspect of some of these risk-parity portfolios—I prefer to think of it as investing in risk premia— is that the capital asset pricing model (CAPM) is a very simple, one-factor model, and we realize that the actual world is much more complex and that there are many risk factors that are priced. On the other hand, the risk premia do vary over time. So in practice, a number of considerations go into the ways you allocate risk across those different premia, and Black-Litterman is a tool that allows you to do that.

MICHAEL DIESCHBOURG: There seems to be a lot of interest in looking at downside risk protection first and not using just volatility and expected return, but adding a third factor to try to figure out how to minimize drawdown. A number of previous risk-parity products have really taken a beating in 2013 because they don't have those same types of protection on the downside, and now new products are coming out. What's your view about factoring in volatility, but also adding in downside protection versus expected return and volatility?

ROBERT LITTERMAN: I'm not sure about the downside protection. Many of those risk-parity products have significant equity allocations, and if they have a significant positive allocation to equities, they've done okay in 2013. If they have a particularly large allocation to fixed income, maybe they've had a little bit of trouble. However, if you think about downside protection focusing on equity, it's a very expensive protection to buy. I'm not sure that it makes a lot of sense to both create exposures to equities and then try to hedge the downside. In fact, as you probably know, I wrote an article in the *Financial Analysts Journal* a few years ago (2011), where I talked about the fact that a better approach might be to reduce an equity allocation and sell some downside protection, where you really get paid significantly for providing that insurance. The point of that article was that some investors are more sensitive than others to the particular environment where downside protection pays off. They probably should be buyers of the protection, and those who are not particularly sensitive should be sellers.

■ ■ ■

> [S]ome investors are more sensitive than others to
> the particular environment where downside protection
> pays off. They probably should be buyers of the protection,
> and those who are not particularly sensitive should be sellers.

LUDWIG CHINCARINI: You talked about your work at Kepos. Many people believe the quant crisis[7] was caused by crowding and other sorts of problems of that nature. How has risk management either at Kepos or other firms evolved since then, or has it?

ROBERT LITTERMAN: First of all, I think the quant crisis was very much a crowding event, and basically there was a run for the exits. It was a combination of the fact that there was a tremendous flow of assets and risk capital into the quant space, and many of those portfolios were investing in the same risk factors, if you will, the same well-known quantitative factors. Then you had the financial crisis that caused significant demand for liquidity and risk reduction, and folks in the quant space got scared because they correctly anticipated that there was very significant leverage in some of those portfolios, and they tried to get out. So that was indeed the essence of what happened. As to what has happened since then, first of all, the space has deleveraged to a very dramatic extent. The amount of assets being managed in those quantitative portfolios is a very small fraction of what it was at the peak. You asked about what we've done at Kepos. We've moved out of the quant equity space virtually completely for that reason, and we're pursuing a set of strategies that we think are much less crowded and less subject to exactly those phenomena for that reason. I think that's true of many of the folks who had been in that space.

RONALD KAHN: Other than moving out of the quant equity space entirely, do you think there are lessons for people who decided to stay in the quant equity space?

ROBERT LITTERMAN: There are a number of lessons there. I would say first of all, the lesson about the ability of things to spill over. When the financial crisis began, and I guess I first started seeing it in 2006, I sat on the Goldman Sachs risk committee at that time, and we could just feel the tensions rising in one space after another, particularly in the spring of 2007. It was one of those things where, week after week, there was a mantra of "avoid crowded trades, don't take a lot of risks, stay close to home, make markets but don't be a hero," and I didn't think that had anything to do with the business I was managing. So I didn't see it coming. But obviously, as it progressed, we all realized that these things do tend to spill over. So what was happening in the mortgage market and then the credit market started showing up in the money markets and auction preferreds. Then in July and August 2007, it completely caused a run in the quant space. The interesting thing about that was how quickly it ended. You know, it really only lasted a few days, but it was certainly enough to cause a huge problem in the quant space. So I think a big lesson is how things like this can spill over into seemingly unrelated areas.

Another lesson is that you really have to monitor the stresses in financial markets and the connections. The crowding itself is difficult to quantify, but particularly for me, one of the lessons was not to think about crowding in terms of the level of assets but rather the flows of assets. We knew the quant space was crowded in some sense because there was so much money being managed that way, but as long as flows were continuing to go into the space, the returns were very positive. So through June 2007, our hedge fund was up very sharply for the year. Although the space seemed crowded in terms of the amount of assets, it was the change in flows—and obviously the fact that those flows could accelerate exponentially as people got scared. So that was another lesson. In addition, leverage—that is, the dangers of leverage in that situation—was emphasized. There are many, many other lessons about risk management and so on, but those are some of the big ones.

MARK ANSON: Were there any instances, let's say at Goldman Sachs, where risk management had to have a faceoff against the asset managers? Could you relate one of those instances, and who won the faceoff? Was it the asset-management team or the risk-management team?

ROBERT LITTERMAN: When I was head of firmwide risk at Goldman (1994–1998), we instituted a weekly risk committee meeting. One of the issues concerned who would attend that meeting. The asset management division basically argued that it didn't belong in the meeting, and we agreed with that to some extent because we felt there should be a separation between the risks that the firm faces on its capital account versus the risks that are being taken on behalf of clients in the asset management division. On the other hand, we also had each of the divisions come before the committee once a year and talk for an hour about how that division thought about managing its risk. So the question was whether we should bring the asset management division into that, and my boss, John Thain, who was chief financial officer at the time, thought that was probably a good idea. So, in the end, we did have the asset management division come before the firm's risk committee. I think this probably happened a couple of times, and they gave an overview of how they thought about risk management. However, they didn't have a risk manager in the asset management division. Then at the end of 1998, the firm asked me to move into the asset management division and take over the quant business after Cliff Asness left as well as to create a risk-management function. In 1998, that was a rather new idea. There weren't many asset management businesses that had a position titled "risk manager." So part of what we had to figure out was what does that person do, and how does that function in the context of asset management? It was—and is—very different from the broker-dealer side, because there are tradeoffs between, for example, covering positions and the transaction costs of moving in and out of positions. All of those kinds of decisions have to be the responsibility of the portfolio manager. You can't have a risk manager overriding a portfolio manager and telling him to sell positions. You can't have mixed responsibility for the results of the portfolio.

Our view was that the role of the risk manager is primarily to identify risks, to quantify risks, and to highlight those risks to the folks who are responsible. On the broker-dealer side, that chain of responsibility goes all the way up very quickly to senior management. On the asset management side, that responsibility lies with the portfolio manager, and really the only decision that management has is whether or not they have confidence in that portfolio manager. So it's a little bit different, although obviously the main role of the risk manager in both cases is to identify and quantify the risks and pass that information on to the appropriate people.

EDWARD BAKER: You mentioned that you're now pursuing some new kinds of strategies, away from more-quantitative strategies. Could you elaborate a bit on what you're finding to be novel and interesting?

ROBERT LITTERMAN: Let me be clear about Kepos—it's a totally quantitative shop. So what we've moved away from is the quant equity space. I don't know if you want me to go into too much detail, but it's basically what we would call macro statistical arbitrage. It's still totally quantitative, but it's basically focusing on the liquid markets, futures, swaps, and so on; for example in equities we trade primarily equity index futures, not individual equities; in terms of basic markets we trade fixed income, currencies, and commodities, equities, and volatility. That's in our primary strategy, which is an alpha strategy. Then as I mentioned before, we also have what we call an exotic beta strategy where, again, we're not using individual equities. However, exotic beta is very different, much slower moving. Basically, we create exposures to risk premia in different venues around the world. The main difference, I would say, between what we used to do in macro at Goldman Sachs and what we do at Kepos is in terms of the time frequency. The average holding period at Goldman in our macro fund was on the order of months, whereas our average holding period at Kepos is really a matter of days. Rather than looking primarily for value and momentum factors, as we did at Goldman, at Kepos we're much higher frequency and shorter term. It's not high frequency. It's not in and out in a matter of microseconds. That's certainly not our specialty, but it's really looking at the patterns across markets and over relatively short periods of time and trying to take advantage of those. So from an economic point of view, I would say it's primarily liquidity provision.

LUDWIG CHINCARINI: Since you had a formula at Goldman that worked, what made you jump to this shorter horizon? It seems like getting out of your comfort zone.

ROBERT LITTERMAN: In terms of portfolio construction and in terms of what quants actually do, it's all very similar: It's about forecasting and incorporating those forecasts into a portfolio that will benefit if those forecasts turn out to be accurate. So it's all the same tools, but it's really a question of which factors you look at and in which markets you apply them. We decided that this was a relatively less crowded space, and that's exactly why we moved there.

EDWARD BAKER: Is the risk-management framework similar or substantially different, and if different, how so?

ROBERT LITTERMAN: The main difference is in terms of how you think about transaction costs, because when you're moving assets around much more quickly, over the course of a year there's much more buying and selling per dollar invested, so that's one of the differences. Also, the risk management is much more sophisticated. For example, for many, many years at Goldman, most of the time I was there, as part of managing assets we targeted a particular volatility. We told clients that's what we were aiming at, and we tried to achieve it. So that meant if volatility in the marketplace went down, we expanded the sizes of our exposures to maintain that volatility. Of course, that volatility can change overnight, particularly when it's been low, and that's exactly what we saw during the quant crisis. At Kepos, we recognize that you do have to adjust your volatility, and we try to adjust it appropriately. We also try to figure out which of the strategies and risk factors are going to do well in a stressful environment versus an environment where the stresses are lower. We look at a huge variety of factors. When we were at Goldman, we had to a certain extent optimized a covariance matrix in terms of a decay rate. I'd say one of the lessons of risk management is that you can't really use any one model and depend on it that way. So we have lots of different covariance matrixes with different decay rates that we use. We use what we call flexible probabilities, where rather than simply looking at observations based on how old they are, we look at observations based on whether they were from a period of stress similar to what we have today. In other words, we've put more weight on observations from a similar environment. Currently, our measure of financial stress is quite low, so we look at observations from low stress periods and give them more weight. In a period of high stress we would put more weight on previous periods of high stress.

■ ■ ■

I'd say one of the lessons of risk management is that you can't really use any one model and depend on it that way.

Basically the bottom line is that we look at half a dozen different models and what they say, and sometimes they give very different answers. Obviously, we look at lots of stress tests, we look at measures of diversification in the portfolio, we look at the beta of the portfolio, and we look at the portfolio's correlations, both in terms of risk factors and also in terms of other quantitative hedge funds. We monitor the decomposition of risk, not only in terms of volatility but also in terms of contribution to tail risk. The number of factors we look at is an order of magnitude larger than what we were doing when we were at Goldman, and it's driven by the advances in risk management as well as lessons learned from events during the financial crisis.

EDWARD BAKER: How do you measure transaction costs for the asset classes that are over-the-counter (OTC) and spread-based, such as currencies and commodities? You said those were an important part of your framework.

ROBERT LITTERMAN: They are. How you trade and how you measure transaction costs are incredibly important when you get into the higher-frequency space. I would say that in the over-the-counter market, we've actually developed some very interesting auction techniques. When we're trading instruments such as variance swaps[8] and other OTC instruments, we have an auction, and we get bids and offers automatically from broker–dealers. We have a good sense of the spreads in those markets, and we don't reveal ahead of time which way we're trading.

EDWARD BAKER: Do you capture those spreads and somehow model what you might have gotten versus what you did get?

ROBERT LITTERMAN: Absolutely, every time. We have huge amounts of data because we capture that data and save and analyze it. You could say that every day we have a forecast of what we expect to see, and then we have actual data on what we did see. So there's a lot that can be done in terms of modeling transaction costs. We are very cautious about when we transact, how we transact, and how we build those costs into our models.

GEOFFREY GERBER: Regarding asset allocation, we see many public pension plans, foundations, and endowments thinking about or already beginning to reduce their target rate of return. I was just wondering, given your outlook on equity, fixed income, and alternative rates of returns over the next ten years or so, do you think it's a prudent idea to be lowering the target rate of return?

ROBERT LITTERMAN: I do think it's appropriate. Basically, the rate of return for institutional investors is going to be the real risk-free rate plus some risk premia, depending on the exposures that they have, plus some expected inflation. We're currently in a very low real interest-rate environment with low expected inflation, and the risk premia are really rather hard to predict. We've had a great year in equities in 2013 but, looking forward, it's realistic to recognize that nominal returns are likely to be lower. I think it's appropriate to build that into the expectations rather than try to take more risk in order to increase those nominal returns.

EDWARD BAKER: Pension plans are now using alternatives as part of their allocation, so obviously that would tend to bring expected returns down as well, would it not, for the overall framework?

ROBERT LITTERMAN: I think that alternatives, to the extent that they capture risk premia other than the basic equity premia, are a good way to diversify and reduce the amount of risk in the portfolio while at the same time increasing—or at least not lowering—the expected returns. However, the point is that investors do have to be realistic. It does seem that over several decades there has been a decrease in the Sharpe ratios[9] and net returns coming from alternatives.

MICHAEL DIESCHBOURG: Many pension plans are looking at being more dynamic in their decision making, and it sounds like at Kepos your modeling now is more active—or what some people might call market timing. What would you recommend for advisors and consultants on how to answer the question about the importance of being active and dynamic in today's markets versus just static as in the old days?

ROBERT LITTERMAN: Actually, I think there's been a trend over the years, especially with institutional investors, toward recognizing that it's difficult to add a lot of value through active management. In other words, a recognition that asset allocation is really the dominant determinant of returns in the long run, a recognition that perhaps you can improve the overall risk and return of the portfolio by diversifying across different sources of return, but in a relatively passive way. Certainly there have been huge increases in allocations to index funds, exchange-traded funds, and other passive approaches. So I think that's the bigger trend. There's always going to be a role for asset managers like ourselves who try to create value through active management, because someone has to make the markets efficient. However, in terms of the impact on the overall portfolios of large institutional investors, active management has perhaps been decreasing and will continue to do so.

MARGARET TOWLE: Related to that, Meir Statman, who was unable to join us today, passed along a question about investors' understanding of that trend, particularly in public equities where markets are really quite efficient. He referred to Ken French's study that estimated U.S. investors would save more than $100 billion a year if they abandoned their attempts to beat the market and used low-cost index funds (French 2008). Now, Meir is of the behavioral finance school, but assuming that investors are aware of the benefits of investing in index funds, why don't advisors and individual investors switch to these low-cost funds?

ROBERT LITTERMAN: I think many of them are switching, and I think more of them should switch. It's probably basically a question of education on the benefits of reducing transaction costs. To the question of why they haven't switched more quickly, I suppose I'll leave that to the behavioral finance guys to explain. However, I would also say there's a little bit of an incentive problem here, because it's not always in the advisor's best interests—or self-interest, let's put it that way—to create a low-cost product for clients.

■ ■ ■

> I think many of them are switching, and I think more of them should switch. It's probably basically a question of education on the benefits of reducing transaction costs.

MARGARET TOWLE: What is your view on environmental, social, and corporate governance investing (ESG),[10] especially considering the mixed performance results of this type of investment strategy?

ROBERT LITTERMAN: I don't think of myself as an expert in ESG or sustainable investing. I think of that as being more a part of the fundamental space. There probably are characteristics of firms that might be considered associated with sustainability or good governance with which it might be possible to forecast returns, and maybe there are managers who can use those to that effect. However, I don't think it really lends itself very well to quantitative investing. I don't think those metrics are that well-developed, and we don't have enough history to look for publicly available metrics that are clearly associated with positive results.

LUDWIG CHINCARINI: On a different topic, it seems to me that there are currently two camps of thought: One camp believes that the Federal Reserve's buying programs are actually good because we're in a deflationary environment, while the second thinks that we're going to have high inflation, with bubbles popping up everywhere. Do you have any thoughts on this and what you think might happen?

ROBERT LITTERMAN: I worked at the Fed for five years back in the 1980s, so I guess my views are tempered by that experience. I'm not a Fed watcher, but from my perspective, the Fed did an incredibly good job of handling the financial crisis. They certainly created a huge increase in the money supply, and I'm actually rather surprised and gratified that we haven't seen more inflation. However, I think that lack of inflation is, in large part, a reflection of the hard-won credibility that the Fed developed during the period under Paul Volcker,[11] and we've been a beneficiary of that credibility. Now, having said that, that credibility can be lost, and I think the

Fed has a tough job here in terms of reining in its quantitative easing. In the long run, you can't separate monetary policy from fiscal policy, so it's really not just Fed credibility, it's really the credibility of government policy. Right now the government is not behaving in a way that would tend to shore up its credibility. So I think the Fed is in a difficult position going forward, but I wish them all the luck in the world in being able to unwind this easing program without creating inflation.

GEOFFREY GERBER: You mentioned that twenty years ago, very few asset management firms—and plan sponsors—had a risk-management department. Today, they are much more common. How do you see the focus and importance of risk-management departments changing over the next ten to twenty years?

ROBERT LITTERMAN: Risk management has become a well-developed science, so to speak, and many areas need to be pushed further over the next twenty years, particularly the area of systemic risk. We've got a fairly good handle now on ways that individuals can manage their own portfolios and that traders can manage their positions, and so on. However, when you think about systemic risk, that's an area where there are network effects[12] and spillovers that are hard to identify. So there's a lot more room for progress to be made there. The other area that I've been very focused on has been pricing carbon emissions. That's also really a risk-management problem. Going forward, society as a whole needs to make a lot of progress on incorporating and pricing catastrophic risk appropriately.

MARGARET TOWLE: I agree. Given all that we've talked about today and your comments on systemic risk and so forth, what do you see as the appropriate role for investment consultants and advisors, both for institutional investors and individual investors? Do you see consultants fulfilling those roles today?

ROBERT LITTERMAN: Consultants have a number of roles, and of course there are many different types of consultants, and they operate at many different levels. For individual investors, there is a lot of opportunity for consultants in the area of online capabilities, in terms of enabling people who have very different circumstances—very different risks, liabilities, and so forth—to structure appropriate portfolios and to advise them on ways to do that. In terms of institutions, with the smaller institutions—$50 million to $500 million—there is an important role for consultants to help in terms of risk management, asset allocation, and providing information and access to high-quality managers. There has been a large move into that sort of outsourced chief investment officer space, if you will. I think that's a very important role.

MARGARET TOWLE: In terms of what the future holds for the investment industry, given some of the things that you've talked about, where do you see the industry headed, either within the context of regulation or new investment ideas or just generally the direction we're taking?

ROBERT LITTERMAN: Clearly we're going through a period of evolving regulation. I think, appropriately, a lot of risk taking is going to move out of the "systemically important, too big to fail" institutions into hedge funds and private equity firms and so on. The asset management business is going to be focused on creating low-fee products for individuals and for institutions as well. So there is going to be fee compression in the industry. Maybe I'll leave it there.

■ ■ ■

ENDNOTES

[1] Rational expectations is an economic theory that holds that investors make financial decisions based on several factors, including a rational outlook, all available information, past experiences, and their own best interests.

[2] Thomas J. Sargent (1943–) is a U.S. economist specializing in the fields of macroeconomics, monetary economics, and time-series econometrics. Christopher A. Sims (1942–) is a U.S. econometrician and macroeconomist.

[3] Lars Peter Hansen (1952–), the David Rockefeller Distinguished Service Professor of Economics at the University of Chicago, is a macroeconomist who focuses on the links between the financial and real sectors of the economy.

[4] Fischer S. Black (1938–1995) was a U.S. economist, best known as one of the authors of the famous Black-Scholes equation. Professor Black taught at the Massachusetts Institute of Technology from 1975 until 1984, when he joined Goldman Sachs, where he worked until his death.

[5] The Black-Litterman model is a mathematical model for asset allocation developed at Goldman Sachs by Fischer Black and Robert Litterman in 1990 and published in 1992.

[6] Bayesian refers to methods in probability and statistics named after Thomas Bayes (1702–1761), an English mathematician and minister, particularly methods related to statistical inference.

[7] The quant crisis of August 2007 occurred when most quantitative long-short equity funds experienced short-term losses far greater than their risk-management systems predicted could occur.

[8] A variance swap is an over-the-counter financial derivative that allows one to speculate on or hedge risks associated with the magnitude of movement, i.e., volatility, of some underlying product such as an exchange rate, interest rate, or stock index.

[9] The Sharpe ratio provides a method for measuring risk-adjusted performance.

[10] Environmental, social, and corporate governance (ESG) refers to the three areas that serve as the major factors in measuring the sustainability and ethical impact of an investment in a company or business. Another term for the criteria used in socially responsible investing, ESG covers issues such as climate change, hazardous waste, nuclear energy (environmental); diversity, human rights, consumer protection, animal welfare (social); and management structure, employee relations, executive compensation (corporate).

[11] Paul A. Volcker, Jr. (1927–) was chairman of the Federal Reserve during 1979–1987. He is widely credited with ending the high levels of inflation seen in the United States during the 1970s and early 1980s.

[12] A network effect (also called network externality or demand-side economies of scale) is the effect that one user of a good or service has on the value of that product to other users.

REFERENCES

Black, Fischer S., and Robert B. Litterman. 1990. *Asset Allocation: Combining Investor Views with Market Equilibrium*. Goldman Sachs & Co. Fixed Income Research (September).

———. 1992. Global Portfolio Optimization. *Financial Analysts Journal* 48, no. 5 (September/October): 28–43.

French, Kenneth. 2008. The Cost of Active Investing. *Journal of Finance* 63, no. 5 (August): 1,537–1,573.

Litterman, Robert B. 2004. The Active Risk Puzzle. *Journal of Portfolio Management* 30, no. 5 (September): 88–93.

———. 2011. Who Should Hedge Tail Risk? *Financial Analysts Journal* 67, no. 3 (May/June): 6-11.

———. 2013. What Is the Right Price for Carbon Emissions? *Regulation* (Cato Institute) 36, no. 2 (summer): 1–6.

Litterman, Robert, and Goldman Sachs Asset Management Quantitative Research Group. 2003. *Modern Investment Management: An Equilibrium Approach*. New York: Wiley Finance.

Litterman, Robert, Robert Gumerlock, Goldman Sachs, and SBC Warburg Dillon Read. 1998. *The Practice of Risk Management: Implementing Processes for Managing Firm-Wide Market Risk*. London: Euromoney Institutional Investor PLC.

This interview was published in its entirety in *Journal of Investment Consulting* 15, no. 1, 2014.

CHAPTER 8

BURT MALKIEL:
RANDOM WALKER WITH A CRUTCH

BURTON G. MALKIEL, PHD

Chemical Bank Chairman's Professor of Economics, emeritus, senior economist at Princeton University; dean, Yale University School of Management and William S. Beinecke Professor of Management Studies; appointee, Council of Economic Advisors under the administration of U.S. President Gerald R. Ford; author, *A Random Walk Down Wall Street* and *From Wall Street to the Great Wall*, among others and numerous articles in academic journals.

Burt Malkiel was ahead of his time when it came to incorporating innovative ideas into the mainstream of investment management. The 1973 first edition of Malkiel's *A Random Walk Down Wall Street* was published three years before the first index fund appeared. Now in its tenth edition, the book is still relevant for today's investors and today's markets. Malkiel holds that, although the principles of investing may remain persistent, the tools available to implement investment strategies, such as ETFs, are constantly changing. Malkiel refuses to rest on his laurels and continues to be at the forefront of the industry. At the age of 81, he recently assumed the post of chief investment officer at Wealthfront, a so-called "robo advisor" that is revolutionizing the delivery of investment advice.

■ ■ ■

EDWARD BAKER: We're delighted that you accepted our invitation to be our first Master. We've all reviewed your recent paper in the *Journal of Economic Perspectives* and found it to be a great read, as always. It certainly stimulated a lot of thought and questions. So let's get started.

RONALD KAHN: To put our discussion in some perspective, I would like to begin by asking how you think the markets have changed since *Random Walk* was first published in 1973, and have these changes affected your view of market efficiency?

BURTON MALKIEL: For one thing, the markets have become more and more institutionalized. Institutions are now responsible for 90 to 95 percent of trading. In recent years, the influence of hedge funds has increased, and it's been estimated that, at certain times, most of the trading has been done by these funds. The markets have also changed because of the variety of new derivatives being used by both institutions and individual investors.

Essentially, I think that, if anything, all of these factors have made the markets more efficient. For example, hedge funds are trying, on a leveraged basis, to make a nickel because an underlying stock is mispriced relative to the derivatives contract or because the market has not yet caught up to an event such as an earnings surprise or stock split. Based on this information, these funds come right into the market and quickly take a position. In this way, the hedge fund is ensuring that new information is reflected in the stock price without delay. Factors like this have changed the market, and I think the result of the changes is that the market is more efficient today than it was in 1973.

MEIR STATMAN: In your recent article, you make the distinction between market efficiency from the perspective of "price equals value" in individual stocks and market efficiency from the standpoint of investors' collective judgment, in that some participants may become less than rational in trying to beat the market (Malkiel 2003a). According to your definition, the markets can be efficient even if they sometimes make errors in valuation, which was certainly true during the Internet bubble of 1999–2000. But is it possible that hedge funds and others sometimes act in a way that increases the gap in price and value? Aren't we losing something by confusing those two notions of market efficiency?

BURTON MALKIEL: As you know, people differ with respect to the degree of efficiency they believe exists. I refer to myself as a random walker with a crutch. I'm willing to admit that the markets make mistakes. However, Eugene Fama wouldn't agree with me. He would not use the word "bubble," and in the latest edition of *Random Walk*, I refer to the 1999–early 2000 period as the biggest bubble of all time. Multiple trillions of dollars were lost, and I agree with you that, in this instance, the institutions and hedge funds were actually guilty of making it worse. It appears to me from the data I've seen that hedge funds, to the extent they were market-timing, were momentum-driven and therefore couldn't be counted on to sell short the Internet stocks that, in retrospect, were obviously over-priced. So I admit the market gets it wrong sometimes. However, what always brings me back to the concept of efficiency is the fact that nobody can know in advance when the market has it wrong.

■ ■ ■

> As you know, people differ with respect to the degree of efficiency they believe exists. I refer to myself as a random walker with a crutch. I'm willing to admit that the markets make mistakes.

This might be an appropriate point to talk about market timing. This strategy now has backing among many academics—John Campbell and Robert Shiller, for example—so should investors try to market time? My answer is very simple: Never! Here's the problem. Bob Shiller argues that the market was irrationally exuberant in 1992. When Alan Greenspan later made his famous speech using that phrase, the Dow was at the 5,000 level. Between the time of that speech and now, the market has returned annually close to 8 percent. So, while I'm willing to admit that the market gets it wrong sometimes and occasionally overshoots, investors never know until after the fact when it has crossed that point into irrational exuberance.

MATTHEW MOREY: Speaking of irrational exuberance, did the market events of the 1990s—like the Internet bubble—change your definition of market efficiency? Do you think an efficient market can provide a way to valuate stocks rationally?

BURTON MALKIEL: The Internet bubble was clearly concentrated in one part of the market—the high-tech sector—and you might argue that what happened in that sector supports the idea of an irrational market, that is, prices did not accurately reflect value during that period of time. As a result, too much capital flowed into Internet-related stocks. So the stock market may have temporarily failed as an efficient allocator of capital. Fortunately, instances like this are the exception rather than the rule. One of the problems with rational valuation—that is, pricing stocks as the present value of the expected future income stream—is that it's not easy to do, particularly when there's no technology that can estimate the future growth rate of a company with any degree of precision.

For example, if eBay goes down $3 or $4 in trading today, does that mean that eBay was in fact in a bubble earlier in the week? Will it eventually bounce back? I don't think we can know. The price of eBay stock obviously reflects investors' view that the company will grow at a substantial rate. In fact, this is a question I use on exams: Is eBay overpriced or underpriced? If we assume that eBay is appropriately priced, what is the implied growth rate of earnings per share likely to be? It's difficult to predict future growth rates, and the market will continue to make mistakes.

However, the fact that we know in retrospect that the market made a mistake during 1999–2000 doesn't mean that the market is inefficient—or that we should change our definition of efficiency—because we didn't know beforehand that the market was going to make a mistake. I don't think anybody can prove definitively whether eBay is appropriately priced or not today. If next year, however, eBay is selling at $10 per share, people will say, "Boy, what a bubble!" How could you assume that eBay could grow at 23 or 24 percent a year for the next ten years? It's simply not possible for anyone to say with precision what the right growth-rate estimate is.

Again, I think this is an area where people such as Gene Fama wouldn't agree with me. During early 2000, one could have argued that market prices were crazy. I actually said this in an op-ed piece in the *Wall Street Journal* published at that time. I looked at the growth rate implicit in Cisco's price, which I estimated had to be 15 to 25 percent a year for twenty years in order to justify the price. If the gross domestic product (GDP) grew at 5 percent annually over this same period, then in twenty years, Cisco would be bigger than the GDP. So it was easy to see that the growth rate implicit in Cisco's price was just unreasonable. In that sense, I argued that Cisco was inappropriately valued when it had a market cap well above $500 billion in early 2000. So that's where I'm a random walker with a crutch—I'm willing to say that, at certain times, prices appear to be wrong even before the fact. Any reasonable analyst would have agreed with me about Cisco and, in fact, it was the momentum—the feedback loops that Bob Shiller talks about—that was responsible for the market prices. I'm distinguishing price from value here. Again, this gets back to the admission that the market can be wrong.

MARK ANSON: While we're on the subject of market mistakes, one of the observations I've made in looking back at the stock market crash of 1987 was the extremely low implied equity risk premium in the market at that time. Back then, investors thought stocks were virtually riskless compared with long-term Treasury bonds. Many of those investors had portfolio insurance, and I believe that's part of the reason why the equity risk premium approached zero. If you have insurance, you don't have to worry about risk. Then we all saw what a failure portfolio insurance could be. Was it rational for the market to believe so strongly in portfolio insurance?

BURTON MALKIEL: I think this was actually another instance of temporary market inefficiency. In fact, we got too smart for our own good. We really did think that sophisticated derivatives could take some of the risk out of the market. That was a mistake, because we later realized that everyone can't get out of the door at once, and when everybody tries to get out of the door at once, nobody gets out. It was an irrational period, and we recognize now that it was irrational. One of the effects of 1987 is that portfolio managers today don't use portfolio insurance the way they did then because they know now that portfolio insurance doesn't work the way they thought it did. It was a learning experience. It goes back to the fundamental premise we started with: The market is not always right. However, when we learn of systematic things we've done wrong, we don't do them again.

MEIR STATMAN: In earlier editions of *Random Walk*, you talked about picking stocks. One of your examples involved the fact that you had noted a rise in the rate of burglaries, which resulted in increased buying of home security stocks. So, do you dabble in stocks? Did you buy the home security stocks as a result of your observation? Given your earlier example, did you sell Cisco short? Or do you stay away from making bets on individual stocks?

BURTON MALKIEL: Nobody who spends a lifetime working on Wall Street, serving on boards, and studying these issues as an academic does so without some sort of a gambling instinct. While the stock market may be somewhat of a casino, it's a lot better than Atlantic City or Las Vegas, because the odds really are in your favor— that is, there's a long-term uptrend in the stock market. So, do I buy some individual stocks? Yes, I do. I also go to Las Vegas and Atlantic City—I like to gamble. But as a trustee for family trusts, or a member of the investment committee for various foundations, and in my own 403(b), I believe in indexing stocks, bonds, and real estate. Essentially all of my investments are indexed. This is a direct consequence of my belief that the markets are efficient and that, therefore, investors holding broadly diversified portfolios indexed to the market should earn returns equal or superior to that achieved by the experts. Then, on the side, I buy individual stocks simply because it's fun.

When *Random Walk* was originally published in 1973, I couldn't advise investors to buy index funds, because index funds didn't exist at that time. In fact, one of the things I said in the book was there ought to be index funds. So I advised buying closed-end funds. That was my favorite strategy then—and not because I thought the managers of these funds were going to outperform. I actually thought that would not be the case. Instead, I thought that if you could buy assets at sixty cents on the dollar, your portfolio would benefit. I thought that presented an inefficiency that could be exploited.

There's an old joke about efficiency—the professor and the graduate student find a $100 bill on the ground. The graduate student stoops to pick up the bill, and the professor says, "Don't bother. If it really were a $100 bill, it wouldn't be there." My advice is a little different—I say to pick it up right away because it surely won't be there for long. With respect to closed-end funds, the discounts have largely closed. The ones that still are trading at discounts usually also have very high expense ratios, so it's not clear that there's any inefficiency left to exploit. As a result, I don't currently see a benefit in closed-end funds. I also don't think there are a lot of individual stocks that appear to be crazily priced right now. My advice today to investors in search of better performance would definitely be to buy a very broad-based index fund.

MATTHEW MOREY: What about anomalies such as the January effect? Don't they represent some inefficiencies in the market that could be exploited?

BURTON MALKIEL: I think that anomalies, like the $100 bill, don't last for long. To the extent they do exist, they are soon corrected, and I believe this is true of most of the so-called predictable patterns and anomalies that have been discussed in the literature, such as the January effect or the differences among asset classes like small cap/large cap or value/growth. There are always mistakes to be made. However, if the market were to systematically make mistakes, if it were systematically irrational, then we should be able to find some professional investment managers who could consistently exploit these patterns and consistently win. However, the professionals don't win every time, and they weren't even a countervailing force in the Internet bubble. The pros—and even the hedge funds—became momentum investors who perpetuated the bubble, rather than counterbalancing it.

EDWARD BAKER: In my personal experience in the active management industry, I've seen a number of professional managers who have consistently added value, maybe not every year, but over the long term; that is, managers and teams that are able to provide consistently superior performance, even on a risk-adjusted basis. If the markets are indeed efficient, how do you explain the estimated $6 trillion invested in actively managed equity strategies? What is the place of active management in an efficient market?

BURTON MALKIEL: Let me take the initial part of your statement first, because I don't agree with you. The area where we have accurate, complete data on performance is mutual funds. Obviously, this data doesn't include all the private funds, but I've been on enough investment committees and seen enough consultant reports to believe that my view holds true there as well. The fact is that if your strategy is to buy the mutual fund with the best return last year—or over the previous two or three or five years—you cannot find any one single strategy that consistently outperforms. There simply is no consistency in performance. In fact, it is quite the contrary, at least in the mutual fund area.

To illustrate, in the latest edition of *Random Walk* I ask, "What would have happened if, at the beginning of 2000, you had bought the twenty best-performing funds, that is, the twenty funds that outperformed in 1997, 1998, and 1999?" These were the funds written up in all the financial magazines. As we know now, while these funds performed twice as well as the S&P 500 on the way up, their losses were about three times worse on the way down. There's no question in my mind that a little bit of performance persistence does exist. In the area of style, for example, value will be in for a couple of years, then growth may be in after that. However, this persistence is not dependable. I don't find that there is any way to consistently pick the best mutual fund. It's like finding a needle in the haystack. My view is that investors should just buy the whole haystack.

■ ■ ■

> There's no question in my mind that a little bit of performance persistence does exist. In the area of style, for example, value will be in for a couple of years, then growth may be in after that. However, this persistence is not dependable. I don't find that there is any way to consistently pick the best mutual fund. It's like finding a needle in the haystack. My view is that investors should just buy the whole haystack.

So the next part of your question is: If the markets are efficient, why is $6 trillion actively managed? First of all, as I understand it, about 25 percent of institutional money is indexed and about 10 percent of individual investors' assets. Now, why is only 10 percent of individual money indexed? That's something I've spent my life trying to change. The reason the figure is only 10 percent is a rational one: It's more difficult for individual investors to find a broker willing to sell low-cost index funds, rather than actively managed funds, because of the difference in commissions to be made on the sale. On the institutional side, am I disappointed that it's just 25 percent? Yes, but on the other hand, given the lag between academic discovery and events in the real world, I'm actually thrilled that it's 25 percent. These things take time.

RONALD KAHN: Is there a *right* number for the amount of money institutional funds should have indexed? Should it be 100 percent?

BURTON MALKIEL: That's the paradox about market efficiency. If the market were 100-percent indexed, who would do the active management to make the market efficient? I don't know the answer to your question about the *right* percentage, but I would say if 95 percent of the market were indexed, I'd start to worry. However, with only 25 percent of institutional money and 10 percent of individual money indexed, I don't worry at all. In fact, I think it could easily be 50 percent, maybe even 75 percent.

Again, this paradox—often called the Grossman/Stiglitz paradox—says markets can't be perfectly efficient, or there would be no incentive to uncover the information that drives market prices. Someone has to be quickly taking positions to ensure that the new information gets into the market in a timely fashion. That's where I think active management, especially of hedge funds, serves a very useful purpose. To get back to Ed's question about the place of active management in an efficient market, there definitely has to be some active management in order to make the markets efficient.

RONALD KAHN: Don't you think there's a price that every investor in aggregate should pay to make sure that markets are efficient, or reasonably efficient?

BURTON MALKIEL: Absolutely. For example, the hedge funds that are doing merger arbitrage have costs. These funds have experts researching and reviewing issues such as the likelihood of the SEC [Securities and Exchange Commission] or the FTC [Federal Trade Commission] nixing a specific merger, or the European Commission coming down like a ton of bricks on a multinational merger. The hedge fund managers have to pay for this expertise, so there's no question that there must be enough profit to cover this expense.

MARK ANSON: At CalPERS, we're besieged by people from active-management shops offering us products. Every day it seems there are more and more actively managed products for pension funds to consider. Is it inefficient for these managers to believe they can beat the market, or is it inefficient for us as investors to put our faith in their ability to beat the market?

BURTON MALKIEL: It's inefficient for you as investors to put your faith in the managers. It's certainly not inefficient for the managers—they are well paid for their efforts. From my experience serving on the Princeton investment company board and working with endowments, here's how I would advise institutional investors: Investors get paid for accepting illiquidity. There's no question that the private markets and the real estate markets tend to be less efficient. While CalPERS can't invest in the same ways Princeton does because it doesn't have the same infinite time horizon, Princeton has only a minority of its holdings in marketable common stocks. Most of the holdings are in nonmarketable assets because we know we will be paid for accepting illiquidity. That, to me, is not an inefficiency in the market. Looking for these types of opportunities is where I think institutions ought to spend their time, not in trying to get the best active managers.

MARK ANSON: Let me follow up on that. For nonmarketable securities—real estate, private equity, venture capital—are you saying that it's not that they're inefficient as much as the fact that there's an additional risk premium for the lack of liquidity?

BURTON MALKIEL: Absolutely. However, I think they also tend to be inefficient in the sense that thousands of people are trying to judge whether a specific stock is appropriately priced. On the other hand, only a handful of people may be looking at whether this office building is appropriately priced. In that sense, the market for some of these securities is probably also less efficient.

MEIR STATMAN: As we know, lotteries provide negative alphas as well as risk. Isn't it possible that some people buy actively managed funds for the same reasons they buy lottery tickets?

BURTON MALKIEL: That's right, and I think actively managed funds are a better deal than a lottery ticket. The way I explain it is that it's like telling people Santa Claus doesn't exist. Some people just want to believe, and for those people—leaving aside the issue of fees for a moment—active funds are a better product than a slot machine. They are better than anything Atlantic City or Las Vegas offers, and it's certainly better than going to the racetrack, where the expected return is a negative 20 percent.

■ ■ ■

> I think actively managed funds are a better deal than a lottery ticket. The way I explain it is that it's like telling people Santa Claus doesn't exist. Some people just want to believe, and for those people—leaving aside the issue of fees for a moment—active funds are a better product than a slot machine. They are better than anything Atlantic City or Las Vegas offers, and it's certainly better than going to the racetrack, where the expected return is a negative 20 percent.

Here's another thought: Take my wife's portfolio, for example. She inherited a sizable amount of Merck stock from her grandmother, and the cost basis is essentially zero, so she's not too keen about selling it. Now, if she is going to invest an IRA [individual retirement account], she probably shouldn't choose a stock index fund, because she doesn't need a fund that invests in everything. Instead, she should invest in something that would help to diversify a portfolio overbalanced in health care. That's possibly another case where an actively managed fund would be of value.

RONALD KAHN: Don't you agree that this situation would also be a good role for a financial advisor, because it's more of a tax and diversification issue?

BURTON MALKIEL: Yes, it is, and that's really what I see as the appropriate role. I tell the story in my new book about a woman who worked at Enron. She was absolutely delighted because she was smart enough to put her entire 401(k) in Enron stock. There she was, in her mid-fifties with almost $2 million and ready to retire and travel. Then Enron went bankrupt, and she lost her job. She had the income from her work, her livelihood, and her entire portfolio invested in the same company. Helping people to understand risk and its ramifications and to avoid situations such as this—that's an appropriate role for an investment advisor. My point again, though, is that the woman would have been even better off if, had she chosen to consult an advisor, she had been advised to diversify with an index fund rather than a mutual fund.

MEIR STATMAN: This raises the question of whether an asset-pricing model should include factors other than proxies for risk. Do factors such as social responsibility and the propensity of investors to buy the so-called admired companies play a role in determining correct asset pricing?

BURTON MALKIEL: With respect to an asset-pricing model, there absolutely ought to be other factors. My first candidate, as I indicated before, would be liquidity or marketability, because there's no question investors get paid for bearing illiquidity. I also think "admired" companies could play a role, but you should be very careful about that. Remember, Enron was one of the most admired companies in the country, and Ken Lay was considered a mastermind.

MEIR STATMAN: Actually, I was referring to the negative relationship between admired companies and expected returns.

BURTON MALKIEL: Well, I'm not sure you should do that either. Some companies may be justly admired, and others may not be. I'm sure there are other factors that should be a consideration in an asset-pricing model, but it's not easy to determine what they are. Liquidity is something I'm virtually sure about.

EDWARD BAKER: If factors other than the fundamental characteristics of companies and risk factors influence asset pricing, wouldn't that introduce the potential for active managers to add value?

BURTON MALKIEL: If you take what I'm virtually sure exists, which is the premium for illiquidity, I think there's no question that if you're Princeton University—or Yale, Harvard, or Stanford—and you have a long time horizon, and you want to exploit this premium, then you do need active managers. On broadly diversified mutual funds, there's a spread of maybe 400 to 500 basis points that encompasses the performance of almost all of the portfolios. When you're in the private markets, these spreads are much wider. That's why I believe these markets are much less efficient. If you want to try to get a premium for illiquidity, you definitely want the best active manager you can find.

■ ■ ■

REFERENCES

Malkiel, Burton G. 1973. *A Random Walk Down Wall Street*. New York: W. W. Norton & Company, Inc.

———. 2003a. The Efficient Market Hypothesis and Its Critics. *Journal of Economic Perspectives* 17, no. 1 (winter): 59–82.

———. 2003b. *The Random Walk Guide to Investing*. New York: W. W. Norton & Company, Inc.

This interview was published in its entirety in *Journal of Investment Consulting* 6, no. 2, Winter 2003–2004.

CHAPTER 9

HARRY MARKOWITZ: FATHER OF MODERN PORTFOLIO THEORY

HARRY M. MARKOWITZ, PHD

Recipient of the 1990 Nobel Memorial Prize in Economic Sciences; Professor of Finance at the Rady School of Management, University of California, San Diego; author, *Portfolio Selection: Efficient Diversification of Investments* and numerous articles in academic journals.

At the University of Chicago in the early 1950s, Harry Markowitz was undecided about his dissertation topic in economics. While waiting to meet his advisor, he chatted with the fellow sitting next to him—a stockbroker—who suggested that Markowitz use the stock market as the focus of his research. Markowitz said it was the best advice he ever got from a stockbroker. He used the market to devise the tenets of modern portfolio theory (MPT), where he applied mathematical and statistical models to analyze risk and return. The approach was so novel that Milton Friedman, one of Markowitz's advisors, argued that MPT was not an appropriate application of economic theory. Fortunately, Markowitz prevailed, paving the way for the incorporation of risk into the investment equation.

■ ■ ■

EDWARD BAKER: Harry, it's nice to talk to you. We've been looking forward to this conversation. Let's start out by asking you about the major factors that shaped your career, helped you evolve your thinking, and contributed to your major achievements.

HARRY MARKOWITZ: My first insight into mean-variance portfolio theory happened while I was working toward my PhD degree at the University of Chicago. I was reading John Burr Williams' book, *The Theory of Investment Value*. Williams asserts that the value of a stock should be the present value of its future dividends. Where the present value is uncertain, it should be the expected value of future dividends. The thought went through my mind that if you're only interested in the expected value of a security, you must only be interested in the expected value of a portfolio. If you're only interested in the expected value of a portfolio, you maximize that by putting all of your money into whichever security has the greatest expected return. But that didn't make sense, because everybody knows you're not supposed to put all of your eggs into one basket. What Williams' theory was lacking was the impact of risk. I'd also read Wiesenberger's *Investment Companies*,[1] and I saw that investment companies were being paid for diversification. I figured that investors diversified because they were interested in minimizing risk—which I formalized as standard deviation—as well as in earning high expected returns.

So I had two quantities—risk and return—and I was a budding young economist. So I drew a tradeoff curve with expected return on one axis and risk on the other, and thus had the first efficient frontier.[2] At the time I was taking a course in activity analysis at the University of Chicago under Tjalling Koopmans.[3] He distinguished between efficient and inefficient production allocation. I clearly had efficient and inefficient portfolios. Over the course of one afternoon, while reading Williams' book, the basic concepts of efficiency came to me, which I published in my 1952 paper, "Portfolio Selection." This still left the problem of how to compute the efficient frontier, which I worked out and published in 1956. During 1955 and 1956, I spent nine months at the Cowles Foundation.[4] There I thought through the relationship between mean-variance efficiency and the expected utility and personal probability of the theory of rational behavior under uncertainty. By 1959, I had worked out in my mind and put on paper portfolio theory as I viewed it. That was it for me for the time being.

EDWARD BAKER: If you could whittle down your career into one major achievement—I know there are so many—what would you underscore? What makes you feel particularly proud?

HARRY MARKOWITZ: I've made contributions in three or four areas of which I'm proud. One is portfolio theory. In the area of linear programming, I developed sparse matrix techniques that are used to solve very huge mathematical optimization equations. In simulation, I created a computer language called Simscript that is still in use. I also have a relationship to behavioral finance in terms of my other 1952 article entitled "Utility of Wealth." There is a recent contribution to the basic problem of the dynamic programming of large systems of which I feel very proud. I'm not one of your one-shot Nobel Laureates who can only work in one field.

EDWARD BAKER: That's a very impressive list. How about your biggest mistake or disappointment? There must have been one along the way that you found educational or valuable.

HARRY MARKOWITZ: My biggest disappointment is that I've never been able to get Simscript II developed as I had planned it, including database entities as well as simulated entities. Mistakes? You make lots of mistakes. I remember my successes and I forget my mistakes.

EDWARD BAKER: That sounds very typical.

HARRY MARKOWITZ: It's very behavioral.

RONALD KAHN: I'd like to follow up on portfolio theory and ask what you thought the impact of mean-variance analysis might be and how that compares with what you've seen.

HARRY MARKOWITZ: At the time I developed the theory, I thought this was something that investors could use. But, at the moment of discovery, I really wasn't thinking about its impact. I had no idea that I would eventually get a Nobel Prize for it. I did think I would get a PhD degree. When I published in 1952, I put forward a proposal I thought people could use, and it never struck me that hundreds of billions of dollars would be invested this way if my idea was taken seriously.

MEIR STATMAN: I don't know if you've seen the January 2009 issue of the *Journal of Financial Planning*, but your name is on the cover page. It's a very short question that asks, "Is Markowitz wrong?" The author of the article says that we know now that diversification is dead. How do you defend yourself?

HARRY MARKOWITZ: Usually that's accompanied by a statement that all correlations have gone to one.

MEIR STATMAN: Let me just add that the author says—and you've heard this before, of course— that market timing should be substituted for diversification because there are times when it is obvious that some asset classes are overpriced and you should move out of them. So the article says that strategic asset allocation or diversification is dead and it is time to move on to tactical asset allocation.

■ ■ ■

It's yet to be shown that anybody has the capability to market time successfully, and it's certainly yet to be shown that billions of dollars' worth of pension funds could be successfully market-timed.

HARRY MARKOWITZ: It's yet to be shown that anybody has the capability to market time successfully, and it's certainly yet to be shown that billions of dollars' worth of pension funds could be successfully market-timed. Let's go back to the basic questions: Do all correlations go to one? Is diversification of no value? The simplest way to describe what's going on would be to pretend as if covariances were subject to the one-factor model. Then the return on a security would be its alpha plus its beta times how the underlying factor—let's say the market—does, plus idiosyncratic risk.

Of course, if you take any short period of time when the factor has had an extreme move, then over that short period of time, all of the correlations are indeed very close to one. However, a priori, you have different estimates of the betas for different asset classes. For example, the emerging markets asset class has a higher beta than large-capitalization U.S. equities. In fact, in 2008, emerging markets did move down much more than the Standard & Poor's 500 Stock Composite Index. Now, it is not true that all of the idiosyncratic risks went to zero. It's just that there was a big move in the underlying factor so that, more or less, asset classes and, to a certain extent, stocks moved in proportion to their betas. This swamped their idiosyncratic terms.

If you had put all of your money into one security, like credit default swaps, you could have lost everything. I understand there were municipalities in Australia that put all of their money into credit default swaps—not buying them, but writing them—and they were wiped out. Compare that with a person who put his 401(k) in a 60/40 mix of stocks and bonds. Let's say he had $600,000 in equities and $400,000 in a mix of government and corporate bonds: the $600,000 became $400,000, and the bonds would have stayed at $400,000. So his $1 million became $800,000. He's not happy about that, but he hasn't jumped out of any windows. Certainly putting all of his money into one asset class, or trying to time the market, would have been a foolhardy idea.

MEIR STATMAN: Do you think that mean variance, or really the optimization, is being oversold in the sense that both professors and financial advisors explain it in the language of negative correlations where one asset goes up and the other goes down, rather than in the realistic language of positive correlations where both assets go down but one asset goes down more than the other?

HARRY MARKOWITZ: It may be that people say that they can find negatively correlated securities—and perhaps there are some rare negatively correlated securities—but most securities and most asset classes have positive betas. It would be misleading to pretend otherwise.

MEIR STATMAN: So why are people so shocked when both U.S. and international markets go down during the same period? Your explanation is fairly straightforward. Why do people fail to understand it?

HARRY MARKOWITZ: That seems to be a behavioral question, so I'd have to ask you for the answer, Meir. It may be that there's a tendency to oversell anything. For example, financial engineers speak of risk control, as if you can control risk, whereas I've never said you can control risk. I say there is a risk-return tradeoff. If you go higher on the frontier, you're exposed to more risk. If you come lower on the frontier, if you want less exposure to risk, you have to be willing to accept less return. It's just part of the mean variance risk-return paradigm that if you stick your neck out and things go badly, you may get your head chopped off.

RONALD KAHN: I have a question that's slightly different, but related. When I think of your work on mean-variance optimization, it seems like that was the first time we saw a financial analysis that required more detailed mathematics and computers to perform. You can draw a line—maybe not a straight line—to today, where people are building collateralized debt obligations and very nontransparent investments. Do you see that as a straight line, or perhaps an inevitable path—something that started out fairly simple, but has evolved with many aspects that you wouldn't necessarily have expected?

HARRY MARKOWITZ: I give a talk called "Portfolio Theory versus Financial Engineering, and Their Roles in Financial Crises." It has to do with what I consider fairly straightforward mean-variance analysis—especially supported by a top-down asset-class view that has done reasonably well through these crises, versus analyses that have become very complicated, very obscure, and somehow have encouraged a great deal of leverage. These types of analyses are based on many assumptions. If any one of these fails the whole thing comes tumbling down. So I make a distinction in my mind between, on the one hand, good old-fashioned mean-variance analysis as it has evolved with the Brinson[5] asset class view, Ibbotson[6] data, the use of Monte Carlo simulation[7] to help investors pick out where they should be on the frontier, and so on, and, on the other hand, these—people would say very sophisticated, but I believe obscure is a better descriptor—analyses, which have been a source of big trouble lately.

EDWARD BAKER: How important do you think it is that investors try to understand the time-varying nature of some of these risk relationships? Isn't that really one of the problems with correlations, that is, they do change so much, and what you think you might have in terms of diversification in one context differs from what you have in another context? How does one really account for that successfully?

HARRY MARKOWITZ: Let me go back to the notion that, ex-ante, you don't know whether you're going to go into a very quiet time or a very wild period. If you look at it in terms of the one-factor model, ex-ante you don't know whether you're going to have a big move in the underlying factor and the idiosyncratic terms are all going to be rather irrelevant, or if you're going to have a small move in the underlying factor and the idiosyncratic moves will be the largest source of variance. During periods when the common factor has large moves, correlations are high. When the common factor has small moves, correlations are low.

EDWARD BAKER: So perhaps one solution to the problem is to always be conservative and force your correlations to be above their historical averages, if it's really the outlier or the ugly periods that you're concerned about?

HARRY MARKOWITZ: The simplest way to explain this is in terms of the one-factor model. Shall we be conservative and assume that the average beta is greater than one? I don't think so, because the average beta has to be one. We can up our estimate of the variance of the underlying factor. For example, if you look at the 1930s, the volatility of the market was generally much greater than in the 1950s. While it seems to be very difficult to predict the expected return over the next period, there does seem to be certain persistence in volatility. So it's probably a fair guess that 2009 might be more volatile than the 1950s, but not as volatile as the 1930s. Again, going back to the one-factor model, you should use judgment looking forward, rather than just historical statistics looking backward. It's perfectly reasonable for you to say that, on average, my beta estimates are one and I think my idiosyncratic risks are perhaps right, but my estimate of the volatility of the underlying factor should be greater when I look toward 2009 than it would have been in 2005.

MEIR STATMAN: Is it possible that investment managers and advisors are simply pushed to promise too much? It seems that Ed was saying that we need to be able to forecast the future a bit better, and I think clients are pushing toward that. Shouldn't investment managers push back and tell them that it is impossible?

HARRY MARKOWITZ: Let me contrast two different people. One I know well; the other I just saw across the room. The first is Roger Gibson,[8] who served on an advisory board with me. One of the things he does is interview prospective clients three or four times before he accepts them as clients. During these interviews he tries to determine the prospect's comfort with various asset classes. He also tries to determine how a large downdraft in their portfolio would cause them to chicken out of the program. If they seem risk-averse, then he suggests putting in a little more fixed income and a little less equity. I spoke to Roger recently and asked him if his clients were sticking with him, and he said that yes, they were sticking with the program. Some have decided not to rebalance just yet, but they are sticking with the program. So that's an example of a person who tells it as he sees it, and his clients are loyal.

The second person is someone I don't know. My wife and I were dining in a small Italian restaurant, and I could see two women conducting business at a table near the window. The woman who was selling said, "Yes, the program you just chose *will* give you a 10-percent return." I thought to myself, "It's misleading to tell a client that she *will* get a 10-percent return." One of the things William Sharpe does at Financial Engines, and we do at Guided Choice, my 401(k) advisory service client, is Monte Carlo analyses to show investors that there is a probability distribution of what can happen. I think people should be taught that there is no certainty about investment.

EDWARD BAKER: Let me go down a slightly different path. Many people are arguing that distributions aren't normal, that tails are fatter than for normal distributions and that we should expect to see these bad events more often. In other words people are just misassessing probabilities. Do you think that's true? If it is, what does that mean for portfolio theory?

HARRY MARKOWITZ: Nilufer Usmen and I did a Bayesian analysis of the probability distributions of daily moves in the S&P 500. We found that subjective probabilities should shift very heavily away from a normal, or Gaussian, distribution toward a Student's t-distribution[9] with between four and five degrees of freedom, which is very fat-tailed. We did this analysis before October 1987 and submitted the article to a finance journal, but it was rejected. The article subsequently was published in the *Journal of Risk and Uncertainty* (1996), but had it been published before October 19, 1987,[10] we could have said, "We told you so." As far as daily moves go, I believe in black swans.[11] However, if you take 250 trading days or so, i.e., a year's worth, of Student's t-distributed random samples, and you add those observations together for a year's worth of return, they become very normal looking. So, I believe in black swans on a daily basis, but not on an annual basis.

For example, people who are leveraged and marked-to-market can get wiped out in a day, whereas look at what happened in 2008. The S&P 500 had a little less than a 2.5-standard deviation downward move. If the distribution was normal, then you would expect a more than two standard deviation downward move to happen with 2.5-percent probability. So once in forty years you would expect a move down of more than two standard deviations. You have to be prepared for those. You shouldn't invest in a way that will wipe you out if there's more than a two standard deviation move. So the answer to your question is yes, I believe in fat tails for the day, but not for the year.

RONALD KAHN: You were quoted some time ago talking about the advantages of semivariance over variance. What are your current thoughts about that?

HARRY MARKOWITZ: Well, they're both my children, and I hate to pick among my children. Typically I use mean variance, although if someone said that he wanted to use mean semivariance, I certainly would not try to talk them out of it. The reason I personally use mean variance is twofold: One has to do with the disadvantages of moving away from mean variance, and the other is the disadvantages of staying with mean variance. I'm willing, for practical purposes, to go with the view of von Neumann and Morgenstern[12] and Savage[13] that rational decision making should consist of maximizing expected utility using probability beliefs where there are not objective probabilities. A paper by Haim Levy and me (1979) addresses mean-variance approximations to expected utility. If your probability distributions are not too spread out, say mostly between a 30-percent loss and a 40-percent gain for the period, then if you know the mean and variance of a return distribution, you can guess very closely what its expected utility is. As long as you're talking about diversified portfolios—and portfolios that are not highly leveraged—then mean-variance approximations are quite good, quite robust. A number of experiments subsequent to ours in 1979 have come up with similar conclusions. I don't see much loss in using mean variance. The problem with moving away from it is that the estimation becomes more complex. For example, with mean variance, all we need to estimate are expected returns, variances and covariances, or—maybe better still—we could use a factor model instead of trying to estimate individual covariances. With semivariance, it's not that way. You can't just use one set of statistics, like semi-covariances, and have a relationship between the semivariance on the portfolio as a whole and this one set of statistics. You have to go through historical distributions or maybe Monte Carlo analysis. I don't come out strongly on either side of this issue, although I do use mean variance myself.

EDWARD BAKER: Do you think investors are really more loss averse than they might confess to being when you're describing a probability distribution? When we're in a world such as we are now, and losses are rather acute, do you think the pain and regret are much greater than people anticipated?

HARRY MARKOWITZ: Yes, I've heard from more than one source that when it is explained to investors how much a two standard deviation move is and that they can have even more than a two standard deviation move one year out of forty—I've been told by investment managers and financial advisors who level with their clients about this, that when this happens, the clients are not happy, but they want to stick with the program. I think if you just simply say that here's the mean and here's the standard deviation and you don't really spell it out somehow, investors will underestimate the pain. You have to be conscientious about spelling out what would happen, for example, if the market went down 30 percent or 40 percent and asking if they want a 50/50 mix so their portfolio moves down 15 percent to 20 percent, or do they want to be in 100-percent equities and move down 30 percent to 40 percent, understanding that if they have 50-percent stocks and 50-percent bonds then over twenty or thirty years, they won't do as well as if they were in 100-percent equities. It is an effort to try to make people understand what it means to be exposed to that much standard deviation, but I think investment managers who make that effort are rewarded in the long run in terms of keeping their clients.

■ ■ ■

I think if you just simply say that here's the mean and here's the standard deviation and you don't really spell it out somehow, investors will underestimate the pain.

EDWARD BAKER: Is there an important message there for financial advisors and consultants who are trying to help individuals put together their portfolios?

HARRY MARKOWITZ: Yes, they should look at histograms of the S&P 500 and realize that 2008 was not unique. If I remember correctly 1937, 1932, 1907—those are some of the other years when you had those kinds of moves. You have to educate your clients so that they understand they have to establish a mix of stocks and bonds that they can live with.

EDWARD BAKER: Should people be using hedging strategies more than they do? In general, what's your opinion about derivatives and their role in the investment process?

HARRY MARKOWITZ: One of the results of Black-Scholes (1973) is that puts and calls are redundant, that you could do the same thing by shifting back and forth between cash and a security. That was the idea behind portfolio insurance,[14] which was popular until October 1987. In that, you're essentially moving up and down the frontier, with the aim of trying to guarantee that you could not lose more than a certain amount. There are two problems with that. One, let's suppose that you have a portfolio strategy where, depending on anything, you spend half the time in cash and half the time in stock. On average you are 50/50. Compare that with a strategy where you periodically rebalance to a 50/50 mixture. It can be shown that the expected return for a given level of variance is less with this going back and forth and back and forth than just rebalancing to the 50/50 point. I used to consult for a man named Richard Brignoli.[15] Before 1987, Richard would debate Mark Rubinstein of Leland O'Brien Rubinstein Associates about the wisdom of their portfolio insurance strategy. One argument against it was that you have greater expected utility, or greater geometric mean for a given variance, if you just rebalance to a certain point rather than go back and forth. The other argument was that it was causing positive feedback that would eventually wreck the market.

As far as puts and calls go, I was in the convertible arbitrage business for three years, and I made a modest but rather steady return for my clients. You could make a decent return when things were properly priced. If you're writing covered calls and you get a decent return on your money, that can juice up the return on your portfolio. If you're buying calls and the guy on the other side is making money, then on average you're losing money. Buying calls is a way to borrow and leverage and satisfy a desire to have a small chance at a very large gain, because your utility function is like that. But on the average, over the long run, that's not going to make you money. The problem is that it's very hard to value puts and calls. You need a computer and a model, and if you buy them at the wrong time at the wrong price, on average you're going to lose.

MEIR STATMAN: What about a product like an immediate annuity, where you put in $100,000 and you receive a promise of getting, say, $8,000 a year for life, however long you live?

HARRY MARKOWITZ: You are insuring against your longevity. That seems a reasonable bet. It's very hard to evaluate the combination of annuities, fixed income, equities, and consumption rate (as a function of how well the market is doing) that is best for you. I can't do it, but with Monte Carlo I can help. Immediate annuities certainly should be considered as part of your spending strategy post-retirement.

MEIR STATMAN: So this has the characteristics of a structured product with characteristics resembling a put option?

HARRY MARKOWITZ: Well, it's a life insurance policy, but it's not one that pays off if you die. It's one that pays off if you live. Since one of your concerns is to not become a bag-lady before you die, it's certainly a reasonable thing to consider for your portfolio. That's different than wondering if you should be buying puts on your portfolio.

MEIR STATMAN: But why not buy a put? Let's say you have a 60/40 portfolio. Why not buy puts on the equity portion of your portfolio?

HARRY MARKOWITZ: That's certainly a possibility. However, if the puts are overpriced, you'd be better off just going with a 50/50 or a 40/60 mix.

EDWARD BAKER: Certainly, though, there are costs of transacting to get there, so that one always has to trade off one set of costs relative to another, which is another somewhat tricky thing to do.

HARRY MARKOWITZ: There are costs to turning over the puts, and there are costs to moving once from the 60/40 mix to the 40/60 mix. So if you're going to be at that 40/60 mix for a long time, you can, perhaps gradually, move toward the place on the frontier where you feel more comfortable. If the market falls, and the value of your portfolio goes down, then maybe again you want to shift down the frontier, just because now the motivation of protecting yourself from further declines outweighs the motivation of having returns over the long run. Again, it depends on prices.

MEIR STATMAN: When we spoke with Eugene Fama,[16] we asked him about the state of finance. He suggested that the peak in our sense that we had it all figured out was sometime around 1975, when we had portfolio theory, a capital asset pricing model (CAPM) that seemed to work, and market efficiency. Nowadays, he said, we have an empirical asset pricing model that we don't really fully understand. How would you assess the state of finance?

HARRY MARKOWITZ: I would say that the highlight, the peak of our understanding—and I'm being only slightly facetious—was somewhere around March 1959.... Now, you know I don't really believe that. Let's distinguish between portfolio theory as advice to a single individual investor or institutional investor and the capital asset pricing model or the Black-Scholes model as hypotheses about the world. So we have Markowitz (1959) versus Sharpe (1964). In the area of more recent developments in portfolio theory as applied to one investor, we have the notion of asset classes, top-down strategy, and Ibbotson data. There's certainly been a filling out of the Markowitz view by many other people besides Markowitz. That's one train of thought. The other is the Sharpe-Lintner-Mossin Capital Asset Pricing Model,[17] which became the Black-Scholes model in continuous time. Those have had two different histories. With the CAPM, if it were true, expected returns would be a linear function of betas. Fama-French (1993) says those returns are functions of everything except betas—well, a couple of things other than betas. The more sophisticated calculations that have been based on Black-Scholes have become increasingly obscure and troublesome.

EDWARD BAKER: In an answer to a previous question, you talked at length about the high points in the history of financial market theory and investment theory. What do you think might happen in the future? Have all of the great and/or useful ideas already been discovered and played out, or is there something new that you think could come in the future?

HARRY MARKOWITZ: I don't see much hope in our actually being able to develop financial models that can predict future market moves very well. Hopefully we can develop financial models that will help us understand what is going on, but not to the point where we can say that this stock will go up and that asset class will go down. Naturally the areas where I expect progress are the areas where I'm working, because obviously I wouldn't work in areas where I don't expect progress. Let me tell you about two areas that I think can be of value. First, one of the problems on the portfolio management side is what to do about illiquid assets and changing probability distributions. If assets are perfectly liquid, it's easier to figure out the optimum move to make now, because we don't have to worry about potentially incurring more costs than it was worth if we move now and then want to move back. There's a paper by Erik Van Dijk and myself (2003), and a more recent one by Kritzman, Myrgren, and Page (2009) that have heuristics for how to handle this that seem to work out very well. The problem of illiquidity and changing probability distributions always has been a sticky one for portfolio management, and I think we have a handle on it. The second area I'm working on is the problem that our models—our hypotheses about the world—tend to be very simplistic. Economists' models tend to consist of a few equations and a few unknowns, and that's supposed to model the world. I think there should be more use of asynchronous, discrete-event simulation models of financial markets. A couple of colleagues—Bruce Jacobs and Ken Levy—and I have done some work about that, some of which we have already published, and there's a forthcoming book where we show our experimentation with asynchronous discrete-event simulation of financial markets. I think those are two areas where we should see progress.

EDWARD BAKER: What sort of applications do you see for that latter area?

HARRY MARKOWITZ: There are at least two kinds of applications: One has to do with government policies, for example, does the uptick rule[18] help markets. The second has to do with investment policies and trading strategies. For example, when should one use market versus limit orders. Such asynchronous simulation is used, for example, in manufacturing simulations, where the world is too complicated to figure out analytically, as well as in transportation and computer simulations and war games. The financial markets are certainly at least as complicated as a war game, and I think we could use these techniques as well.

EDWARD BAKER: Those are certainly very interesting ideas.

HARRY MARKOWITZ: Now here's one question I was waiting for you to ask me. In Jason Zweig's book, *Your Money and Your Brain*, I'm quoted as saying that I split my retirement money 50/50 between stocks and bonds. Just to clarify, that is what I did in 1952, when the RAND Corporation asked how I wanted to split my contributions between TIAA and CREF. Like most people, I split it 50/50. Now I don't do that. I've seen many efficient frontiers, and I know typically people like me are higher on the frontier. I am older than I was in 1952, but I'm also a little wealthier now, so I'm willing to go up the frontier. I split my money among asset classes, like efficient portfolios I have seen. I know I should overweight small-cap stocks as compared with large-caps and perhaps overweight emerging markets as compared with more established international markets and then get a comfortable balance between stocks and bonds.

EDWARD BAKER: I'm impressed also that a lot of your conclusions seem to be judgmental and reasoned, rather than purely based on running an optimization.

HARRY MARKOWITZ: It's a back-and-forth process. For example, one of the things everybody does in using an optimizer is put in constraints, and they'll say: "Well, we don't necessarily believe that input. We've tried very hard, but if the answer comes out more than 10-percent emerging markets, don't buy it. Put in a constraint." So there is a back-and-forth between intuition and calculation. I have absolutely no idea to what extent someone who is not quite as comfortably fixed as I am ought to put money into annuities and where they ought to be on the frontier and how fast they can consume. I think that Monte Carlo analyses really add to your intuition. If they don't add to your intuition, then they are of no value.

EDWARD BAKER: That's a very important message for our readers to take away. It was also interesting to hear your perspective on how you actually build your own portfolio. We knew it wasn't just 50/50 based on what you did in 2008.

HARRY MARKOWITZ: That brings to mind another question that I've often been asked: Isn't equal weighting better? There's a standard answer to that. Suppose somebody is given the choice of stocks versus bonds, then equal weighting would be 50/50. Now suppose somebody is given the choice among large cap, small cap, EAFE, emerging markets, and bonds. Then equal-weighted would be an allocation of 20 percent to each of those, so that ends up being 80-percent equities and 20-percent bonds. Which is right? I think if you push it, equal weighting doesn't work.

■ ■ ■

ENDNOTES

1   *Investment Companies* (now issued as *Investment Companies Yearbook*), an annual compendium of information on investment companies and mutual funds, has been published by Wiesenberger Financial Services since 1944.

2   The efficient frontier, which was first defined by Dr. Markowitz in his 1952 paper that launched modern portfolio theory, examines a universe of potential asset combinations and the expected risk and return for each mix. The efficient frontier is a collection of such portfolios, each of which represents the highest return for a given level of risk. This group forms a convex line in a plot of the portfolios' returns versus their risks, graphically depicting the efficient frontier.

3   Tjalling C. Koopmans (1910–1985) was awarded the Nobel Memorial Prize in Economic Sciences in 1975 for his work in resource allocation, specifically the theory of optimal use of resources.

4   The Cowles Foundation for Research in Economics, founded in 1932, was established to foster the development and application of rigorous logical, mathematical, and statistical methods of analysis.

5   A study of major pension funds by Brinson et al. (1986) concluded that asset allocation accounted for more than 90 percent of the variation in a portfolio's quarterly returns, leading to increased focus on allocation among asset classes as the most important consideration in portfolio construction.

6   Roger Ibbotson, professor of finance at the Yale School of Management, together with Rex Sinquefield, authored *Stocks, Bonds, Bills, and Inflation*, which serves as a standard reference for information on investment market returns dating back to 1926.

7   A Monte Carlo analysis is a sampling method that uses random numbers and probability to compute results, often used when a model is complex, nonlinear, or involves more than a few uncertain parameters. Monte Carlo simulations use inputs randomly generated from probability distributions to simulate the process of sampling from an actual population. The term is a reference to the games of chance popular in Monte Carlo.

8   Roger C. Gibson is founder and chief investment officer of Gibson Capital Management and author of *Asset Allocation: Balancing Financial Risk*.

9   In probability and statistics, Student's t-distribution is a probability distribution that occurs in estimating the mean of a normally distributed population when the sample size is small. It forms the basis for Student's t-tests for the statistical significance of the difference between two sample means and for confidence intervals for the difference between two population means.

10   On October 19, 1987, or Black Monday, stock markets around the world plummeted, with the Dow Jones Industrial Average losing 22.6 percent, the largest one-day percentage decline in U.S. stock market history. Potential causes of the crash—including program trading, overvaluation, illiquidity, market psychology, foreign exchange, and inflation—continue to be debated.

11   The black swan theory describes rare, unpredictable, and high-impact events. In his book, *The Black Swan: The Impact of the Highly Improbable*, Nassim Nicholas Taleb applied the term to events such as the rise of the Internet and the September 11, 2001, attacks on the United States. He also argued that banks and brokerage firms were very exposed to black swan events and major losses. The term comes from the fact that it was commonly assumed that all swans were white until black swans were discovered in Australia in the seventeenth century.

12   John von Neumann (1903–1957) and Oskar Morgenstern (1902–1977) authored *Theory of Games and Economic Behavior* (1944), which, in addition to creating the field of game theory, introduced important concepts such as utility theory and choice under uncertainty.

13   Leonard J. Savage (1917–1971) was a U.S. mathematician and statistician whose 1954 book *Foundations of Statistics* proposed a theory of subjective and personal probability and statistics that forms a basis for Bayesian statistics.

14   Portfolio insurance involves hedging an equity portfolio against market risk by selling equity index futures short or buying equity index put options. This strategy was developed by University of California, Berkeley academics Mark Rubinstein and Hayne Leland and marketed by Leland O'Brien Rubinstein Associates.

15   Richard Brignoli was the founder of Brignoli Models Inc., a quantitative investment firm with the primary task of predicting and measuring the growth rate of various investment strategies.

16   See "Ideas That Changed the Theory and Practice of Investing: A Conversation with Eugene F. Fama, PhD," *Journal of Investment Consulting* 9, no. 1 (fall 2008): 6–14.

[17] Working independently, William F. Sharpe, John Lintner, and Jan Mossin developed a theoretical equilibrium model of market prices called the capital asset pricing model in the mid-1960s.

[18] The uptick rule, also known as the short-sale rule, was a Securities and Exchange Commission (SEC) trading regulation that restricted short sales of stock from being placed on a downtick in the market price of the shares. Short sales could only be permitted on upticks (last trade higher than the one before) or zero-plus ticks (last trade is the same as previous, which was an uptick). The regulation was passed in 1938 to prevent selling shares short into a declining market; at the time market mechanisms and liquidity couldn't be guaranteed to prevent panic share declines or outright manipulation. This regulation was rescinded in July 2007 by decree of the SEC; as a result short sales can occur (where eligible) on any price tick in the market, whether up or down.

REFERENCES

Black, Fischer, and Myron Scholes. 1973. The Pricing of Options and Corporate Liabilities. *Journal of Political Economy* 81, no. 3 (May/June): 637–654.

Brinson, Gary P., L. Randolph Hood, and Gilbert L. Beebower. 1986. Determinants of Portfolio Performance. *Financial Analysts Journal* 42, no. 4 (July/August): 39–44.

Fama, Eugene F., and Kenneth R. French. 1993. Common Risk Factors in the Returns on Stocks and Bonds. *Journal of Financial Economics* 33, no. 1 (February): 3–56.

Fama, Eugene F. 2008. Ideas That Changed the Theory and Practice of Investing: A Conversation with Eugene F. Fama, Ph.D. *Journal of Investment Consulting* 9, no. 1 (fall): 6–14.

Gibson, Roger G. 2007. *Asset Allocation: Balancing Financial Risk*, 4th ed. Hightstown, NJ: McGraw-Hill Professional.

Holton, Lisa. 2009. Is Markowitz Wrong? Market Turmoil Fuels Nontraditional Approaches to Managing Investment Risk. *Journal of Financial Planning* 22, no. 1 (January): 20–26.

Jacobs, Bruce I., Kenneth N. Levy, and Harry M. Markowitz. 2004. Financial Market Simulation. *Journal of Portfolio Management* (30th Anniversary): 142–152.

———. 2010. Simulating Security Markets in Dynamic and Equilibrium Modes. *Financial Analysts Journal* 66, no. 5 (September/October): 42–53.

Kritzman, Mark, Simon Myrgren, and Sebastien Page. 2009. Optimal Rebalancing: A Scalable Solution. *Journal of Investment Management* 7, no. 1 (first quarter): 9–19.

Levy, Haim, and Harry Markowitz. 1979. Approximating Expected Utility by a Function of Mean and Variance. *American Economic Review* 69, no. 3 (June): 308–313.

Markowitz, Harry. 1952. Portfolio Selection. *Journal of Finance* 7, no. 1 (March): 77–91.

———. 1952. The Utility of Wealth. *Journal of Political Economy* 60, no. 2 (April): 151–158.

———. 1956. The Optimization of a Quadratic Function Subject to Linear Constraints. *Naval Research Logistics Quarterly* 3, no. 1–2 (March/June): 111–133.

———. 1959. *Portfolio Selection: Efficient Diversification of Investments*. New York: Wiley.

———. 2009. Proposals Concerning the Current Financial Crisis. *Financial Analysts Journal* 65, no. 1 (January/February): 25–27.

Markowitz, Harry, and Nilufer Usmen. 1996. The Likelihood of Various Stock Market Return Distributions, Part 1: Principles of Inference. *Journal of Risk and Uncertainty* 13, no. 3 (November): 207–219.

———. 1996. The Likelihood of Various Stock Market Return Distributions, Part 2: Empirical Results. *Journal of Risk and Uncertainty* 13, no. 3 (November): 221–247.

Markowitz, Harry, and Erik L. van Dijk. 2003. Single-Period Mean–Variance Analysis in a Changing World (corrected). *Financial Analysts Journal* 59, no. 2 (March/April): 30–44.

Savage, Leonard J. 1954. *Foundations of Statistics*. Hoboken, NJ: John Wiley & Sons, Inc.

Sharpe, William F. 1964. Capital Asset Prices: A Theory of Market Equilibrium under Conditions of Risk. *Journal of Finance* 19, no. 3 (September): 425–442.

Taleb, Nassim Nicholas. 2007. The Black Swan: *The Impact of the Highly Improbable*. New York: Random House.

Von Neumann, John, and Oskar Morgenstern. 1944. *Theory of Games and Economic Behavior*. Princeton, NJ: Princeton University Press.

Williams, John Burr. 1938. *The Theory of Investment Value*. Cambridge, MA: Harvard University Press.

Zweig, Jason. 2007. *Your Money and Your Brain: How The New Science of Neuroeconomics Can Help Make You Rich*. New York: Simon & Schuster.

This interview was published in its entirety in *Journal of Investment Consulting* 10, no. 1, Summer 2009.

CHAPTER 10

ROBERT MERTON: RATIONAL MAN, WITH A BIG "R," BIG "M"

ROBERT C. MERTON, PHD

Recipient of the 1997 Nobel Memorial Prize in Economic Sciences; School of Management Distinguished Professor of Finance at the MIT Sloan School of Management and University Professor Emeritus at Harvard University; author, *Continuous-Time Finance and the Global Financial System: A Functional Perspective* and numerous articles in academic journals.

Robert Merton hails from a family of innovative thinkers. His father, Robert K. Merton, was the eminent psychologist who gave us the concepts of "unintended consequences" and "self-fulfilling prophecy." As a result, Merton gained a solid foundation in understanding the social sciences, especially sociology and functionalism. Among his many accomplishments is Merton's structural credit analysis model, which relates the price of a firm's risky debt to the price of its equity. Merton exemplified perseverance in his career starting with his days as a student. He applied to several doctoral programs, and he was turned down by all but one—the Massachusetts Institute of Technology, which accepted him as a candidate and provided him with a full fellowship.

■ ■ ■

MARGARET TOWLE: First of all, we appreciate your spending time with us today, Dr. Merton. We'd like to start with some general questions that we ask each of our Masters, with the first question focusing on the major factors that helped to shape your career and brought you to where you are today. Your career has obviously encompassed some great achievements, and we would like to hear about these as well as your biggest challenges and disappointments.

ROBERT MERTON: Well, that's a fair question, but it's a bit daunting because the major factors were a combination of my education, of course, and a lot of good luck. I had an engineering education as an undergraduate at Columbia University, and I was able to take many mathematics courses, applied and pure, and explore all kinds of uses for math, including mathematical sociology. I had a wonderful undergraduate education where people didn't interfere with what I was learning. Then, ultimately, I ended up at the Massachusetts Institute of Technology (MIT). In my first semester there, I was advised to take a second-year economics course with Paul Samuelson,[1] even though I had no economics background. That turned out to be a major factor for me because not only did I learn my economics that way, sort of backwards, but I also came to know Paul and became his research assistant. I found out, among other things, that what I had been thinking of as an after-hours sort of pursuit actually could be a part of a day job of serious research in economics. That was a major element. Additionally, Paul happened to be working in some of the financial areas that I knew something about and wanted to pursue. So I would have to say, first, getting to MIT. By the way, I was turned down at every doctoral program to which I applied except MIT, and they gave me a full fellowship, so that was a large piece of luck. And my admission at MIT was dependent on another piece of luck, which was that the admissions person at MIT happened to recognize the mathematical people who wrote my letters of recommendation.

I'm jumping around a little at the very beginning, but I'd say getting a good education and exposure to some great people was important, but there also was an incredible amount of luck. I don't know where I would have ended up had these events not taken place. That was the main driver. Also, the fact that I had earned my master's at the California Institute of Technology, where they had the notion of students "playing" with research, rather than passively learning material, so from the beginning of being a graduate student I was fooling around with research in economics. That gave me a very big kickstart into doing the research that helped move my career forward. I hadn't even thought about teaching in a business school, and Franco Modigliani,[2] one of my other professors at MIT, came to me and said, "How would you like to do that?" So I ended up in the Sloan School at MIT, which is where I've stayed and enjoyed it, and that's a major factor in how I built a career. I've always been involved full-time in academics and full-time in practice—not full-time in practice, but a lot in practice. I found that the interplay between being engaged in a serious practice and doing serious research, each fed a bit on the other, and that was an important factor. It certainly helped me in formulating models, and the models helped me in the practice. Also, my father and I were very, very close throughout life.[3] He was an eminent sociologist, so I grew up understanding a bit about the social sciences, particularly sociology and functionalism,[4] and all kinds of topics that had an influence on my research in finance, especially later on. So that's the answer to your first question.

Probably my major achievement was the work I did in developing ways of modeling the dynamics of financial markets, and securities and optimization under uncertainty. That led to a series of papers, initially, on the lifecycle problem of lifetime consumption and investment, and then those same tools led to the work on derivatives pricing. Long before coming to MIT, I was always involved in derivatives. I used to trade them, and I thought I knew what I was doing, but I didn't really know. So I came in with a lot of market knowledge about derivatives, and that helped me when I decided to work on research in that area. So I'd say the early work of that sort was probably the most fruitful and turned out to have a major impact in the sense that, on the portfolio side, we were able to reconcile expected utility theory[5] and mean-variance theory[6] and then see the real difference between dynamic intertemporal models versus one-period static models.

MARGARET TOWLE: What about challenges?

ROBERT MERTON: In terms of challenges or disappointments, well, on the academic side, for the past twenty years or so, I've been very interested in developing what I think of as a functional perspective on understanding how institutions change endogenously. I'd like to move away from an institutional definition of the anchors of the system to a functional one. While this idea has gotten a fair amount of traction in practice, it's had practically zero effect in academia. So I guess I'd say that's a disappointment. The other is that I had thought that the impact of finance should have been much quicker into the fields of public finance, particularly macroeconomics, but also just the whole idea of understanding macro and monetary and so forth. It is just now beginning to evolve. I've had some very interesting successes in practice, and I've had some rather spectacular failures. Long-Term Capital Management will forever be a part of my life, and I wish that hadn't happened as it did, but that's what happens when you're working in an innovative area.[7]

The other thing is a natural disappointment, so I'd say it's more in the challenge area, and that is, if you're working in financial innovation, you often have to be very patient. For example, take the option-pricing model that Myron Scholes and Fischer Black and I came up with. Myron and I took it to Wall Street in 1971. It was published in 1973. By 1975, I think it is fair to say that everyone in the options market was using that methodology, and largely that same methodology—the methodology, not the formula—is still being used today, and it is still being used as a core methodology for doing much of this type of work. So that was a very fast adaption of something that was conceived in theory and then put into practice. On the other hand, I came up with a debt model, or a credit model, that was published in 1974, and it took twenty-five years before that was widely used in practice, so one has to be extremely patient sometimes in the innovation area.

MARGARET TOWLE: One of the points that you have mentioned a few times is the idea of theory and practice. If we look at the *Journal of Investment Consulting*, it is a fusion of theory and practice for the consulting advisory world, in terms of providing this information in the print medium. Given your perspective and your demonstrated ability to combine these two constructs throughout your career, what do you see as major trends in the investment industry today, and what are the issues that are important looking out into the future? For example, you mentioned the long time horizon required for ideas to take hold, so looking out five, ten, or even fifteen years, what do you see as some of the major issues in the industry?

ROBERT MERTON: I'm not sure if I have a grand vision as to where it's all going. One thing that I think is going to be very important—that remarkably is missing now—is the notion of goals-based investing. This probably won't be for twenty years, but I hope it isn't twenty years. I've been doing a lot of work in the area of next-generation retirement system design and implementation. If you look at that area, amazingly many investment products that are developed don't have a goal. They are a process, like target date funds. I only use target date funds as an example. I'm not trying to trash target date funds or criticize them, but they're very widely used. If you look at what they are, or if you read a prospectus, it says: "Here's a process. As you get older, we're going to adjust the amount allocated between fixed income and equity." They never tell you where you're trying to get or why, and that has a profound effect on a whole range of factors in investing because, if you have an actual goal for investing, you start with that, and then you derive the optimal way to achieve that goal. You'll find that you get a lot different strategies and methodologies and ways of reaching your goal than you do with the open-ended approach. So it's not that finance theory or science hasn't had goals in the sense of preference functions and so forth. It's just that they don't seem to appear in a useful or effective way in practice. At least that's my judgment. So I think goals-based investing is going to be one piece.

■ ■ ■

> One thing that I think is going to be very important—
> that remarkably is missing now—is the notion of
> goals-based investing. This probably won't be
> for twenty years, but I hope it isn't twenty years.

A second piece is the ability to take advantage of all of the information, the so-called big data[8] processing. We'll be able to create much more mass customization of solutions, and we won't have to put people in broad buckets, like age, for example, so that everybody thirty-four-years old follows the same plan, no matter their gender or other factors. That really hasn't been developed yet, but I think it will be a big area. In connection with that, there will be much greater integration of data. We all know, in principle, that to make the optimal choices for portfolios, you really need to look at all of the assets that are relevant and liabilities and the like, and that again isn't generally done. I think you can get huge improvements in practice by being able to carry out a more integrated analysis. That doesn't mean that you control everything, but that you're aware of all of the assets and various liabilities in terms of the optimization, and that's really becoming quite feasible with the technology.

Now, the third piece really goes back to the public sector. Since the great financial crisis, we've been exposed to the focus on systemic risk. If you look at the macro models that are used, even by the Federal Reserve, they're very, very crude, and they're all certainty models to which they then add a noise term. However, the structures of these models inherently omit the fact that risk is an intrinsic part of the system, so they have no options or those kinds of structures associated with structural uncertainty. As a result, they are not likely to be very effective at picking up on the kinds of situations in which systemic risk propagation can happen. I've always thought that finance has a lot to contribute to this area of public finance, and that hasn't happened. However, it's starting to happen, and I think it will be a big area, particularly in other parts of the world, other than the Anglo-Saxon world, where the distinction between the public and private sectors in the financial system can often be blurred. These tools are going to be a big growth area and one that I believe will be for the good.

MEIR STATMAN: You've developed tools for advisors, using the goals-based investing approach. Would you describe these tools?

ROBERT MERTON: Sure. First, a brief background: The retirement function, as you know, is performed partly by government, partly by employer plans, and partly by personal savings. Over the past decade or so, one of the biggest shocks to the retirement function has been to employer plans. These were largely defined benefit (DB) plans, which are no longer. I mean, they're still around, but they're being closed, and no one is starting any new ones. That shock left a void as to what needed to be done. The natural thing to fill that void was defined contribution (DC) plans, because they were the only alternative. They solve the problem of the employers pulling out of DB plans by bounding their risks and making their costs more predictable. However, the problem with DC plans is that they were never designed for core retirement, and they certainly weren't designed for people who were served by DB plans.

■ ■ ■

If I ask a thirty-year-old, a forty-year-old, or a fifty-year-old what they want for retirement, the first question I always get back is, "What should I want?"

So this set up an opportunity to create something new. What I did was to go back to basic principles and ask the question, "What would you do if you had to design a system for individuals to serve this function subject to the constraints of what plan sponsors would be willing to take in terms of risk?" This really meant that it had to be a DC legal structure, because sponsors weren't willing to take the open-ended risks of a DB plan. The way we started was to set a goal. Again, the target user really was working middle-class people in large retirement plans, and so those imposed the kinds of constraints, and then we set up the goal. In setting the goal, first of all, you're not going to be able to really find out what people want. In fact, most people, as I'm sure you know, don't really know what they want when it comes to retirement objectives. If I ask a thirty-year-old, a forty-year-old, or a fifty-year-old what they want for retirement, the first question I always get back is, "What should I want?" They really don't know, and for younger people, it's an abstract concept. So they're not going to tell you what they want, other than to say, "Well, I'd like to have a good retirement." So the goal we set up wasn't very imaginative, but it was definite. When they reach retirement, most people, if you don't know anything else about them, would like to live better if they could, but they certainly don't want to live a lot worse if they have a choice. So we have Modigliani's Lifecycle Hypothesis, in that a good retirement means being able to sustain the standard of living that you've come to enjoy in the latter part of your work life. That became the goal. Then you have to convert that goal to a financial goal, and that conversion essentially was to say that standard of living is probably best defined by income, rather than accumulation of wealth. So the goals were set in terms of income, and that income had to be protected from inflation if it's standard of living and if it's going to take care of retirement for life, and that became the financial goal.

Once you have that, then you can come up with the design criteria that are important. The plan has to be efficient, scalable, and low-cost. Scalable is particularly important. It has to work effectively for participants who are never going to become engaged in the process. That is to say, they don't tell you anything. That's what we call—post the Pension Protection Act of 2006[9]— defaulters,[10] people who are enrolled in plans but who never give you any information. You've certainly written plenty on that, and I experienced it when I was at CREF (College Retirement Equities Fund). There are many people who are not engaged in the process and won't likely become engaged, and even if they were, it's not clear that they know what to do. The plan has to work well for such people, and so that was part of the design. It should be customized, not only individual accounts, but the goal should be individual, not collective. That's doable now, though it wasn't doable in an effective way with the technology of the past. Then you put all of this together, and you end up with a solution. You offer people a solution: The money is going to come in because they're in a plan, they have a goal, and then you optimize. That is, you set up an objective function and optimize to get that goal, which is defined in terms of the standard of living in retirement. You can do that, and you can gather the information you need to customize it if you're clever, without ever talking to the individual.

So that's the core of the solution. Another important thing is, if people do become engaged, which eventually most of them will, that you only give them meaningful information and meaningful choices, and those are very few. Here's an example from the auto industry that illustrates meaningful versus important information. If you were buying a car, you go to the dealer down the street, and then you come to see me, and I'd say to you: "Well, you know, the guy down the street is a good guy. His engine has a 9:1 compression ratio. My engine has a 9.3:1 compression ratio." Now you're smart enough to figure out that first, compression ratio must be fairly important or otherwise I wouldn't mention it, and second, higher must be better or I wouldn't mention it. But can you convert that increase of three-tenths in compression ratio into something that matters to you, such as better gas mileage, faster speed, or more reliability? I doubt it. I can assure you that the compression ratio is important for the function of the car for all of those things, so it's important information, but it's meaningless information to you the car buyer and user. It's not meaningful, so that's the kind of information we wouldn't give to individuals.

In investing, if you have a goal—now think retirement—there are fundamentally really only three ways you can improve your chances of hitting that goal. You can save more, you can work longer, or you can take more risk. I don't think there's a fourth one. If you have one, I'd be happy to hear it.

MEIR STATMAN: You can lower your standard-of-living goal.

ROBERT MERTON: No, because I said we had a fixed goal. So, given the goal, there are only three things you can do, and then of course you can rate that goal against other objectives. But if you accept the notion that when you do engage people, you want to offer only meaningful choices, then really the only meaningful choices for people are those three things, given the goal. Now they may want to change their goal and get feedback and so forth, which this does, by the way. However, the point is, almost all of the other factors that we see, at least risk-return frontiers, asset allocation, glide paths, etcetera, etcetera, no matter how intuitive you make it, are like telling you the components of engines when you're buying a car. To me, it doesn't make sense as a way to approach this on a mass scale.

By the way, DB plans were an institutional way of performing that function. If you're a twenty-seven-year-old who enrolled in the old DB plan, they'd tell you: "You'll work for the company for the rest of your life. When you retire, you'll get an income based on number of years of service and your latter years' level of salary, and that income, combined with Social Security, ought to be adequate for you to sustain your standard of living." That's a thirty-second speech, and the next time you have to think about it is when you retire. Now that's idealized—we understand DB plans have a lot of aspects that don't fit the modern labor force, but the point of it was that you didn't tell people about all of the workings under the hood of a DB plan, all of the investments, and everything else because that's not meaningful to them. So the attempt here is not to replicate a DB plan, but rather to provide a solution and to have the characteristics that make sense. So that's a long-winded answer.

MEIR STATMAN: Just one clarification. In your program, do you allow people to make changes in all of the levers that you mentioned?

ROBERT MERTON: Absolutely. And that's all.

MEIR STATMAN: Yes, and I can see that.

ROBERT MERTON: Okay. So it's very different, in that sense, from what you usually see in a DC plan. Plus it's integrated with other retirement assets, and as you know from portfolio theory, that's very important.

EDWARD BAKER: Is it integrated with other personal assets as well?

ROBERT MERTON: It could be, but as a practical matter, no, because that would mean that you would have to get information from the person. My view is that the system has to work, at the extreme, if you never have any contact with the person. Also, the information that you get from people is often highly unreliable, e.g., what your house is worth, that sort of input. You can do things to fix that, but the answer is, of course, someday, if you have efficient ways of gathering information that's reliable and happens on a regular basis, sure, you'd want to do that. But this is not a financial plan for the entire lifecycle of the person. This is just solving one important piece of it, which is the retirement part.

RONALD KAHN: It sounds like you're focused on, as you said, working/middle-class people, so maybe their house is the other major asset they have, but they're not going to have a lot of other investments.

ROBERT MERTON: That's right. High-net-worth people and even upper-middle-class to well-off people—well, there's lots more to be done for them, but retirement for working/middle-class people was the particular problem for which this solution was designed. It can be used for wealthier people, and you use it in components and so forth, but this was the problem. The challenge was that you suddenly had millions of people around the planet who were receiving this part of financial services through plans that were no longer going to be there and finding a way to fill that void in some efficient way. The technology can be adapted to the most-sophisticated investors, but that's not what this solution is designed to do.

EDWARD BAKER: One of the interesting differences between DB and DC plans is that DB plans define an income level that you're going to receive, whereas the DC plans are focused more on a wealth level. How are your goals specified?

ROBERT MERTON: Income level. Absolutely. That's why this plan was designed with the first step of setting a goal, and the goal is standard of living. For most people, when you press them, a standard of living is defined in terms of income, not by an accumulation of wealth. If you have $5 million, tell me what standard of living you can support. You can't answer that for me, right? With the thirty-year TIPS (Treasury inflation-protected security) currently trading at 30 basis points or so, that's very different from 300 basis points, that is, you can have the same amount of money invested, but very different incomes, and it's not sustainable. So the answer is an income goal. By the way, that's quite important because the risk is measured in terms of that goal, not in terms of your wealth, the way it's normally done, so the risk-free asset is not a Treasury bill. In fact, a Treasury bill is very risky, as we are well aware.

TONY KAO: I used to be with a large corporate pension plan. We all know that DB plans have become less relevant in terms of providing individual retirement. From your perspective, as an academic as well as a practitioner in the DB world for years, looking back, in terms of providing secure income to retirees, what went wrong with corporate DB plans or, as a separate question, with public plans?

ROBERT MERTON: Actually, they are similar problems. I mean—and this is not a Monday morning quarterback description, and I'll even recuse myself from myself—many people have written for a long, long time about the whole process in which contributions were determined in employer plans. Let's just stay within the United States, although there are similar issues in the United Kingdom and elsewhere. First of all, actuarial science is a very strong, powerful science. It was around long before finance emerged as a field, but actuaries' approach to modeling is not a very good one for dealing with financial market risks. The biggest problem is projecting, that is, treating expected returns as if they were a sure thing. A corollary of that is that stocks, or risky assets, in the long run aren't risky. The latter is just not true. I rarely make such absolute statements. It's not true theoretically. It's not true empirically. By the way, if you do believe it's true, do you know where you could best use that idea? I have the following proposal. What has a longer time horizon in the United States than pension funds? The government, right? At least I hope so. So why don't we have the government issue trillions of dollars in debt and take that money and invest it around the world in stock markets and other risky assets? If you really can, in the long run, get higher returns virtually risk-free that way, then you have a money machine, because you borrow at 2 or 3 percent and you earn 7 percent. If you do that on a large-enough scale, you can solve not only the pension problem, but you can fund the entire U.S. government without any taxes. It's the same principle. You laugh, but you have to say, "Hmmm, maybe, even before we get into the mathematics or anything, there's something strange because the principle is the same." Plus, by the way, unlike other long-term investors, the government has a central bank, so if it has any short-term liquidity problems, it can handle those, too.

The reason I bring that up is because, if you look at the accounting, which leads to what the contribution rate should be, that accounting has always, in one way or another, underestimated liabilities. Now it's true that some of the smoothing by actuaries at times overestimated liabilities because, in the days of high interest rates in the 1970s, they were averaging data for the past five or ten years, so there were transitory effects. However, the overwhelming fact is that we didn't put in enough funding, and we treated risky assets as if they were risk-free. The extreme of this, which recently got reaffirmed in the public sector in the GASB (Governmental Accounting Standards Board) and in the Pension Relief Act of 2010,[11] is that you can discount your liabilities at the expected return on assets. Now there's no place in finance where that makes sense. It has an even more perverse effect that says the more risk you take with your assets, the lower the value of your liabilities and the less you have to contribute. So you have a system that feeds off itself. Now I'm not being capricious. I'm saying that, if you look at the whole system, that's the way it evolved, and it works well until it doesn't work. It took the events of 2000–2002 to finally bring it home, as world stock markets fell, world interest rates fell, the weaker industries—steel, autos, and so forth—went bankrupt, and chief executive officers around the world came to recognize they had more risk in their pension plans than they had in their businesses. It was the most leveraged debt on the planet.

■ ■ ■

> ## The reason I bring that up is because, if you look at the accounting, which leads to what the contribution rate should be, that accounting has always, in one way or another, underestimated liabilities.

Just quickly—do you recognize that the risk of a typical corporate DB plan is identical to the risk of entering into a total return asset swap? Say you had $100 in assets and $100 in liabilities, so you're fully funded. If you wanted to have no risk in the pension payouts, you would immunize, right? You'd match funds. I don't say we should do that, but that's the zero-risk benchmark. If the average large corporate pension plan had 60 percent or 70 percent of assets in risk, what's the change in risk from that? Well, you'd be substituting receiving the total returns on, let's say, equities and paying the total returns on fixed income, i.e., long-dated, long-duration fixed-income assets. Well, that's a swap. I receive total return on the stock market, and I pay the total return on long-duration bonds.

You asked me what went wrong. I'm saying that we were taking enormous risks in this industry, huge leveraged bets in our pension system, and in the 1990s when stock prices rose almost every year, that worked very well. In fact, everything was fine. When you make a huge leveraged bet and the markets are up, you win, but when you lose, it's big. Now we have the $3-trillion underfunding of public employees' pension plans, and that's for accrued current benefits, not future. So that would be my answer. In fairness, I think there are additional factors, such as the mobility of the labor force and so forth, but the biggest one was that. I didn't see employees marching on their companies trying to get rid of their DB plans. They're very happy with them.

EDWARD BAKER: May I ask a slightly different question? You mentioned before that you think financial economics is now beginning to influence policy and macroeconomic decision making. Can you comment on how you think that is actually occurring?

ROBERT MERTON: The way I see it, this is driven by need. By the way, a fellow with whom I've written some papers and who over the past decade has devoted his life and passion to this idea is Dale Gray[12] at the International Monetary Fund (IMF). He's written a book and also many, many papers where, in looking at the propagation of macrofinancial risk across and within sectors, he essentially models all of the interchanges, interactions, particularly the guarantees, but not just the formal guarantees. As you know, every debt issue implicitly has a guarantee in it, even if you guarantee it yourself. We've seen formal guarantees given by governments, and we have surely seen huge implicit guarantees. Now, those are options, and options not only are nonlinear in their response to the underlying investment but also, depending on where assets move and so forth, what they call the delta can change dramatically, so the sensitivity of the value of the guarantee to price changes in the assets guaranteed can change dramatically. None of that is embedded in anything that the Federal Reserve or the macroeconomists do because their models are basically certainty models, and options, like all insurance, have no structure, no purpose in certainty models. So they tack onto a certain model some Monte Carlo simulations[13] of error terms, and the effect of that is simply to make every sample path act as if it's certain, in the sense there's no feedback. If volatility goes up in a typical macro model, you don't get a change in value, a change in risk of the various interchanges across this. What Dale Gray and his work have done is essentially model all of that using the notion of contingent claims analysis (CCA),[14] and it's generated a lot of interesting results. It's produced some very dramatic comparisons between this kind of model and the standard macro model for financial stability and risk propagation in terms of showing how much is left out with the standard model.

This notion is beginning to take off. Gray is in perpetual motion around the world, ministries of finance, all of the central banks. Of course, hedge funds are also interested, and other large investors are paying attention because they are interested in how it all propagates. Why? Because of need. People are recognizing that much of what happened in the financial crisis and afterwards was the consequence of not taking account of these factors. At the time they talked about large, highly improbable, and unexplainable shocks that were not anticipated in the assumed distributions—events of ten standard deviations. I don't believe it was ten standard deviations. I believe that the sensitivity of all of these guarantees got much higher because assets fell, and the standard linear models didn't pick that sensitivity change up. What they viewed as a ten-sigma event really was a two- or three-sigma event, but measured with the wrong sensitivity factor. I think that the ways of looking at events like this are finally going to have an impact. These models are informed through market variables as well as inputs, and they promise to be able to do much more serious simulations of what can happen to the system. I'm somewhat hopeful that that's going to happen.

■ ■ ■

Of course, hedge funds are also interested, and other large investors are paying attention because they are interested in how it all propagates. Why? Because of need.

Some other work along this line in which I'm currently involved is understanding the connectivity of all of these entities, sovereigns and so forth, and measuring and creating maps of connectedness. You get some really fascinating results on these maps as to how things looked before the crisis of 2008–2009 versus the way they look after, up to today. There's a lot that can be done using what I would call market-proven techniques such as CCA, tools that are well-understood in finance. We've had a great deal of experience and practice using these tools, and the way you address things in this new application, as far as I can see, really hasn't been used, certainly in policy in the past. I don't see it being used in the sense of predicting GDP (gross domestic product) growth so much as being used to deal with the elements that are missing from the models now, which is structured risk.

GEOFFREY GERBER: You talked about the DB side earlier, so my question relates more to the DC side. I've read your analogy that investors see their retirement programs as similar to a car and that all they care about is the performance and not the inside workings of the car. I know you've done a lot of work at Dimensional Fund Advisors on the whole idea of dynamically optimized portfolio strategies. So, from a fiduciary perspective, do you see the Managed DC approach or the target fund approach really changing the responsibilities from the employer to the employees? How do you see the fiduciary breakdown of that?

ROBERT MERTON: Of course, you understand I've chosen a particular path, so understand that in my response. I didn't design the product by picking something out of a bucket. Just so you understand that this is my opinion and, obviously, I could be wrong, or there could be other views. That said, I truly think that most sponsors want to do the right thing for their employees. Beyond that, if trustees and sponsors are thinking about fiduciary duty, I actually think, in a world of DC, that they are going to be much better off with something like Managed DC. This is a narrow answer to your question.

The main reason Managed DC was designed was to help provide the best services for achieving the good retirement goal, at a reasonable cost for the participants. However, I believe it also offers plan sponsors more protection for fiduciary duty because, if you look at what it does, first of all, it sets income targets that make sense. It looks just like, in that sense, DB or Social Security. It's clear what you're trying to do for people. The goals are always made clear. At the same time, it's an integrated solution, so it shows seriousness in the sense that you're providing a solution, not a bunch of parts left on the driveway for someone, usually the participants, to assemble and, if it doesn't work, that's their problem. That's not going to fly in the world of the future. I'm not a lawyer, but I think any sponsors or consultants who are hanging on to some of these narrowly defined legal ways to say that they are not fiduciaries or they won't be fiduciaries are fooling themselves. Because, as we translate the core of employer retirement plans into DC—this is not tomorrow, but over time—if something goes wrong, if we have general advice that we put everybody into, let's say, some investment strategy that doesn't pan out, and we have a macro problem in the industry (I'm not talking about a few individuals but about a whole generation invested in such a way that they're not going to make it in retirement), the idea that the government and the people are just going to say, "Too bad for that cohort, tough luck," is not likely to be the answer. And I don't think the answer is going to be that the government will say, "We made a mistake." People are going to want to find out, "Who is it?" It's like with asbestos or smoking. It's not what the rules and circumstances were at the time you made the investments. It's what the rules are when disaster happens, and when it happens can be ten or twenty years down the road.

So I think Managed DC really tries to do the right thing for people. It tells them what's informationally useful. It doesn't ask them to read prospectuses or try to make judgments among investment managers or any of the other kinds of things that they're not equipped to do. I don't care if they have 180 IQs and are finance professors or brain surgeons—they don't have the time, interest, or training to do that. So, ultimately, relying on individuals to make those sorts of decisions seems, to me, to be a losing proposition. On the other hand, in our Managed DC plan,[15] for example, we have an alert system for people who have never even been in our offices. When they fall below a certain level of probability of success relative to their goal, they are contacted, and they are told, "You've got a problem, and we can help you address it."

GEOFFREY GERBER: So they can change their allocation as a result?

ROBERT MERTON: No, they don't change their allocation. See, you're already thinking in terms of asking them to make a technical decision about allocation. I'm sorry—maybe you weren't talking about asset allocation.

GEOFFREY GERBER: Right, to different funds, or different targets.

ROBERT MERTON: Different targets maybe. As Meir mentioned earlier, they can change their goal. They can say: "Look, the goals I've set are higher than I'm willing to attempt. I have no way to get there. I'm going to reduce my expectation or reduce my goal." But, principally, as I mentioned earlier, there are only three things they can do to improve their chance of reaching a goal, and that's to save more, work longer, or take more risk. Anything else you ask them to do, to my mind, is dysfunctional, because they're not in a position to translate those decisions into anything useful. So, as a sponsor, if you provide a way of taking all of the technical factors and performing your role, not of guaranteeing anything, but of using yourself and your consultants to work with the provider of the plan, that's where the gatekeeper should be. You may say, "Well, that entails fiduciary duty." Well, you've got fiduciary duty, whether you carry it out or not.

The question is how you perform that duty. The way I see it—and I'm not trying to be an idealist here, I'm being very pragmatic—if I could show there was a process by which we designed a solution, we worked with the best experts we had and our consultants, we made our best efforts there, continued to monitor on an ongoing basis, we're cognizant of all of this, and we give participants the facts and feedback, just the way a doctor's report gives you the facts from your checkup. We don't tell participants goody-goody stories. We don't try to make them feel good. We tell them the facts, and we tell them what they can do to help themselves. If you have all of that, along with the alerts, then you have a record. If you send someone an alert every month for twenty-five years, that's 300 alerts saying: "You know what? You're not going to make it in retirement unless you change what you're doing. Save more or work longer or take more risk." Then they don't make it. It's rather hard to get a legal case out of that. You have a record that you sent them alerts. It's like your doctor saying: "Your cholesterol is 300. You can take statins, exercise, or change your diet. We can fix it." Then you don't do anything about it for twenty-five years, and you drop dead. It's very hard to file a suit against the doctor if you have 300 messages documenting that he or she tried to get you to take action.

That's a fast-pass answer, but I think it's the right thing to do. I also think it's the wise business thing to do, and that's true for consultants helping plan sponsors as well. The idea is that you recognize that you have a fiduciary duty or responsibility that's going to evolve, and if you follow this sort of strategy, that's the best protection. Some people say, "Well, if we get involved in any decisions, that makes us a fiduciary." That's the mindset that got us target date funds. I would love to be on the plaintiff's side when you get up there and say: "Everybody who is age thirty-four should have this same allocation. Everybody who is age forty-two should have that allocation." I would love to adjudicate that, because I'm going to get a forty-two-year-old male who is making $40,000 a year and a forty-two-year-old female making $125,000 a year, and I'm going to put you on the stand and ask, "These really are comparable, huh?" Put it this way. These core retirement decisions are probably the second most-important decisions people have to deal with beyond their health and medical. Would you be willing to go online and get your meds dispensed on the basis of your age, not even taking into consideration your gender?

Retirement funding is a complex problem. In judging target date funds, you can say that you've looked at historical data, and you can show all the facts, but it's really just common sense. Why would you ever think that such a complex problem as a lifetime retirement accumulation could be sufficiently solved with a single variable, i.e., age—and you don't even have a stated goal? I've taken time on this because I think it's a very important point. The industry has to learn and accept, if they don't already, that there is no safe harbor created by turning these matters into mechanical rules and thinking that they can say, "Well, as long as it's a mechanical rule, I don't have any fiduciary responsibility." I think that, first, it's a lousy way to treat people, and that's the first order for getting into trouble, and second, I don't think it's likely to hold up.

■ ■ ■

Retirement funding is a complex problem. In judging
target date funds, you can say that you've looked at historical data,
and you can show all the facts, but it's really just common sense.
Why would you ever think that such a complex problem as a lifetime
retirement accumulation could be sufficiently solved with a single
variable, i.e., age—and you don't even have a stated goal?

ARUN MURALIDHAR: My question probably ties up everything that's been said so far because I've also seen, in the past twenty years, the bad use of finance theory in investment decision making, both on the DB and DC sides. However, I wonder whether the academics also have failed the industry. When I look at reality—and you've hit on one very important point, which is liabilities and Modigliani's lifecycle concept of investing—the second thing that is practically the case in all investment decisions is delegation of investment decision making from principals to agents. I'm wondering whether finance theory for asset pricing should have started with what I call relative asset pricing theory, where it's relative to liabilities and relative to the risk that the principal is willing to delegate to agents. Then the CAPM (capital asset pricing model) becomes a very specialized case of a much more relative theory.[16] Would that have helped avoid some of the problems that we've seen over the past decade?

ROBERT MERTON: There are compound questions within your question. First, the most direct one to answer is on the asset pricing model. Let's not call it an asset pricing model because the asset pricing model, strictly speaking, is how assets price in equilibrium. In the normative space where I'm managing money for you—or would you rather stick with asset pricing? That's a much longer discussion.

ARUN MURALIDHAR: Let's keep it simple.

ROBERT MERTON: Yes, the simplest one, where you would then come to, if you like, an asset pricing model. A normative model simply says that you want to use the goals to begin with, and then from the goals, you derive, if you like, what the liabilities are. The liabilities, in this case, are that I want to have some kind of consumption pattern. Think of it as an Arrow type plan.[17] Then you should measure as numéraire,[18] or—if you like—all risk and return, in terms of that metric. So the risk-free asset, for example, for retirement would probably translate into an inflation-protected lifetime annuity at the proper level. That should be what you use as the risk-free asset. That's what you should use as numéraire, so what immediately happens is that you transform all of the assets, risk-return characteristics, in some cases quite dramatically. So a Treasury bill, which preserves capital, is the risk-free asset, if your goal is capital preservation. That's a very risky asset in terms of an income goal, so you'll get very different risk-return characterization. However, the bottom line is that you don't have to transform all of the theory that we've developed over the past forty or fifty years. You don't need a new theory. I'll give you a simplified example: All you need to do in that case is change the numéraire. But when I say "all," that could be very important. Your point is that could be very important, because it has very different implications for how we measure risk.

In fact, let me just mention this now. In the area of regulation where I believe most people are truly trying to do the right thing, you are hearing more and more about the idea of putting in floors as a requirement. Certainly in Europe, it's very, very common. Some regulators are saying that investors at least ought to get their principal amount back, and they're defining those floors in terms of wealth preservation. In reality—and I think no one here has disagreed—for retirement, you're interested in income. You're not interested in stability of capital. You're interested in stability of income. If that rule on floors—which, in some regulators' mindset, is a good, prudent thing—is passed, you could not put clients into a U.S. Treasury strategy that matches a long-duration annuity, which is the risk-free asset. Why? Because if interest rates go up, the value of that investment could fall below par, in which case you would have violated the rules. So do you see the irony? In the name of trying to make things safer for people, you have ruled out putting them in what everyone would normatively agree is the risk-free asset, by using the wrong measure, the wrong numéraire. So that's a dramatic—simple, but very dramatic—example of well-meaning legislation that well-meaning people think is a wise idea, and in reality, they've just ruled out the possibility of putting people in the asset that's the safest.

This is the kind of area where, to answer your question, I think academics can be very important in pointing out the irony, and the industry ought to, also. They ought to help regulators understand that some of the things that seem intuitively good maybe aren't. So I think your question is rooted correctly, but I'm not sure that it takes any kind of revolutionary transformation of finance science. It takes the transformation of the implementation of that in practice and regulation and so forth.

MARGARET TOWLE: That's a great point. Dr. Merton, is there any area that we have not covered that you would like to discuss, or do you wish to make any concluding comments?

ROBERT MERTON: Since I point this out to every group, Myron Scholes and I did not get the Nobel Prize for the Black-Scholes formula, but for our work with the late Fischer Black on a new methodology to evaluate derivatives. So the first point is the formula was not the important contribution, even though everyone talks about it. The formula was a very special case of the methodology, and today the formula is rarely used for anything other than standardized measures in practice because, in more than forty years, the methodology has developed much more sophisticated ways than the simplified assumptions underlying the formula. That's one part.

But now we come to the broader issue that I wanted to touch on. That is the issue of models. You've heard people talking about the crisis, about bad models, or about how we have to get rid of the models. I would just say that I don't believe that "Is something a good model?" is a well-posed question. I think you have to look at a triplet. You have to look at the model, who is using the model, and what the application is. What you will find is, even in as tightly defined an area as derivatives, that if I'm making a nanosecond-to-nanosecond market in derivatives, I use a very different model than if I'm performing an evaluation of the capital structure of a firm or evaluating employee stock options. The reason is that all models are abstractions from complex reality and therefore incomplete. You have finite resources, so you put more weight in the model on the parts that are most important for the application. The reason I'm going through this is the abstraction issue in modeling, but I think that's often forgotten. You can't evaluate a model in the abstract. You have to evaluate it in the context of both the user and the application, and that approach will help clarify and identify what are so-called good and bad models. Since the topic of models keeps coming up, I thought that might be worthwhile to mention.

■ ■ ■

> You can't evaluate a model in the abstract. You have to evaluate it in the context of both the user and the application, and that approach will help clarify and identify what are so-called good and bad models.

MARGARET TOWLE: I've often heard the quote, "All models are wrong, some models are useful."[19]

ROBERT MERTON: Well, yes, models are wrong because they're abstractions. Just as an aside, an example of this that comes to mind involves a trip I took to Geneva last year. When the plane hit the runway, it was a beautiful landing. The pilot came on and said: "Ladies and gentlemen, I just wanted to tell you that I did not land the plane. The computer system here did, but I thought I'd wait until you were on the ground to tell you." I thought about it, and I said, "Would I fly in a plane without the pilot?" and I said, "No." Then I thought longer about it, and I still said, "No." The precise reason is that, as good as that computer model was, it's a model and thus incomplete, and therefore there will be situations that are outside the bounds of that particular model. That's the reason we put a pilot in the plane, because that's the best thing we can think of to deal with that unstructured situation. However, the key here is—and it goes back to what I just said to you about models—how do we determine what's a good pilot? A good pilot is not Tom Cruise in *Top Gun*. A good pilot is someone who understands the computer model better than anyone and can make the judgment about when he or she has to intervene. I think there's something to be said for that in terms of the statements as to what we should do going forward.

■ ■ ■

ENDNOTES

1   Paul Samuelson (1915–2009) was an economist and the first American to win the Nobel Memorial Prize in Economic Sciences. Dr. Samuelson spent his career at the Massachusetts Institute of Technology, where he was instrumental in creating a world-renowned economics department by attracting other noted economists to join the faculty.

2   Franco Modigliani (1918–2003) was an economist at the Massachusetts Institute of Technology Sloan School of Management and MIT's Economics Department. He was awarded the Nobel Memorial Prize in Economic Sciences in 1985 for his work on household savings and the dynamics of financial markets.

3   Robert K. Merton (1910–2003) was a distinguished American sociologist who taught for more than forty years at Columbia University, where he attained the rank of university professor, Columbia's highest academic rank. In 1994, the elder Merton won the National Medal of Science for founding the sociology of science and for his pioneering contributions to the field.

4   Functionalism, a major theoretical perspective in sociology, interprets each part of society in terms of how it contributes to the stability of the whole society.

5   The expected utility of an entity or aggregate economy is calculated by taking the weighted average of all possible outcomes, with weights assigned according to the probability that a particular event will occur. The expected utility theory posits that, under uncertainty, the weighted average of all possible levels of utility best represents the utility at any given point in time.

6   The mean-variance theory approaches risk and expected return mathematically by evaluating potential investments based on the expected value and variance of possible outcomes to find maximum return for minimum risk.

7   Dr. Merton served as a principal of Long-Term Capital Management (LTCM), a hedge fund established in 1994 that reached $7 billion under management by the end of 1997. The highly leveraged fund was designed to profit from combining academics' quantitative models with traders' market judgment and execution capabilities. In August 1998, following the Russian financial crisis and an ensuing flight to quality, the fund lost substantial amounts of capital and was on the brink of default. The threat of a systemic crisis in the global financial system led the Federal Reserve to orchestrate a $3.5-billion takeover by major U.S. banks and investment houses in September 1998. In December 1999, LTCM fully repaid the banks that had prevented its collapse. The fund closed in 2000.

8   In information technology, big data is a collection of datasets so large and complex that it becomes difficult to process using database management tools or traditional data processing applications.

9   The Pension Protection Act of 2006 was the most comprehensive reform of U.S. pension laws since the enactment of the Employee Retirement Income Security Act of 1974. It established new funding requirements for defined benefit pensions and included reforms affecting cash balance pension plans, defined contribution plans, and deferred compensation plans for executives and highly compensated employees.

10 Defaulters are employees who participate in employee benefit plans by default and contribute according to default investment allocations rather than making individual investment decisions.

11 The Pension Relief Act of 2010 provided retroactive pension funding relief for single-employer and multi-employer defined benefit pension plans that suffered significant losses in asset value due to the steep market slide in 2008.

12 Dale Gray, senior risk expert in the International Monetary Fund's monetary and capital markets department, has developed macro financial risk frameworks linking finance, risk management, and macroeconomics.

13 A Monte Carlo simulation is a sampling method that uses random numbers and probability to compute results, often used when a model is complex, nonlinear, or involves more than a few uncertain parameters. Monte Carlo analyses use inputs randomly generated from probability distributions to simulate the process of sampling from an actual population. The term is a reference to the games of chance popular in Monte Carlo.

14 Gray et al. (2007) adapted contingent claims analysis (CCA) to the sovereign balance sheet in a way that can help forecast credit spreads and evaluate the impact of market risks and risks transferred from other sectors.

15 Dimensional Managed DC is a trademark of Dimensional Fund Advisors.

16 The CAPM is a model that describes the relationship between risk and expected return. The CAPM says that the expected return of a security or a portfolio equals the rate on a risk-free security plus a risk premium.

[17]   Kenneth J. Arrow (1921–) is a U.S. economist and the Joan Kenney Professor of Economics and Professor of Operations Research, emeritus, at Stanford University. In 1972, together with Sir John Hicks, he won the Nobel Memorial Prize in Economic Sciences for his pioneering contributions to general equilibrium theory and welfare theory. See Arrow (1950, 1951).

[18]   Numéraire is a basic standard by which value is measured, or a unit of account. A numéraire is used to measure the worth of different goods, services, and assets relative to one another, i.e., in same units, to identify which goods, services, and assets are worth more than others are.

[19]   This quote is attributed to British statistician George E. P. Box (1919–2013), in his 1987 book with Norman R. Draper, *Empirical Model-Building and Response Surfaces* (Hoboken, NJ: John Wiley & Sons, Inc.), page 424.

REFERENCES

Arrow, Kenneth J. 1950. A Difficulty in the Concept of Social Welfare. *Journal of Political Economy* 58, no. 4 (August): 328–346.

———. 1951. *Social Choice and Individual Values.* New York: John Wiley and Sons, Inc. http://cowles.econ.yale.edu/P/cm/m12/index.htm.

Black, Fischer, and Myron Scholes. 1973. The Pricing of Options and Corporate Liabilities. *Journal of Political Economy* 81, no. 3 (May/June): 637–654.

Bodie, Zvi. 1998. *Investment Management and Technology: Past, Present, and Future.* http://ssrn.com/abstract=178629 or http://dx.doi.org/10.2139/ssrn.178629.

Bodie, Zvi, and Robert C. Merton. 2000. *Finance.* Upper Saddle River, NJ: Prentice Hall.

Bodie, Zvi, Robert C. Merton, and David Cleeton. 2009. *Financial Economics.* Upper Saddle River, NJ: Prentice Hall.

Crane, Dwight B., Kenneth A. Froot, Scott P. Mason, Robert C. Merton, A. F. Perold, Zvi Bodie, E. Sirri, and P. Tufano. 1995. *The Global Financial System: A Functional Perspective.* Boston: Harvard Business School Press.

Gray, Dale F., Robert C. Merton, and Zvi Bodie. 2006. A New Framework for Analyzing and Managing Macrofinancial Risks of an Economy. NBER Working Papers 12637, National Bureau of Economic Research, Inc.

———. 2007. Contingent Claims Approach to Measuring and Managing Sovereign Credit Risk. *Journal of Investment Management* 5, no. 4 (4th quarter): 5–28.

Mason, Scott P., Robert C. Merton, A. F. Perold, and P. Tufano. 1995. *Cases in Financial Engineering: Applied Studies of Financial Innovation.* Upper Saddle River, NJ: Prentice Hall.

Merton, Robert C. 1969. Lifetime Portfolio Selection under Uncertainty: The Continuous-Time Case. *Review of Economics and Statistics* 51, no. 3 (August): 247–257.

———. 1970. A Dynamic General Equilibrium Model of the Asset Market and Its Application to the Pricing of the Capital Structure of the Firm. MIT Sloan School of Management, Working Paper #497-70 (December).

———. 1971. Optimum Consumption and Portfolio Rules in a Continuous-Time Model. *Journal of Economic Theory* 3, no. 4 (December): 373–413.

———. 1973a. Theory of Rational Option Pricing. *Bell Journal of Economics and Management Science* 4, no. 1 (spring): 141–183.

———. 1973b. An Intertemporal Capital Asset Pricing Model. *Econometrica* 41, no. 5 (September): 867–887.

———. 1974. On the Pricing of Corporate Debt: The Risk Structure of Interest Rates. *Journal of Finance* 29, no. 2 (May): 449–470.

———. 1990. *Continuous-Time Finance.* Cambridge, MA: Basil Blackwell, Inc.

Samuelson, Paul A., and Robert C. Merton. 1969. A Complete Model of Warrant Pricing That Maximizes Utility. *Industrial Management Review* 10, no. 2 (winter): 17–46.

This interview was published in its entirety in *Journal of Investment Consulting* 14, no. 1, 2013.

CHAPTER 11

MYRON SCHOLES: INTELLECTUAL FATHER OF THE CREDIT DEFAULT SWAP

MYRON S. SCHOLES, PHD

Recipient of the 1997 Nobel Memorial Prize in Economic Sciences; Frank E, Buck Professor of Finance Emeritus at Stanford University Graduate School of Business; author, *Taxes & Business Strategy* and numerous articles in academic journals.

In collaborations with Fischer Black and Bill Sharpe, Myron Scholes defined option pricing as the uncertainty of the outcome, providing us with a quantitative perspective on risk. The Black-Scholes model is an important and useful tool that prompted professional investors and ordinary people alike to frame choices as options. Once aware of optionality, we see options everywhere. For example, optionality allows an executive to view a corporate liability as an option, a private equity investor to see a follow-on investment as an option, or a hedge fund manager to consider an incentive fee as an option. Scholes has modestly stated that in research, sometimes you don't realize what you have and where it will go. For Scholes (and Sharpe), it led to the Nobel Memorial Prize in Economic Sciences.

■ ■ ■

MARGARET TOWLE: Dr. Scholes, your career has been extraordinary, including the Nobel Memorial Prize in 1997 and your academic career with the influences of Milton Friedman,[1] Merton Miller,[2] and others. In turn, you have influenced the lives of so many, in terms of the research you have done, in teaching, and so forth. We are especially interested in the factors that helped to shape your career and bring you to where you are today. Perhaps you could also talk about what you consider your biggest achievement and your biggest mistake.

MYRON SCHOLES: Actually, what shaped my career was a little bit of luck and a little bit of skill. I intuitively came to the conclusion that I should try to go to school where the best people were, because I would be able to steal as much as I needed from them, or as much as I could. That led me to the University of Chicago. I realized that I would have to be good myself to keep up with the people there, because if you are with the best, you have to try to be the best yourself. I was then fortunate enough to become a computer programmer at the University of Chicago at a time when virtually no one knew what a computer did, or how to program one. I provided programming assistance to a number of professors and fell in love with their enthusiasm for their research. As a result, I decided that this is a wonderful area, a wonderful experience. I went on to get my PhD, and I fell in love with research and ideas. The rest is history.

One of the things that shaped my career, and continues to shape my career to this day, is my love of the combination of theory and experience. I've always felt that theory alone—without experience—is not very valuable, and the converse is also true. Just experience, or being experiential without putting a framework around it, also is not valuable. I've always loved the idea of learning the details, trying to understand in depth what I need to know, and then trying to conceptually think about how all of the pieces fit together. I figured out a long while ago, and still use to this day, the fact that you have to gather data—you have to be inductive and gather data—but you have to make the decision to stop and then deduce something important and sustainable from the data you've accumulated. It's fun to do that, and I've enjoyed it.

I think, as you said in the introduction, that my major achievement has been a body of research, not the least of which is the crown jewel, which is the option pricing theory[3] and its applications. This research has had a great effect on others, and they have used it to extend their thinking, their understanding, and their applications of research to practice and theory. Also, for those who didn't like parts of my research, it led them to go in different directions and make new discoveries. I think the biggest mistake or disappointment was when I was in practice with Long-Term Capital Management.[4] Although I was a partner, I relied too heavily on others for the risk control piece. If I had taken a more proactive role, as opposed to a more consultative role, then I may have been able to step in earlier to reduce risk. That was, if you want to characterize it as such, a major disappointment.

■ ■ ■

> My major achievement has been a body of research,
> not the least of which is the crown jewel, which is
> the option pricing theory and its applications.

EDWARD BAKER: I remember when I first learned about the option pricing model many years ago when I was a student. I was very impressed by the thinking behind that. When you did that work, did you have any idea how important it would become?

MYRON SCHOLES: No, we always thought that it would be applicable to existing contracts such as call options or warrants or corporate bonds. I never thought that others would take the technology and the intuition behind the option pricing theory and build new products and conduct new research or use it in ways that were far afield from our original thinking. It was really exciting for me to watch those developments. I mean, for example, I never thought of real options as a research field.

MEIR STATMAN: I think the option pricing model and options, or derivatives more generally, have been used for good. However, covered calls continue to be advertised as free lunches. You railed against that as far back as an article you wrote in 1978 (Merton, Scholes, and Gladstein 1978). Do you see cases where options are being used to obscure? Of course, we cannot think about the market events of the past couple of years without thinking about the role of derivatives in what happened. The real question is whether people, even the people who designed those derivatives—the credit default swaps and the like—understood themselves what was involved, let alone could explain it to people who were not as immersed in derivatives as they were.

MYRON SCHOLES: Well, yes. Science might not be applied correctly. Obviously, appliers of technology can apply it incorrectly or obscure benefits and costs. For example, Porsche designed a highly efficient and powerful car. Drivers who don't know how to drive it, however, might have many accidents. I think we believe that there is value in using technology and ideas, and we understand that mistakes will be made. If everyone knew exactly which way to go and what was the correct way to apply technology, it already would have been done or we would find that it is boring and find new applications. Your question is a broad one. The first part involves investors who make mistakes using covered call options to generate extra income, forgetting that they lose if stocks fall in price (and giving up on the upside as well). There are no excess returns to be made in call-selling strategy unless the calls that are sold are overvalued. I agree with you. And, the mistake in believing that call-selling strategies provide excess returns is common in many different investment activities. For example, floor traders on the options exchanges might sell options to generate income, or investors might sell other forms of embedded options in financial contracts thinking they're garnering extra income such as buying high-yielding products. High-yielding products have risk of loss as clearly shown during the recent financial crisis. Take for example, the ubiquitous "money market fund" or "bank deposit." Although money market funds invested in higher-yielding paper to garner extra current yields for investors, they promised their investors that they would always receive one dollar back for each of their shares. But that was an impossible promise to keep unless the government stepped into their shoes and guaranteed the investments. The call-writing strategy is prevalent in one form or another across the investment spectrum. The problem is offering stable value products that provide higher income most of the time but can't really guarantee that investors will receive their principal back. Those who run the money market funds are knowledgeable and aware of this problem; they feel, however, that investors want the illusion of stable value or maybe they believe that the government will provide the option protection, if needed. Similarly, insurance companies offer stable value products such as annuities that promise investors they'll at least get their money back plus a 2-percent or 3-percent minimum return. At the same time, however, the insurance companies invest investor proceeds in higher-yielding bonds or equities to provide extra returns most of the time; at other times they have gone broke as markets moved dramatically against them—for example, Equitable or AIG. There are myriad cases where investors, or even institutional managers, sell options, creating seemingly higher returns for their investors while guaranteeing principal, and as a result worry—or maybe don't worry—about the consequences of an investment defaulting and having to take losses on the initial investment. The same is true of investment banks and banks. They earn higher current income on holding illiquid inventory. They report higher earnings to shareholders as long as they don't need to liquidate this inventory. From time to time, maybe during a crisis, they are forced to liquidate this illiquid inventory to reduce debt and risk at a large loss. They can't guarantee the principal of their shareholders. All of these are equivalent to our discussion on call-writing strategies; all of these products have options embedded in them. Now, all of these faults existed before the Black-Scholes model. They existed in myriad forms. And, our research points to these faults and how to correct and understand them.

MEIR STATMAN: I'm surely not going to fault the Black-Scholes model. However, using your current example of an automobile, we have speed limits on the highway, rather than leaving that up to the drivers. I was just wondering what you think about the role of government regulation and to what extent government should stay out of things and leave it to the market? Or is there a role for government in saying, for example, whether money market funds where prices are not marked to market should be prohibited?

MYRON SCHOLES: That is an excellent question. I don't think that we should prohibit money market funds. Although we know that speed limits don't work all of the time, society does believe that they constrain speeding and reduce the external costs caused by these accidents. Is it better to prohibit money market funds, or is it better to allow them, and, therefore, occasionally society will have to step in and guarantee their net asset values? I believe that we should restrict "excess speeding" and police it. We must decide, however, how to put meat on the bones. Up until now, we've taken the view that if banks fail, we bail them out. I believe that we shouldn't bail out the debt holders. They have to bear the risks. If they do, bond yields will reflect this and constrain bank risk-taking activities. And, we must decide on what constraints to impose on bank activities and capital that will not destroy the productivity of our society and will not prevent any bank failures, etc., but will limit the costs of systemic failures on society. We must find the proper balance. I think that's a societal decision—at the extreme whether to be proactive or just reactive to each crisis.

MARK ANSON: To build on Meir's question for a moment, one proposal has been to have a central clearinghouse for over-the-counter contracts: options, swaps, and other derivatives. I'm not certain it's feasible, but just in general, without trying to pin you down, what are your views on that?

MYRON SCHOLES: For all contracts that can be moved to a central clearing corporation, I think that idea obviously has a lot of benefits, for the cost of clean-up of all of the existing bilateral contracts is reduced dramatically. Right now, if a hedge fund or another entity wants to unwind its obligation, it needs to negotiate with the entity from which it undertook the contract. The cost of doing so, however, might be greater than entering into an offsetting contract with another entity. As a result of all of these offsets and the cost of eliminating outstanding contracts, the notional amount of derivative contracts grows dramatically. And, at times of crisis, the clearing corporation can offset contracts and eliminate counterparty uncertainty and risk efficiently since all contracts are effectively back-to-backed with a clearing corporation. (For example, theoretically, if Lehman had back-to-backed its over 2 million contracts with a clearing corporation, on its bankruptcy all of its contracts could have been netted and closed efficiently at mid-market pricing, reducing the dead-weight settlement costs and risks associated with default.) So I think that would be a great benefit to allow for a way for contracts to settle efficiently, especially in times of crisis.

On the other hand, the issue is to what extent and how many contracts can be migrated to exchanges or clearing corporations and how that should be done, because clearing corporations don't want to go broke themselves. Therefore they need to understand the underlying contracts, and they don't have the skills to understand idiosyncratic or complicated contracts. To date, only standard-form contracts have been cleared on clearing corporations or options exchange clearing corporations. And, these contracts settle each night since as values change entities post more collateral. Over-the-counter derivatives don't have readily observable market prices. A clearing corporation will not know how much collateral to demand at the end of the day to protect itself on other than standard-form contracts. And, during the crisis interest-rate swaps were not the problem. Other hard-to-understand structured products that are difficult if not impossible to clear were the difficulty. As we see, if we constrain activities such that all contracts need to be cleared on clearing corporations, the number of innovations, experiments, and idiosyncratic solutions for clients would be eliminated. Maybe others would claim that to be beneficial, but I've always thought that the intermediation process had value for society, in part, because it handles specifically what the customer needed by fashioning idiosyncratic solutions for the client. As these solutions become standard, they could be cleared.

■ ■ ■

> ## As we see, if we constrain activities such that all contracts need to be cleared on clearing corporations, the number of innovations, experiments, and idiosyncratic solutions for clients would be eliminated.

Since a clearing corporation is a separate legal entity, users would worry about all of the cross-margining problems that exist among contracts that might be cleared with the clearing corporation that are hedged by using swaps or other derivative contracts that are not cleared there. The actual margin required to post with each entity might far exceed the theoretical margin; that is, the margin that is actually necessary to assure performance if all contracts were cleared on one platform. This extra margin might make the clearing corporation prohibitively expensive for users needing to post excess collateral because their borrowing costs might far exceed the rate paid on collateral at the clearing corporation.

We must start on the details of over-the-counter derivatives. Overall, I would say yes to the idea of clearing corporations but there are major difficulties that I think should be solved prior to its implementation. That is, in bankruptcy, how do these over-the-counter contracts settle? Even today, the Lehman Brothers estate has 1.5 million outstanding contracts that have not settled or unwound. When Lehman went bankrupt[5], the firm had something like $21 billion of asset value and $15 billion of liabilities in its derivatives program. The $21 billion has shrunk to only $4 billion, while its liabilities have shot up from $15 billion to approximately $100 billion. This has been caused by the time delay, lack of understanding of the contracts, and the lack of incentives to conserve value. It's in the details. The bankruptcy mechanism is really the main issue; it imposes the bigger cost on the financial system and creates the most uncertainty. Regulators and practitioners should figure out how to make the system more efficient. I have argued that at the default of either a clearing corporation or a bank, all contracts are unwound at mid-market terminations within a period of three to five days. Entities would be able to recontract with nonbankrupt entities. In addition, mid-market settlement would greatly reduce the need for collateral and reduce cross-margining costs. On the other hand, without mechanistic redesign, a clearing corporation bankruptcy would create another mess.

EDWARD BAKER: Taking a more academic point of view, I'm thinking again that when I studied Black-Scholes, I was impressed by the power of the no riskless arbitrage principle in finance, which was part of the beauty of the whole derivation. I wondered how important you think that principle is broadly and why it doesn't get more attention? How important is it for markets to allow mechanisms that push in that direction?

MYRON SCHOLES: You are correct. I used that principle even in my doctoral thesis forty years ago, in which I introduced the theory of substitution versus flows in financial markets into the academic literature. If assets with similar risk-return characteristics are priced differently, then intermediaries have an incentive to close the market and bring the prices back into line. As you point out, in the Black-Scholes world, the option and the underlying security were perfect substitutes. Substitution versus flows is the primary tradeoff that all intermediaries face. Markets function because intermediaries assess values and buy assets that they think are cheap relative to other assets that they sell to hedge their risks, believing that substitution will bring security prices back into line. If flows, however, overwhelm substitution, intermediaries might not be able to hold their positions long enough or worry that they no longer understand valuation. Finance compresses time. If an investor wants to buy something today and there's not a ready seller for it, an intermediary steps in to provide it until the seller comes forward. However, the intermediary can't intermediate unless he believes in a valuation to supply the inventory outright or he can hedge and reduce its risk and show either through arbitrage or through hedging that he was correct in his valuation. In the press and in academic circles there is the belief that the Black-Scholes technology was developed using the concepts of efficient markets. It was not based on efficient markets.

EDWARD BAKER: No, not at all. It was based on arbitrage pricing theories.

MYRON SCHOLES: That's correct—on the idea that if a derivative and its underlying security are perfect substitutes, then one can be priced relative to the other and the expected return does not play a role in the formulation. Efficient markets says something about the mean and the process underlying the evolution of the returns from equilibrium values (for example, not mean reverting or trend following); option prices have something to say about volatility and nothing to say about the mean. I think this idea of arbitrage, or hedging or risk management, is a primary part of financial markets and how markets become efficient.

GEOFFREY GERBER: You've talked about measuring risk, and you've talked about bank failures. You've also been quoted as saying that while any one bank can measure its risk, the real problem is that it also has to know what risks are being taken by other banks in the system at any particular point in time. How would they go about that?

MYRON SCHOLES: To me, that may be the key role of the proposed systemic risk regulator.[6] I worry that the systemic risk regulator will by necessity have to figure out where asset bubbles are at any moment, and that's an extremely difficult task for anyone. Where are the asset bubbles now in the system? And, there are so many that naturally arise and disappear without consequence.

MARGARET TOWLE: I love your terminology—the Fed.com bubble. That's great.

MYRON SCHOLES: Well, thank you. We don't want to observe a future scenario wherein the systemic risk regulator can't find any asset bubbles over a period of time, and, as a result, investors and institutions take more risk. To follow on from the risk aggregation question more directly, the systemic-risk regulator should aggregate risks of the various banking institutions and maybe hedge funds and others in the so-called "shadow-banking system" and disseminate the risks (short-term risks, the so-called "greeks," and scenario risks, etc.) to the financial community in aggregated form. The financial community will be able to adjust its own model assumptions and its own risks more efficiently on learning about the aggregated risks in the system and, in my view, act to reduce systemic risk in the system.

■ ■ ■

> We don't want to observe a future scenario wherein the systemic risk regulator can't find any asset bubbles over a period of time, and, as a result, investors and institutions take more risk.

GEOFFREY GERBER: You bring up hedge funds, and obviously hedge funds in 2008 were a major disappointment at one level because, contrary perhaps to some investors' priors, they did have a beta component. What do you think about hedging strategies going forward?

MYRON SCHOLES: Beta theory is incomplete. It was developed under the assumption that investors liquidate and reconstruct their portfolios at the end of each period without cost. And, the opportunity set is assumed to remain unchanged to measure beta and performance using historical data. I think there are at least two functions that generate the returns on securities. One is an evolutionary process, wherein returns are created by generating factors and idiosyncratic risks. Hedge funds can hedge factor risks and create zero-beta portfolios. The second function is a liquidity process. Since at least 2000, in papers I've written and talks I've given—at times of liquidity shocks, or when all intermediaries stop intermediating because they can no longer calibrate their models or assess valuations correctly, asset prices that appeared to be uncorrelated most of the time become highly correlated. I have called the provision of liquidity and risk-transfer services, "Omega." Most hedge funds and alternative investors earn returns by providing

Omega services. They earn returns by buying less-liquid assets and those assets that investors do not want to hold at a particular time. They hold these assets until they are able to liquidate them when Omega prices change in their favor. In 2007–2009, Omega providers lost as asset classes fell in value—even though they had a zero beta in a classical sense—as all asset classes seemed to move together since Omega prices moved against them. As a result, measured correlations increase. Stocks fall, bond prices increase, interest rate curves steepen, and volatility increases as flows caused by investors wanting to convert to cash to reduce risk overwhelm substitution until intermediaries have time to recalibrate their models and to discern new valuations. As a result measured betas increase dramatically.

■ ■ ■

I think a great direction for future research is to understand the value of liquidity, ways to measure it, and the implications for society, as well as why the intermediation business fails and what we can do to mitigate failure, if anything.

Basically, I think that at the time of a shock like we had on different occasions over 2007–2008, and, in particular, at the time of the Lehman failure and the aftermath thereof, everyone was trying to reduce risk and liquidate, and the market intermediation process stopped. In finance volatility and time are the same. When markets are quiet, everyone has more time to think and more time to act, and it takes longer for things to evolve or to change by very much. As volatility increases, however, market participants are forced to act more quickly. When volatility becomes extreme, time stops. With large shocks, volatility becomes extreme because so many decisions have to be made quickly and without an ability to evaluate and incorporate all of the information available. As a result, intermediaries withdraw capital and reduce their Omega provision in markets. I call that the "Heisenberg uncertainty principle of finance,"[7] because, as soon as investors no longer know value or liquidity needs or who's selling (their fixed point), the flows (velocity) overwhelm the power of substitution. At that moment, two things happen: liquidity dies and asset prices jump. Market participants need time to reestablish value and separate price movements attributable to value and liquidity price changes. That functionality produces a very high measured beta, but it's not the beta of the Sharpe capital asset pricing model sense,[8] or the market model sense. The market model assumes draws from the same urn. Mixing market model evolutionary process returns with those of a liquidity process generates distributions that have fatter tails.[9] So it's liquidity in the intermediation business that really needs to be understood going forward. I think a great direction for future research is to understand the value of liquidity, ways to measure it, and the implications for society, as well as why the intermediation business fails and what we can do to mitigate failure, if anything. Providing liquidity and risk transfer has been a service provided by hedge funds and other intermediaries in the past. If we do not allow banks to do so in the future, who will provide the intermediation function so important to making markets efficient?

EDWARD BAKER: There are some new techniques being developed for managing risk when you do have fat tails. Have you looked at that literature at all, and do you have any comments?

MYRON SCHOLES: I have read the extreme value theory literature. There are others who assume that fat-tailed distributions can be used to model risk in the extreme. Most of these approaches, however, use reduced-form marginal distributions without trying to understand and model the underlying economics. That is why I and others are trying to model and understand the intermediation process and when and why it breaks down. When it breaks down, we observe extreme price movements and although we are unable to predict when these will occur, we are able to predict their direction and magnitude. We know that liquidity is akin to a put option. We don't know, however, the form of the option necessary to protect us at times of shock. That is why the degree of flexibility in operating and financing policies is a business decision at the option of management. For example, we know that with shock asset values fall and to reduce risk banks must sell assets or issue equity to reduce risk. If banks issue equity, however, the lion's share of the benefit is transferred to its debt holders because the extra equity protects them against default. As a result, banks are forced to liquidate assets to reduce risk and to do so in an illiquid market wherein value and liquidity needs are difficult to discern quickly enough. Leverage is akin to cancer in the sense that it is necessary to do something to get rid of it. There are more efficient ways to rid banks of their debt cancer than having taxpayers bail them out. We have to figure out automatic ways to rid us of that cancer. For example, if the debt of financial institutions converted into a certain fraction of the equity of the firm at the time of a systemic event, it would give intermediaries time to recalibrate their models, to revalue assets, and to make new flexibility decisions without needing government intervention or a wholesale liquidation of assets at fire-sale prices. This forced conversion would mean that we would not need governments to bail out financial institutions; they would bail themselves out. And, if debt holders suffer loss, they would be more cautious and, as a result, reduce the possible magnitude of a crisis.

EDWARD BAKER: That would certainly change the game for the stockholders. Presumably that would impose a greater standard of governance and risk measurement on the part of management.

MYRON SCHOLES: That's right. Why not? That goes back to my earlier point. Society has a choice: Should we be reactive and pay the price after the crisis? Or do we think of measures that are proactive, and the price is paid over time, and, as a result, build more flexibility into our financing decisions? Our decision to date has been to bail out institutions. Over time these decisions have increased moral-hazard problems. The recent collapse of our financial system and resultant bailouts has led to anger and calls for the "heads" of the bankers and could lead to extreme constraints on their activities. Perhaps now is the time to be proactive and make changes in advance that will constrain activities but allow market participants to make choices. We might not be able to write rules that prevent crisis. We can, however, change contractual forms to protect society in the event of a shock. We have to think of mechanisms that are self-correcting, as opposed to trying to regulate the rules of the road. I agree with Meir that we need speed limits in place, in the sense that banks need additional capital that would reduce leverage. However, leverage is only one part of the speed-limit constraints. Banks can reduce flexibility not only by using a lot more leverage but also in many other ways, such as concentrating very heavily in one activity (such as Lehman's illiquid real estate investments), or reducing bonds in their portfolios or cash reserves (as Bear Stearns), or selling off businesses that are cash-cow businesses and then investing in growth activities. Even after restricting leverage, there are myriad ways that banks and other intermediaries can reduce flexibility in the system. This needs study and the cooperation of academics and practitioners.

■ ■ ■

Society has a choice: Should we be reactive and pay the price after the crisis? Or do we think of measures that are proactive, and the price is paid over time, and, as a result, build more flexibility into our financing decisions?

EDWARD BAKER: In part it's a matter of asymmetric incentives on the part of the management. They do well when the risks pay off, and they aren't really hurt that much when the risks don't pay off.

MYRON SCHOLES: That's correct. There is the "trader" model or the "investor" model. The trader model is one in which the trader says to the boss, "I don't need very much capital to run my business because I'm hedged, I have no beta risk, I just have pure profits ahead of me." And the boss says, "No, you need capital because you're not going to be right 100 percent of the time, nor are you going to be right immediately." Traders want as little capital allocated to them as they can possibly get away with for they realize high returns on capital and are paid well accordingly, most of the time. When a shock occurs, however, the trader loses money and runs to the boss and says, "My opportunities are the best I've ever seen, but I need more capital because I am broke." Heads traders win; tails the firm losses. If I leave home and I carry my umbrella—thereby creating flexibility—and it doesn't rain, then I've paid the price—I've carried the umbrella. On the other hand, if I leave the house without the umbrella and it does rain, I have to scurry around New York City to find an umbrella on a street corner, or I get wet. So there's a tradeoff. Flexibility—both financing and operating flexibility—is a business decision. I think the trader model tends to move toward "Let me be reactive; I need little capital because I am hedged, and I am able to make more money if I don't provide for the possibility that I will need more capital at times of shock." The investor model requires that managers have enough capital to sustain their positions at times of shock. There is no "boss" to call at that time for extra capital.

MARK ANSON: So let's say you walk out of your house without your umbrella, it rains, and you have to buy an umbrella on the street, but now you're going to have to pay a premium to buy that umbrella on the street. So you still have to pay for that optionality one way or the other.

MYRON SCHOLES: You're right. That it is why it is a business decision. If bankers come to the conclusion that shocks are unlikely or that carrying the extra capital is too much of a drag on reported earnings, they prefer to be reactive, and, if needed, buy the umbrella on the street corner. That's a business decision. And, it might be easier to make that decision with the possibility of a government bailout. For example, a venture capitalist might invest in a start-up that needs $10 million in expectation of finishing research and development and marketing the project before the start-up becomes self-sufficient. However, six months later we often hear: "Things are going great, but we need more capital." To make the correct investment decision, the flexibility option has to be valued before the fact and added to the direct cost of making an investment, to compute the correct return on capital; maybe the correct investment is not $10 million but $15 million. If too little capital is allocated to a project, investors, bank management, and others cannot make the correct allocation decisions. We need to learn how to make dynamic adjustments. This is the future for bank (and other) investment allocation decisions.

Endowment funds, for example, in recent years decided that they did not need a reserve against shocks or liquidity crises. They reduced their bond holdings to maybe 3 percent of their portfolios. Why? They felt that their time horizon was very long and that they did not need flexibility in their investment allocations. This turned out to be incorrect. Or pension funds have invested a large fraction of their portfolios in equities. Why? Because they have a long horizon and equities are nearly certain to outperform bonds over a long horizon. The problem, however, is that although in expectation stocks outperform bonds over a long horizon, the longer the horizon the greater the possibility of a shortfall when the money is needed to pay beneficiaries. The value of a chooser option, the maximum of stocks or bonds over a thirty-year horizon might represent 40 percent of the value of the portfolio. Once again, volatility, optionality, or the value of flexibility must be part of the investment decision-making process. And, adding to the problem—and I'm responsible for it as are others—is that we assume that the world is putty-clay-putty.[10] Investors start with putty today, make investment decisions, putty into clay, and at the end of the investment period, convert clay back into putty, and start over again without cost. But, the world does not work that way. At times of shock, for example, converting illiquid assets to cash to build flexibility is very expensive. Finding an umbrella in a rain storm might be impossible or very costly.

MARGARET TOWLE: Could we switch gears a little bit and go back to something you said earlier that I found interesting? You said that you really love the combination of theory and experience. I know that you've recently spoken on some contemporary topics such as the rally in junk companies and the metrics that people are using to measure that. Are there ideas about looking at what's currently going on in the markets that are well-known or understood by professionals, but not by individuals?

MYRON SCHOLES: Yes, certainly. By definition we've had myriad managers who are trying to make money by understanding the complexities of various arrangements that are impossible for individuals to do on their own. For example, how does the typical investor value Lehman bonds or their outstanding other claims? No one can do that without diving into it and spending the countless hours necessary to try to figure out and understand all of the game-theoretic approaches to value those instruments. The same thing is true in many other instances in finance. Division of labor is very important. Markets become efficient or move toward efficiency because of individuals who are willing to take the time to actually evaluate situations and to act on those evaluations because they believe they have found opportunities that will earn them money for the capital they need to employ and the time necessary to hold assets before realizing returns.

MARGARET TOWLE: I was thinking of my question in the context of a large part of the audience for this publication, that is, investment consultants, in terms of their role with institutional clients and individual investor clients.

MYRON SCHOLES: Consultants and intermediaries are extremely important, and even more so as the number and complexity of investment choices have increased over the years. In the investment world, we know that an index fund (or equivalent) has the lowest costs and also the lowest monitoring costs. It's very easy to measure the shortfall from what an index fund alternative might be. If one invests in a hedge fund, which doesn't take factor exposures, the monitoring costs are much greater. Intermediaries are needed to help investors decide among all the alternative hedge funds and the myriad alternative investment vehicles. And, consultants and advisors are necessary to plan for liquidity needs and asset allocation decisions. Clients are moving to wanting investment solutions.

■ ■ ■

Consultants and intermediaries are extremely important, and even more so as the number and complexity of investment choices have increased over the years.

The interesting evolution in finance that we've seen over the last forty years or so is a movement in responsibility down to individuals to make investment decisions and away from governments and corporations. In the past, individuals were not very heavily involved in the stock market. For their retirement and savings, they relied on their defined benefit pension plans, their homes, and to some extent Social Security. But, without choice, individuals had limited flexibility in their retirement savings programs.

The analogy I like to use is that when I was young, we had a radio in our home, and it was a big box—all of those woofers and tweeters and so forth were right in that big box. Later on, I could buy components and put together my own system. The same thing has happened in the investment world. We left the world of the big-box solution and we forced individuals to make all of the decisions about ways to allocate savings, saving for the education of their children, saving for retirement, saving for health care, life insurance, health insurance, living too long, dying too soon, risk tolerance, human capital, etc. We can't make all of these decisions ourselves—we need advisors and consultants that help us put all of this together. Their advice is very valuable and will continue to be so. Their importance continues to grow because making these decisions will become more complicated; we need their expertise to figure out how to put the components together to make the system work.

We've moved to the next steps in the stereo component world. A few years ago, when I wanted to put a new system into my home, my stereo person told me that he'd come to the house and discuss what I wanted in my new system. Although I asked him about specific component parts, he told me to forget about that. That was his job. He wanted to know my tastes in music, television, etc. When it was completed, I had a media center. It was the box I had as a kid, but it was my own box now, not that "one size fits all" system, but one designed just for me. That will happen with investment programs in the future. An advisor will analyze client needs and then design solutions, or media centers, that suit that client's needs. Now, obviously, the media center was a reconstructed radio; the stereo person took the components and built a better system for me. A year or so later, I wanted to buy an iPod, and it didn't fit into my media center, so solutions deconstruct and reconstruct over time. Note that the difference here is that the components of the media center are less important than their output. The same will become true of investments. And, depending on adjustment costs, the program will be flexible because with volatility we keep learning and our tastes change. It takes technology, know-how, experience, and methods to understand client needs and how those needs can be satisfied. Clients don't have the ability to do so on their own.

MARGARET TOWLE: That goes back to some of the ideas of financial innovation. In October 2009, you spoke at Pace University.[11] I didn't hear the talk, but I believe you were defending contemporary financial innovations.

MYRON SCHOLES: I had not wanted that talk to be a debate about financial innovation; I was very much against a format that required that I defend financial innovation. Debaters point to individual events to try to prove that innovation is costly, which I agree it is. We know that innovation must lead infrastructure that monitors and controls innovation. And, we know some innovations fail. However, when the benefits of innovation are diffused across a spectrum of activities, it is difficult to marry all those benefits together to compute the total value, especially when one can point to individual instances of failure or specific instances of great cost. One of the reasons the Securities and Exchange Commission was put into place in 1934 was that during the hearings following the stock market crash of 1929, regulators heard from a parade of individuals talking about specific instances wherein people had been hurt by investment advisors. It is hard to argue against failures. On net, I claim that successful innovations survive the test of time. And, we have had myriad financial innovations in that category. Even credit-default swap contracts, such as those that brought down AIG, have survived and provide valuable credit-pricing signals and hedging instruments.

MARGARET TOWLE: Speaking of innovations, and we've touched a bit on this already, can you give us some of your thoughts about major trends in the investment industry today, specifically those that you think will still be around in five years, or twenty years?

MYRON SCHOLES: I think we're going to see more and more of a movement to customized solutions for investors, where advisors play a more and more important role. In addition, intermediaries will work to devise products that satisfy client needs and do so in a way that is more service-oriented or client-oriented. Individuals think in terms of activities. They think about transacting, about saving for the future, about investing in large projects, about risk management, etc. Entities tend to think in terms of products, that is, a growth fund or a high-yield product. The growth area in the investment future is to put the client's wants first and then work to figure how technology—whether it's computing or telecommunications or financial or a combination of all of these—can help satisfy the client's demands. To me, that must be a growth industry because it's very confusing for individuals or even entities to figure out all of this on their own. We're in a world of second best,[12] and we have to realize that's the case. In the world of second best, advice is valuable and investors are willing to pay for it. It's not just return-based; that is, informing the client that he can make the most by investing here, or investing there. It's really much more than that; it is understanding the client's horizon, liquidity needs, other contingencies, risk tolerance, human capital constraints, and other wants that have to be satisfied and figuring ways to achieve the desired program.

■ ■ ■

> I think we're going to see more and more of a movement to customized solutions for investors, where advisors play a more and more important role. In addition, intermediaries will work to devise products that satisfy client needs and do so in a way that is more service-oriented or client-oriented.

EDWARD BAKER: We already touched on the recent economic crisis, but if you had to point to one important lesson that you learned from this, what would you say?

MYRON SCHOLES: We don't know the riskiness of the state of the world in which we live. It seems that in recent years we had come to the conclusion that risk had been permanently reduced. And, this turned out to be incorrect. Over time we became convinced that the economy was under control. We must realize that it is difficult to know whether the recent period is the best indicator of the future. How do we know the real state of the global economy? Macroeconomists told us that they could dampen business cycles, the so-called "great moderation." We learned that Mr. [Alan] Greenspan[13] and others claimed that risk transfer dampened the effects of shocks. And with the shocks of the recent past, we were told, "Well, the fundamentals of the economy are strong." And, we had recovered without much consequence from the myriad shocks since the 1950s. The big problem is that the inherent volatility in the economy is unknown. If investors deem volatility to be low, they take on more risk. When volatility is low, the value of the flexibility option is low. Individuals buy bigger homes, they don't save, they believe that they will make money on their house as it appreciates in value and need little income to support it. We think our human capital is secure, so we borrow using credit cards, we borrow against our cars, and save little. The fundamental question is whether there are warning systems that will be built to provide a better picture of the true state of the risks in the economy.

EDWARD BAKER: Is that any different, though, than simply misassessing risk?

MYRON SCHOLES: Well, yes, we're always going to misassess risk. How do we know the true state? It's a time series world.[14] We only have one run of history. The problem is that the converse is also true. If the world were actually calmer because we had learned to manage and to understand risk, the actions we took would have been just fine. With less underlying risk, we take more risk on personal account. However, it turned out the world wasn't as calm as rating agencies, bankers, and others came to believe. There are some who argue that as the economy strengthens we should save for a rainy day by adding to capital requirements. However, we don't know if the economy will continue to get stronger. Therefore, we saved for a rainy day, and it turned out to be costly to do so because no rain came. What we need to learn is not to "data mine" and weight recent experiences too heavily.

GEOFFREY GERBER: From mid-September 2008 through March 2009, the New York Stock Exchange experienced twenty-seven (thirteen best and fourteen worst) of the forty (twenty best and twenty worst) most extreme daily returns since January 1966. The shocks seemed even more extreme than the 1987 one-day shock. Do you think that this is because people keep taking more and more risk, so that when volatility hits, it just hits wider and wider?

MYRON SCHOLES: I think that there was a lot of information to adjust over a short period of time. What was the government going to do? What were international governments going to do? How much support was the Federal Reserve going to provide to the financial markets? What was the value of assets in financial entities, automobile companies, etc.? How were financial institutions going to save themselves from collapse? Obviously, with this shock in a complex global environment there was so much information to digest and the adjustment costs were large. Generally, I would like to see more volatility in the markets. Small shocks remind us that a bigger shock might occur. And, we protect ourselves to some extent. Governments try to protect us against volatility. For example, every time there's been a flood on the Mississippi River, we build a levee or a dam and then we tell people that it's all right now, you can go back to your homes. But the levees fail from time to time and homes along the Mississippi continue to flood, and occasionally we get a gigantic hurricane or rain storm that destroys vast areas such as the effects of Hurricane Katrina. We have built homes in Los Angeles in areas where they theoretically should not have been built. As we put out fires, the underbrush grows, and each subsequent fire is larger and harder to put out. Will we be able to allow small fires to burn in the financial sector to burn out the underbrush? I don't think so. And, it takes a long time to return to where we are cautious about risks and cognizant that we are subject to shocks. Now we have a new generation that has been burned so badly by this recent economic crisis that they will take too little risk. Or are we going to tell people not to take any risk, or will rules and regulations be put into place such that we take too little risk, and, as a result, it's going to take a long time for the economy to recover? There is a need to gain more understanding about the effects of people's beliefs about volatility on their behavior.

MEIR STATMAN: There appear to be two kinds of errors: One is taking too little risk, and the second is taking too much.

MYRON SCHOLES: Yes that is true. It's an ex-post error, but not necessarily a before-the-fact error. But, as you say, it could be a before-the-fact error as well.

MEIR STATMAN: The question is really whether it is an ex-ante kind of error. The bias of investment companies is to go toward too much leverage, rather than too little. Should there be an entity that pushes in the other direction?

MYRON SCHOLES: If your assumptions are correct, then it's worth study. I'm not saying that I know for sure, but, for example, let's look at a hedge fund. If the fund takes on too much leverage or too much risk and it loses a lot of money, then it doesn't have its business any more. There's a tradeoff between staying in business over the long haul by taking less leverage and making a little money each period versus taking a lot of risk for an opportunity to make a lot of money over a few periods but with a high probability of being out of business. Both strategies are possible. The government and the press are discussing compensation policies at banks, arguing that employees should be compensated in stock to dampen risk-taking. However, it did not help Lehman Brothers that Mr. [Richard] Fuld[15] had a billion dollars in Lehman stock and lost it all. So perhaps rules that were put into place in 2001 about taxing executive compensation very heavily—above a million dollars in cash compensation—induced so many firms to give their executives stock that the executives started to take more risk because they figured out that if the company makes money, they can make a billion dollars for themselves. What behavioral implications or incentive implications do we create by the policies we put into place? A shock like we've had opens people's eyes and minds and encourages them to discuss and think about alternatives in light of what could happen. Hopefully we'll see evolution that is beneficial going forward. I hope that we don't shut off discussion too early for the sake of populist solutions to our problems.

■ ■ ■

> ## The world is complicated; it's very, very complicated. Figuring ways to digest all of the information around us and come to the correct conclusion is very difficult. We can, however, use finance theory to help.

EDWARD BAKER: Listening to you, it sounds like these crises are just a natural part of market evolution, and perhaps we just have to know that they're going to happen periodically, and there is no way to avoid them.

MYRON SCHOLES: I agree. The world is complicated; it's very, very complicated. Figuring ways to digest all of the information around us and come to the correct conclusion is very difficult. We can, however, use finance theory to help. Requiring greater capital, putting risk management on the same footing as producers within firms, encouraging better-trained risk managers, realizing the limits of our models and the inputs to models, providing for more control and measurement at the level of the board of directors, and warning of risks and measuring the effects of optionality are all steps that might dampen the consequences of these inevitable shocks. We shouldn't, however, attempt to build a moat around our city and pretend that that solves the problem. As we know, occasionally foreign invaders breach the moat and the city collapses.

MARGARET TOWLE: Dr. Scholes, this has certainly been a very enlightening discussion, and we appreciate your willingness to share your insights with us.

MYRON SCHOLES: My pleasure. One point that I would like to make in closing is new misunderstandings of the meaning of efficient markets. I think many people have come to the conclusion that if prices change by a lot that means that markets were inefficient. Efficient market theory does not claim that the price is 100-percent correct. I've always believed that if a stock is selling for $100 today, it might be worth $140 or $80. What efficient markets theory tells me is that unless someone has information about the error or has a better model for understanding value, her best guess as to value would be the $100 price (even though it is inaccurate). Other people have interpreted it in different ways—that efficient markets have failed, or that our belief in efficient markets has led to the wrong decisions. I don't think that link is correct.

■ ■ ■

ENDNOTES

1   Milton Friedman (1912–2006), a U.S. economist and statistician, was awarded the Nobel Memorial Prize in Economic Sciences in 1976. He served on the University of Chicago faculty from 1946 to 1977, helping to build an academic community of economists known as the Chicago School of Economics.

2   Merton Miller (1923–2000) was a U.S. economist who shared the 1990 Nobel Memorial Prize in Economic Sciences with Harry Markowitz and William Sharpe for pioneering work in the theory of financial economics. He was a faculty member at the University of Chicago from 1961 until his retirement in 1993, and he served as doctoral thesis advisor for Dr. Scholes in the late 1960s.

3   In 1973, Fischer Black and Myron Scholes published their option pricing theory, designed to calculate the value of an option by considering the stock price, strike price, expiration date, risk-free return, and standard deviation of the stock's return. Later that year, Robert Merton expanded the theory and coined the term "Black-Scholes model." As described by Dr. Scholes, the model is "an equation that prices options on common stock and provides a methodology to value options on securities generally. It can be used to measure risk and transfer risk." In 1997, Scholes and Merton received the Nobel Memorial Prize in Economic Sciences for their pioneering formula for the valuation of stock options. (Because the prize is not awarded posthumously, Black, who died in 1995, was ineligible. However, the Nobel Prize committee noted Black as a key contributor to this work.) The Black-Scholes model, which represented a major contribution to the efficiency of the options and stock markets, remains one of the most widely used financial tools.

4   Myron Scholes served on the board of directors of Long-Term Capital Management, a hedge fund established in 1994 that reached $7 billion under management by the end of 1997. The highly leveraged fund was designed to profit from combining academics' quantitative models with traders' market judgment and execution capabilities. In August 1998, following the Russian financial crisis and an ensuing flight to quality, the fund lost substantial amounts of capital and was on the brink of default. The threat of a systemic crisis in the global financial system led the U.S. Federal Reserve to orchestrate a $3.5-billion bailout by major U.S. banks and investment houses in September 1998. The fund closed in 2000.

5   Lehman Brothers declared bankruptcy on September 15, 2008. With more than $600 billion in debt, it was the largest bankruptcy filing in U.S. history.

6   As outlined by the U.S. Department of the Treasury, a systemic risk regulator would be "a single entity [with] the ability to supervise, examine, and set prudential requirements for critical parts of our financial system." These "would not be limited to banks or bank holding companies, but could include any financial institution that was deemed to be systemically important in accordance with legislative requirements" as well as critical payment and settlement systems.

7   In 1927, Werner Heisenberg (1901–1976) published his uncertainty paper (within the context of subatomic particles) which states that "the more precisely the position is determined, the less precisely the momentum is known in this instance, and vice versa." In non-scientific terms, the principle postulates that the more accurately we try to measure something, the less we can be sure of it since the very act of measuring it disturbs the subject. The uncertainty principle has interesting applications in chaotic financial markets since there is present an unavoidable element of unpredictability and randomness in markets due to outside influences, such as market analysts, the media, etc.

[8] The CAPM is a model that describes the relationship between risk and expected return. The CAPM says that the expected return of a security or a portfolio equals the rate on a risk-free security plus a risk premium.

[9] In a normal bell-shaped distribution of portfolio returns, the majority of returns can be found in the "bell," which centers around the weighted average return for the entire market. The ends, or tails, of the curve represent returns that are either extremely bad (left) or extremely good (right). Larger-than-normal tails are called "fat tails," indicating more data on the extremes than expected. Fat tails indicate that extreme market moves were more likely than would be predicted by normal distributions.

[10] The basic idea of putty-clay is that, before a choice is made, a wide range of options is available (i.e., the putty can be molded any way one chooses). Once that choice is made (i.e., the putty is baked into clay), the options become fewer. In economics, putty-clay describes an attribute of capital in financial models. Putty-clay capital can be converted from capital into durable goods, but cannot be converted back into reinvestable capital. This contrasts with putty-putty capital, which can be transformed from capital into durable goods and then back again.

[11] On October 16, 2009, Dr. Scholes participated in a discussion on the pros and cons of restricting the ability of financial institutions to create innovative products and the impact on the opportunity for world growth, held as part of the first annual Buttonwood Gathering at Pace University in New York, NY.

[12] The "theory of the second best" is a term used to describe a situation where one or more optimality conditions in an economic model cannot be achieved. Lipsey-Lancaster (1956) proposed that if one optimality condition cannot be satisfied, reaching the second-best solution involves changing all of the other variables from those assumed to be optimal. According to this theory, if two or more markets are not perfectly competitive, efforts to correct only one of the optimality conditions may drive the economy further from efficiency.

[13] From 1987 until 2006, Alan Greenspan (1926–) was the chairman of the U.S. Federal Reserve Board, which oversees the Federal Reserve Bank.

[14] A time series is a sequence of data points, typically measured at uniform time intervals, such as the daily closing value of the Dow Jones Industrial Average. Time series forecasting predicts future data points based on known points in the past, for example, predicting the opening price of a stock based on historical daily values.

[15] Richard S. Fuld, Jr. (1946–) was the chairman and chief executive officer of Lehman Brothers Holdings Inc. from 1994 until 2008, when the firm declared bankruptcy.

REFERENCES

Black, Fischer, and Myron Scholes. 1973. The Pricing of Options and Corporate Liabilities. *Journal of Political Economy* 81, (May/June): no. 3: 637–654.

Lipsey, Richard, and Kelvin Lancaster. 1956. The General Theory of Second Best. *Review of Economic Studies* 24, no. 1: 11–32.

Merton, Robert, Myron Scholes, and Matthew Gladstein. 1978. The Returns and Risk of Alternative Call Option Portfolio Investment Strategies. *Journal of Business* 51, no. 2 (April): 183–242.

Scholes, Myron. 1969. A Test of the Competitive Market Hypothesis: The Market for New Issues and Secondary Offerings. PhD thesis, University of Chicago.

Scholes, Myron, and Mark Wolfson. 1991. *Taxes and Business Strategy: A Planning Approach*. Upper Saddle River, NJ: Prentice Hall, Inc.

This interview was published in its entirety in *Journal of Investment Consulting* 11, no. 1, 2010.

CHAPTER 12

BILL SHARPE: GODFATHER OF INDEX FUNDS

WILLIAM F. SHARPE, PHD

Recipient of the 1990 Nobel Memorial Prize in Economic Sciences; STANCO 25 Professor of Finance, Emeritus at Stanford University School of Business; author, *Portfolio Theory and Capital Markets* and *Asset Allocation Tools* and numerous articles in academic publications.

Bill Sharpe is well-known for his work in developing the capital asset pricing model (CAPM), but he also created the reward-to-variability performance ratio, also known as the Sharpe ratio. Early in his career, Sharpe met Harry Markowitz, who was working at the Rand Corporation. In Sharpe's words, he "fell in love" with Markowitz's work, and he began drawing heavily on Markowitz's insights to inform his doctoral dissertation. As Sharpe's career evolved and he gained valuable practical experience, he later admitted that the early CAPM model may have been too simplistic—but then he would quickly add that all good models are simple. Sharpe says that, despite its simplicity, CAPM offers two indispensable messages: First, diversify, diversify, diversify; and secondly, costs matter—especially over the long term.

■ ■ ■

EDWARD BAKER: Thank you for agreeing to be part of the *Journal*'s Masters Series. We, of course, are all familiar with your work and excited about the opportunity to discuss it with you. Matt, you wanted to start off with a question about the capital asset pricing model (CAPM).

MATTHEW MOREY: Given all that has happened in the world of economics and finance since you first developed the CAPM forty years ago, how relevant do you think the model is today?

BILL SHARPE: It seems to me that two major conclusions came out of the CAPM and that those two conclusions are still relevant today. The first of these is what I call the market risk/reward theory, which basically says that an investor can achieve a higher expected rate of return only by taking more market risk; that is, the irreducible risk that remains even if the investor diversifies holdings all over the globe using all types of investments. The corollary of that theory—or the second major conclusion—holds that investors shouldn't take nonmarket risk unless, for example, they need to hedge human capital or they are capable of making predictions superior to those already embedded in market prices. So if we go back to the first, very simple CAPM, those are the two major conclusions: Expected returns are related to beta, and investors need to diversify broadly so that they bear only beta risk.

I think those are still very good conclusions and continue to be relevant today. Someone would have to come up with a strong argument to counter them. Do I think these conclusions can be obtained in more realistic or broader contexts? Of course. While the CAPM/mean-variance paradigm is not my model of first choice these days, it still produces—with some caveats—reasonable results on asset pricing. It does produce results that are obviously inconsistent with reality when it comes to portfolio choice predictions; that is, which investments investors will choose and in which proportions. However, that doesn't mean the CAPM has become irrelevant for asset pricing.

MEIR STATMAN: By way of rejoinder, what about the multibeta model you wrote about many years ago? Is it still the case that a risk that can be diversified is not priced, or would a multibeta model imply that some of those nonrisk factors will be priced?

BILL SHARPE: That raises two issues: First, the research of Eugene Fama and Kenneth French, which—to oversimplify—says that, relative to their beta values, small capitalization equities perform better than large capitalization, and that value stocks outperform growth stocks. I recently commented on this research in the second lecture for my latest book (Sharpe 2006), arguing that these conclusions, even in the long historic period, were predominantly an artifact of relatively small stocks in a small corner of the market. Second, many models—assuming rational, informed investors—can yield premiums for something other than beta relative to the whole market. However, that's not what we see in the Fama-French model, which argues that these factors affect expected returns and is agnostic as to whether they reflect risk premiums or not.

MEIR STATMAN: Do you think that the mathematical elegance of CAPM has created such a high standard that we will always feel as if we are "princes who have been chased out of the land," i.e., when other models are introduced, they are always found to be too messy or too difficult to calculate, or have too many variables, etc. Would we be better off with less elegant models that are closer to the real world?

BILL SHARPE: First of all, I'm not sure that the CAPM is all that elegant—it's fairly simple. Be that as it may, in my new book I rely quite heavily on simulations; that is, I create people, give them securities to trade, and tell them to check back when they're finished. Then I see what prices they have set and what the true probabilities, risk, and returns are. It's both simple and elegant, and I find that teaching people using a framework like this is very easy. Some of the more complex models can be quite trivial in this format. I think that this approach can be elegant but also allows for generalities in important ways. That being said, once you get into cases involving disagreement or complex utility functions, you have to keep hammering away and doing more simulations. If you continue to get qualitatively similar results, the weight of the evidence causes you to think that you may be on to something. I think there's a lot to be said for this approach, for both pedagogical and research purposes. We've got computers now—why not use them?

RONALD KAHN: How do you view all of the so-called anomalies that academics have brought up over the past ten years or so?

BILL SHARPE: An easy answer to that is to say, referring to the old aphorism, if you torture the data hard enough, it will plead guilty to anything you like. To demonstrate this, I ask students to set up a spreadsheet in which the market as a whole has, let's say, a risk premium over cash of 5.5 percent and a standard deviation of 18 percent, so you know exactly what the risk premium of the market as a whole is—not just a piece of the market, but the whole thing. Then I ask them to generate a series of fifty years of data randomly from that distribution and compute the average historic premium. After repeating that step 1,000 times, they can see what a fifty-year record might look like in a world where the premium is truly 5.5 percent. Of course, as we all know, you can easily generate plenty of scenarios in which you observe 0 percent, or 2 percent, or 20 percent over fifty years. The moral of the story is that even if the gods are kind and distributions never change—which is improbable—and even if you have lots of data, you can still be far off on the premium for the whole market. Anyone who thinks that looking at empirical data will produce a resolution to the question of whether the premium on small growth stocks is different from that of large value stocks with any degree of precision is just kidding himself. I'm very skeptical of the findings in historic data related to averages. As a result, I'm fairly dismissive of much of the anomaly literature. I like to think I know something about this topic, because I understand how frail empirical averages are as indicators of historic expectations and, *a fortiori*, current expectations.

RONALD KAHN: So is your argument that returns are so "noisy" that it's almost guaranteed that historical data will find what look like anomalies?

■ ■ ■

When one thinks about the amount of investigation of historical data that has been conducted, and the tiny, tiny percentage of results that have been published, one has to realize that this percentage can't be a purely random sample.

BILL SHARPE: When one thinks about the amount of investigation of historical data that has been conducted, and the tiny, tiny percentage of results that have been published, one has to realize that this percentage can't be a purely random sample. We know what the selection bias is: Results that look like anomalies get published. That's not to say we shouldn't read the literature, think about it, and ask ourselves if there's some reason why, in a reasonably competitive market, one should expect this "anomaly" to happen in the future with sufficient certainty to actually justify putting clients' money into a particular strategy.

MEIR STATMAN: How do you address the argument that this cuts both ways; that is, if you cannot reject theories because of noisy returns, theories become religion, where faith replaces scientific inquiry?

BILL SHARPE: I think that's a valid argument—one that I don't dispute. If you look at the studies done by Gary Brinson et al., broadly diversified portfolios of risky securities within countries and, even more important, across countries have performed better on average over the long term than portfolios that have no risk. To some extent, if you take stocks, bonds, and cash, there is at least an ordering of the long-term average returns. I think that part of the theory is reasonably secure. We know, of course, that much of the argument for diversification can be made just with arithmetic. That is, the return on the average dollar—or yen or euro—is the same before cost whether actively or passively managed, and the return after cost is greater for the average passively managed dollar than for the actively managed dollar just because the costs are higher for the latter. So simple arithmetic gives you at least some reason to diversify and also to be skeptical about putting too much of your money in active management or chasing anomalies.

EDWARD BAKER: Does that lead you to the conclusion that the markets are efficient?

BILL SHARPE: No, I don't think we'll ever know the answer to that. It does lead me to the conclusion that in giving investment advice, it's probably a good idea to assume that the markets are reasonably close to efficient. Of course, you have to define what you mean by efficient. In the sense we've been discussing, I think that assumption is worth making.

RONALD KAHN: When we think about potential reasons that we might believe the markets are inefficient, behavioral finance certainly seems to provide the primary arguments. What is your view of behavioral finance?

BILL SHARPE: I've been a great fan of behavioral psychology for many years, as well as the resulting work in behavioral economics and behavioral finance. In fact, I've been working with colleagues on some experimental studies in a portfolio context with real subjects—about 250 people. I think some wonderful work is being done in this field. But it is important to differentiate between the expectation that behavioral finance is going to tell us new things about asset prices and the expectation it will tell us new and useful things about portfolio choice—both how people do make portfolio choices and how you can help people make better choices. People at my company, Financial Engines, are working not only to understand how people select investments based on the ways various alternatives are framed, but also how to improve the way the alternatives are framed so that people can make decisions that are in their best interests. Certainly behavioral finance is crucial to this. In his book The *Wisdom of Crowds*, James Surowiecki makes the argument that a market full of partially informed, somewhat irrational investors can't yield the same prices—and therefore the same risks and rewards—as a market full of fully informed and extremely rational investors. Robert Merton and Zvi Bodie recently published a paper in which they talk about their idea of building financial institutions into models endogenously, but they take the position that financial institutions will do their best in the pursuit of profit to make the markets close enough—in asset pricing terms—to what you would get in a simple, frictionless market, even though the institutional setting doesn't even exist in most asset pricing models. Do I think that twenty years from now we're going to say, "Aha! Because of behavioral finance, we now have a different model of asset pricing"? I'm not sure, because as we all know, you can pick one part of the behavioral finance literature and predict one asset pricing result, then pick another part of the literature and predict the opposite. It's not as if there's a body of behavioral theory that leads you to a particular asset pricing model.

EDWARD BAKER: What about venture capital investing in a world where the only risk taking that's rewarded is systematic, say, a venture capitalist who puts all his focus on one opportunity? Is that complete folly?

BILL SHARPE: Venture capital is an incredibly important part of the whole engine that creates value, productivity, and social welfare. I also think it's well enough organized that while general partners may have concentrated positions, if you take a realistic look at the fact that each partner may be in several partnerships and each partnership has several companies, even general partners are not all that concentrated. However, they are certainly more concentrated than, say, the General Motors pension fund.

EDWARD BAKER: But surely, at a certain level, some people have a concentrated risk?

BILL SHARPE: Well, for example, I have a concentrated risk in my company. There are clearly situations where there is a benefit to having people take concentrated positions. When you look at venture-financed portfolio companies, you see some people with seriously concentrated positions for good reasons—those people presumably can affect the value of their company, especially in the early stages. The point is to find the right trade-off between bad investment policy and good incentive policy.

TONY KAO: Over the past twelve months, we've had a lot of discussions in our business about policy portfolios. Driving this discussion is the issue of the way we use optimization. Obviously, constraints are necessary, but on the other hand, they can drive the results, which form the policy portfolio. What is your view of how practitioners use optimization, and how does this apply to individual investors?

BILL SHARPE: I have a term that I may have invented in this context called "macroconsistency." The idea is that you have a set of estimates—for example, in the mean-variance context, expected returns, risks, and correlations. The question is: Are the estimates macroconsistent? What I mean by that is if everyone in the world used those estimates, in whatever way they chose, would the markets clear? In a simple CAPM setting, a set of forecasts is macroconsistent if expected returns are proportional to beta values. However, it's a much broader idea. Most boards, when they set policy, or financial advisors, when they establish a policy for an individual investor, are doing so in a long-term, efficient-market context. With some exceptions, they say, "If we were investing in index funds and the markets were efficient, here's what we would do." In that hierarchical scheme, however, they'd then say, "Well, we're not investing in index funds and the markets really aren't efficient," so all of the variations that come from those ideas tend to come back to the policy portfolio. If you take the premise that the policy portfolio ought to reflect an index-fund, efficient-market kind of allocation, then it seems to me you have to argue that the predictions should be macroconsistent.

TONY KAO: How does this framework differ from that of Fischer Black and Robert Litterman?

BILL SHARPE: It doesn't. Fischer and Bob started with the CAPM, and then they perturbed that based on an individual's views about market inefficiency. They dealt more with predictions than preferences. That was the starting point, and I first did some of that "reverse optimization" back in the early 1980s. The point is that most institutional policy portfolio studies and many personal financial planning exercises don't impose the criterion of macroconsistency. Here's a simple way to tell if this criterion is being used: Ask the question, "Do the forecasts take into account the current market values of the asset classes?" If they don't, the forecasters cannot even know whether the forecasts are macroconsistent. In other words, macroconsistent forecasts must have the character that total demand equals total supply for each asset. Since we measure everything in terms of value, we have to know the current value of the stocks in Japan, the values of the U.S. equity market, the U.S. bond market, and so on. That's how we express our policy. You have to know current asset market values before you can make a set of macroconsistent forecasts.

MEIR STATMAN: Are you saying that you should start with the allocation of the overall global portfolio and, from there, infer expected returns? That differs from the traditional way of using the mean-variance framework; that is, Harry Markowitz advised investors to begin with estimates of expected returns, variances, and covariances and use the mean-variance optimizer to identify the optimal asset allocation.

BILL SHARPE: Remember that Markowitz's work was all normative; that is, if you have predictions, here's what to do with them. I'm talking about using equilibrium theory, be it a version of the CAPM or the approach of Arrow and Debreu, to make predictions to be used in normative work. In other words, for advising people on portfolio choice you should take into account relationships from a positive model as to how prices are set. As I said, the simple test is to ask the person who has produced the set of items intended to go into your optimizer, "In producing these forecasts, did you take into account the current market values of these asset classes?" If the answer is "No," or even "Not explicitly," then neither of you has any way to know if the forecasts are macroconsistent. Now let me add a caveat to my answer to Meir, and that is, am I saying that you should just take the world market portfolio and back off expected returns from the CAPM relationship? You can, but I prefer to use a more complex equilibrium approach to make sure that expected returns, risks, and correlations are coherent with one another and take into account the current market values of asset classes on a monthly basis.

MATTHEW MOREY: Since you mentioned policy setting and asset allocation, I wanted to ask if you think the advice provided by the financial services industry adds value for investors in the long run?

BILL SHARPE: Again, you always have to ask, "Compared with what?" Needless to say, those of us involved in the financial advice or management business for individual investors tend to compare ourselves with the most horrible alternatives. Basically, I think financial advisors add value in two areas. First, they can help an investor be adequately diversified—if you will, move up to Markowitz's efficient frontier. Second, advisors can help investors get to the right places on the frontier for their circumstances or, using terms from the Markowitz world, get to the right risk-reward combination for their risk tolerance. In the real world, of course, financial advisors look at other holdings and additional aspects of the investor's circumstances. A full financial planning situation involves insurance, heirs, medical conditions, employment, taxes, the spouse's investments, and many other factors. In my upcoming book, I characterize investors as having preferences, positions, and predictions: preferences including attitudes toward risk and return, and preferences for spending money now versus leaving it to the children; positions meaning the investor has a certain job, owns a house, etc.; and predictions meaning the belief that a certain company or sector will do well or poorly. I think financial advisors add the most value in dealing with the specifics of an investor's positions and preferences and somewhat less value in bringing superior predictions to the table, because market prices incorporate predictions that are often as good as one can get.

■ ■ ■

> **Basically, I think financial advisors add value in two areas. First, they can help an investor be adequately diversified—if you will, move up to Markowitz's efficient frontier. Second, advisors can help investors get to the right places on the frontier for their circumstances or, using terms from the Markowitz world, get to the right risk-reward combination for their risk tolerance.**

EDWARD BAKER: That brings me to the question of whether, in a CAPM world, risk aversion is really the only issue for a financial advisor?

BILL SHARPE: That's right. The only issue that differentiates investors in a simple CAPM world is that you have one risk aversion, and I have another. It's all about mean and variance, so there's really only one parameter. It can be wealth-dependent, but that's about as much as you can get out of that model.

EDWARD BAKER: Several companies have tried to build so-called "life-style" funds to match certain investors' risk tolerance characteristics. Do you think that's a sensible approach?

BILL SHARPE: Some people define a "life-style" fund as a fixed risk tolerance fund through time, and "life-cycle" or "life-stage" as one where risk tolerance adjusts downward as time goes on. I assume you're talking about the latter, for example, a "retire in 2030" fund. While I think the basic idea is useful, the problem is that it's a cookie-cutter approach, and the question remains whether the investor can do well enough by picking one of, say, fifteen funds, where there are just five age groups and three different levels of aggressiveness from which to choose. I think a better approach performs optimization at the level at which the investor is actually going to invest—for example, the specific mutual funds in a 401(k) plan, and that takes into account as much of the investor's personal information as it's possible to obtain. If the approach is, "You're thirty-five, so here's the fund for you," that may not be nearly personal enough. Even if there is a rich enough menu of life-cycle funds for an investor to find a close-to-optimal strategy, the investor may still need help selecting the right one. However, assuming that the cost can be kept under control, my question would be: Why not get as personalized a strategy as you can?

MEIR STATMAN: Does personalized also mean looking for alphas, or does it mean just tailoring the strategy to investors' financial conditions and needs?

BILL SHARPE: I think the best approach combines an extensive analysis of mutual fund performance relative to the best benchmarks one can build for each fund, and predictions of future performance relative to those benchmarks, taking into account empirical evidence about the relationship between future performance before costs, or gross alpha, and past performance, residual risk, and other factors. Once you have made the best possible prediction of a fund's future gross alpha you can subtract predicted expenses to obtain an estimate of the net alpha to the investor. So in answer to your question about whether personalized includes looking for alphas, yes, certainly in terms of net returns, but they are often negative because of expenses, given the fact that the best estimates of gross alphas tend to be small—sometimes negative and sometimes positive.

EDWARD BAKER: Certainly many people believe it's worthwhile to look for alpha, and there's an industry full of people who try to help investors find such managers. The Sharpe ratio has become widely used as a way to discover those managers and assess whether they will continue to deliver results. Do you think that's a misapplication of this work?

BILL SHARPE: In many cases, yes. Let me define some terms so that we're all talking about the same thing. If you go back to my first paper on this topic, I presented a measure that I called the reward-to-variability ratio. The idea was that if you had two alternatives, in particular, your whole portfolio and Treasury bills, and you could take positions in any size, then you should look at the ratio of the expected difference between the two returns divided by the standard deviation of the difference between the returns. In my 1966 article, the alternatives were your whole portfolio or risky securities or cash, and, given the fact that you could adjust the amount in these alternatives, selecting a portfolio with the highest ratio uniformly produced better opportunity sets than picking any with lower ratios. That idea was enshrined by Treynor and Black, in an article that suggested calling the measure the Sharpe ratio. Today when people use the term "Sharpe ratio," in most cases they mean reward-to-variability using the difference between the return on an investment and that of Treasury bills.

EDWARD BAKER: The term is also often used to mean something minus a benchmark.

BILL SHARPE: That's what I want to differentiate. When the term is used to refer to something minus a benchmark, where the benchmark can be anything, I think that is more commonly called the information ratio. Whatever you call it, an information or reward-to-variability ratio is only as good as the benchmark. I tried to clear this up in a *Journal of Portfolio Management* article in 1994. The whole rationale for using a reward-to-variability ratio is that you can choose the scale. Any time you take the difference between two returns, that's a zero investment strategy because you're long one asset class and short the other. Let's say that you have two alternative investment strategies, and one has a higher reward-to-variability than the other. When choosing between the two, at any scale, you want to pick the one with the higher ratio. That's part of the basic economics behind why this ratio can be interesting. I think many of the conditions, even for an information ratio, may not be met in actual practice. Certainly, if you are evaluating an investment that is intended to be a piece of a portfolio, you want to evaluate it against a passive benchmark that in some sense has the same exposure to relevant factors. If you're looking at historical data, you want to look at not only the average difference, but also the standard deviation of the difference, and if you're determined to have just one number to look at, take the ratio.

It is unfortunate when people use the original version of the ratio—return minus Treasury-bill return—for a fund that's going to be part of a portfolio. Obviously, if you're evaluating fund A, which is going to be put in a portfolio of funds, you should take into account not only its expected return and its risk, but also its correlation with other funds in the portfolio. A measure that has only risk and return can't deal with the correlation as well. So any setting in which the correlations are important can't be summarized in a number that takes into account only mean and standard deviation. The exception would be residual risk. Most models assume that all residual risks are uncorrelated. If this is true, then there are no correlations to be taken into account. Another case arises when a true hedge fund is being evaluated. If such a fund has no factor exposures, the correct benchmark is Treasury bills, and the Sharpe ratio may be a perfectly good measure. However, you must make sure the condition is met, since many hedge funds are in fact correlated with various asset classes.

EDWARD BAKER: Do you think that all of these measures are just a waste of time in trying to identify a manager who can be expected to deliver future performance?

BILL SHARPE: First of all, I think it's imperative that performance is measured, and second, that it's measured relative to appropriate benchmarks. If you say, "Well, if I measure performance at all, that's stupid because, if nothing else, managers incur costs," you still need to find out if they've delivered something for the costs they've incurred. And if you're measuring a small growth manager who never buys anything but small growth stocks, you have to measure him or her relative to a small growth index, or you'll never have any chance of figuring out if his or her performance has been, meaningfully, good or bad.

■ ■ ■

First of all, I think it's imperative that performance is measured, and second, that it's measured relative to appropriate benchmarks.

TONY KAO: Speaking of appropriate benchmarks, when you wrote your article on style analysis, did you have any expectations that this approach would become so widely used in portfolio construction, performance measurement, manager evaluation, and so on?

BILL SHARPE: Let me give you some history that may shed some light on this. In 1986, I set up a small firm to work with pension fund sponsors. I was trying to build a factor model that would apply across all the investments in a typical large pension fund. At the time, there were the Barra models for equities, various models for bonds, and so on, but I wanted to develop one factor model with which we could look at the pension fund, focusing basically on the tasks of the pension staff and board. As I tried to figure out how to approach this, I started with the thought that there was no way that I could build a fundamentals-based model *à la* Barra that could cover everything in a fully consistent way. If Barra hadn't been able to do it, my four employees and I weren't going to do it. So my first answer to the problem was to try regression analysis. I regressed the returns of my clients' managers on indexes of asset class returns that I thought might work well, and I got total garbage—from implied holdings of −300 percent a year to +500 percent. It was meaningless. So I thought, "Well, that's it for that idea. What am I going to do now?" I did know that almost all the managers had only long positions in asset classes, so I decided to add in some lower bounds of zero and run the data through a QP [quadratic programming] model. Voila! Out came results that seemed quite plausible. I started sending the results out to the sponsors, who shared them with their managers, and we entered a period where it just seemed that I could do magic. I even played a game: you send me returns for ten managers, without any identification, and I'll send you my estimates of their styles. Then you see how well they line up with your perceptions. This approach seemed to be working fairly well, and then we conducted several experiments in conjunction with Barra to find useful new indexes that could make the process as informative as possible. Five of the indexes now called the Barra/S&P indexes came out of this work. So much for the early history of style analysis in the 1980s. I must admit that I was then and continue now to be amazed by the quantity of useful information that comes out of this quite simple and parsimonious use of small amounts of data.

In answer to your question about whether I had anticipated that this model would become so widely used, the answer is no. In fact, there was a period when Frank Russell, which shared the rights to use the software that I had developed in 1988, chose not to use it and even published articles suggesting that this was not a particularly useful approach. My view is that there is obviously room for all kinds of analysis, and this quick and not-so-dirty procedure can provide a lot of helpful information. I had been thinking of developing software to make the technique available more widely when Ken Winston showed me software that was already well along in development. My thinking was just that it was great to have it out there and available, which is why I had published a journal article describing the approach in detail. I did have a good notion that it would be used, since it was useful and people were working on it commercially, but I must admit I'm very pleased that it's used as much as it is.

RONALD KAHN: I wanted to ask a follow-up question to Ed's question about the Sharpe ratio. What do you think of the various downside risk measures, and has that been a useful direction for research?

BILL SHARPE: I think you have to differentiate between the portfolio as a whole and a piece of the portfolio. When you deal with a piece of the portfolio, you obviously have a problem in that the downside risk of a portfolio is simply a function of the downside risks of its components. I'm a great believer in getting the whole probability distribution or, in the case of a portfolio, a joint probability distribution. I continue to aspire to show an investor the entire probability distribution for the portfolio, although some would say that ordinary 401(k) investors are overwhelmed by this and that you have to use summary statistics, such as a downside measure, in addition to a threshold measure. If you are going to show investors only two numbers, you must be sure that those two capture elements of both risk and return. Typically, investors want to see the chance that they'll have better than an acceptable or comfortable threshold of retirement living and the chance that they'll have more than a downside outcome at which they'd be fairly miserable. They can select those in various ways, but the latter is certainly a type of downside measure.

EDWARD BAKER: Please tell us about the excitement of winning the Nobel Prize for economics in 1990 and how that has changed your life.

BILL SHARPE: To answer the second question first, it means I get invited to participate in interviews such as this, and it's always fun to share my opinions with others. Would these kinds of opportunities have happened without the prize? I have no way to do an experiment to find out. As far as the excitement, I had figured that based on the record, the Nobel committee would not include financial economics in the domain for the economics prize. So I had virtually dismissed the idea of a prize in my area of work. As a result, I wasn't even paying attention to the timing of the announcement. We were at a conference in Arizona, and the call came at 3:30 a.m. It was completely unexpected and, of course, a heady and phenomenal experience: going to Stockholm, where the Nobel Prizes are regarded as the Super Bowl is in the United States and the prize winners are like rock stars, waving from the back of the limos, people standing at the entrance of the Grand Hotel, trying to get autographs and take photos. How does winning the prize change your life? Needless to say, it doesn't change the attitudes of your colleagues—they are just as critical of you as they ever were. You certainly receive more attention and more invitations, but I like to think that I would have received at least some of the invitations anyway. The simple way to summarize my experience is that if you get offered a Nobel Prize, take it!

MATTHEW MOREY: Looking ahead, what innovations do you see in the financial industry?

BILL SHARPE: We are in this wonderful period when it has finally become academically respectable to work on problems that are important to individual investors. For a long period in my career, that type of work was considered "personal finance," to be dealt with at lower academic levels. Now some of the best minds in financial economics are working in this field. But much remains to be done. What are the problems that we need to address? They are, basically, the problems of investing over time and in particular, since human beings are mortal, the problem of accounting for mortality. At the moment, the good work in the area posits a return-generating process; for example, assuming that returns are independently and identically distributed or that returns of stocks revert to a mean, that the inflation rate follows a GARCH process, and so on. Given such assumptions, people work to determine optimal strategies. However, it bothers me that these return processes don't come from any underlying equilibrium market process, but from empirical data that may or may not be completely germane. We need to get serious about multiperiod equilibrium; that is, how do preferences and productive opportunities come together to determine the behavior of asset prices over time? If we had a better handle on the answer to that question, we could better advise investors concerning the way in which they organize financial affairs over their lifetimes. When I think about the problems of a seventy-year-old, which is easy for me because I have empirical data, the biggest issues concern your investment portfolio, Social Security, Medicare, annuities, and long-term care policies. But what about your house? How does a couple make decisions that take into account possible differences in mortality and illness? And what about possible heirs? Many of these issues loom at least as large or possibly larger than decisions concerning portfolio investment and spending out accumulated wealth. Good financial advisors are aware of this and know how to deal with such issues, but it is complicated, and financial economics can be very helpful in developing better solutions in this area. Financial institutions can help also, and we're beginning to see more response from institutions as baby boomers near retirement and the demographics lead to huge shifts in the location of wealth.

RONALD KAHN: You've addressed academic research issues, but I wanted to ask you about areas where you see deficiencies in financial industry research; that is, what issues need to be addressed, or gaps filled, although there may not be major distinctions between academic and industry research.

BILL SHARPE: Let me use that as a springboard for some final thoughts on an issue that bothers me a great deal. Think about this: Until fairly recently, the way in which we dealt with retirement in this country, and most Western countries, was based on the fact that you worked, you retired, you got your checks from the government and maybe your employer, you died, your spouse got checks, your spouse died, and that was it. Basically, in effect, people in their working years were buying—to put it in simple financial terms—deferred annuities, some of which were indexed, like Social Security, and some not indexed, like certain pension plans, but all of which were essentially fixed annuities. People were well acquainted with this scenario. Then we shifted to a defined contribution environment where people could choose to invest different amounts at different levels of risk and return. Unfortunately, in many cases, people didn't know what they were doing. People now have the option to buy an immediate annuity when they retire, but the evidence from this country and from countries that have done this longer than the United States is that, by and large, they don't. This may be, at least in part, due to the fact that individual annuities are priced to take into account adverse selection, assuming that those who buy payout annuities are likely to live longer than those who do not. So we have had three sea changes as we moved from one regime toward another; that is, the need to determine one's ability to save, the desire to take risk in the pursuit of higher returns, and the decision concerning the extent of annuitization after retirement. Much of the public discussion focuses on the first two aspects, to the neglect of the latter. So the question is: Why are people not buying annuities now when they previously seemed to be comfortable with a system in which they did buy them? Mortality risk seems like the most obvious gain through trade; that is, my death is relatively uncorrelated with yours, so we should both be better off by pooling that risk. If you're asking what the financial industry can do, my answer is that it can think about solutions to this issue, and I'd like to see research in behavioral finance that would help people better understand the trade-offs in the choices they make after retirement.

He likes annuities to retire on

■ ■ ■

REFERENCES

Arrow, Kenneth, and Gerard Debreu, 1954. Existence of a Competitive Equilibrium for a Competitive Economy. *Econometrica* 22, no. 3 (July): 205–290.

Brinson, Gary P., L. Randolph Hood, and Gilbert L. Beebower. 1986. Determinants of Portfolio Performance. *Financial Analysts Journal* 42, no. 4 (July/August): 39–48.

Brinson, Gary P., Brian D. Singer, and Gilbert L. Beebower. 1991. Determinants of Portfolio Performance II: An Update. *Financial Analysts Journal* 47, no. 3 (May/June): 40–48.

Merton, Robert C., and Zvi Bodie. 2004. The Design of Financial Systems: Towards a Synthesis of Function and Structure. NBER Working Paper No. W10620 (July).

Sharpe, William F. 1966. Mutual Fund Performance. *Journal of Business* 39, no. 1 (January): 119–138.

———. 1994. The Sharpe Ratio. *Journal of Portfolio Management* 21, no. 1 (fall): 49–58.

———. 2006. *Investors and Markets: Portfolio Choices, Asset Prices, and Investment Advice.* Princeton, NJ: Princeton University Press.

Surowiecki. James. 2004. *The Wisdom of Crowds: Why the Many Are Smarter Than the Few and How Collective Wisdom Shapes Business, Economics, Societies, and Nations.* New York: Doubleday.

Treynor, Jack L., and Fischer Black. 1973. How to Use Security Analysis to Improve Portfolio Selection. *Journal of Business* 46, no. 1 (January): 66–85.

This interview was published in its entirety in *Journal of Investment Consulting* 7, no. 2, 2005.

CHAPTER 13

BOB SHILLER: MR. BUBBLE

ROBERT J. SHILLER, PHD

Recipient of the 2013 Nobel Memorial Prize in Economic Sciences; Sterling Professor of Economics and Cowles Foundation for Research in Economics at Yale University and Professor of Finance and Fellow at the International Center for Finance at the Yale School of Management; author of *Finance and the Good Society* and co-author, *Animal Spirits*, among others and numerous articles in academic journals.

Bob Shiller was one of the first academics to recognize the benefits of incorporating psychological and sociological factors into the theory of markets. In doing so, he challenged the idea that markets are efficient. A first-rate academic, Shiller left the security and isolation of the ivory tower to explore the real world of investments and finance. He established the Case-Shiller Home Price Indices, perhaps the world's best-known real estate index. His bestselling book, *Irrational Exuberance*, appeared in 2000 and warned that the stock market had become a bubble ready to burst. In 2007, about a year before the collapse of Lehman Brothers, Shiller again warned of an imminent collapse, this time in the housing market. Given his prescience at calling market tops, investors might do well to heed his advice.

■ ■ ■

EDWARD BAKER: Thank you for accepting our invitation to participate in the Masters Series. Your 2003 paper in the *Journal of Economic Perspectives* was an excellent read and provided a great deal of insight into the origins of behavioral finance. Meir, you wanted to start off with some questions about this.

MEIR STATMAN: I don't know if you remember your visit to Santa Clara University in the mid-1980s, back when you were still under attack for your views on excess volatility. It would be interesting to get a sense of what the field of behavioral finance was like in those early days.

ROBERT SHILLER: I do remember that visit. It was the first time that I realized there were a number of allies around, although we seemed like a rather beleaguered and small group at the time. You, Daniel Kahneman, Amos Tversky, Richard Thaler, Werner De Bondt. It wasn't until the late 1980s that Dick Thaler began organizing conferences focused on behavioral finance, so it's interesting to see how the whole field—and the related research—has grown.

MATTHEW MOREY: I'd like to ask a question related to your recent article in the *Journal of Economic Perspectives* as well as some of the observations you made in *Irrational Exuberance*. One argument made in support of the efficient markets theory is that no investor can consistently beat the market. The preponderance of research on mutual funds concludes that they cannot outperform their respective indexes on a consistent basis. How do you reconcile the evidence on the mutual fund front with the idea that the markets are inefficient?

ROBERT SHILLER: The first thing to establish is that I believe market efficiency is a half-truth. The way I view it is that students like to be told that there's a simple, cut-and-dried, easy way to think about the world, so there's a tendency for scholars to go to one extreme or the other to please their students. One way to go is to say that markets are completely efficient, and you can tell a satisfying story, one with lots of examples about how presumed inefficiencies turned out to be wrong. The other extreme would be to say that market efficiency is totally wrong. The challenge is to find where the line is. Obviously, the markets are not completely efficient or completely inefficient, either.

When you look at mutual funds, that's one group of professional investors. It's not the same group as hedge funds or university endowments. Mutual funds are a specific group with a certain homogeneity, since the funds communicate with one another and people move among them. The most telling studies about mutual funds are the ones about persistence of returns. If the markets are inefficient, it would be reasonable to assume that even though you might not be able to predict which mutual fund is going to perform better than others, some of them ought to be consistently doing better than others. If there are smart managers at a certain fund, you would think that the returns should be persistently higher at that fund. However, the literature has found only weak evidence of persistence—there is some, but not very much.

I suppose the lack of persistence reflects a number of issues. It does suggest that, to some extent, markets are efficient. However, lack of persistence also reflects the fact that there's a great deal of randomness in returns so that even a smart investor can't beat the market all the time, and so persistence won't be that strong. It's partly because mutual funds learn from one another and adapt, so if one fund is a success, other funds start doing the same thing. It's partly because a successful mutual fund tends to bring in more investors and, therefore, more assets, and it's harder to invest well when the fund gets larger. That's just part of the normal life cycle. In addition, in most cases, mutual funds may not tend to attract the most talented investment managers because the culture is oriented more to sales than profits. A more talented investment manager might prefer to go to a hedge fund, where there's more freedom and generally better incentives and compensation. All these things combine together to explain why persistence of returns among mutual funds is not stronger.

MATTHEW MOREY: One thing you discuss is that no one can say exactly when the market is going to decline, just that there appears to be excessive enthusiasm or exuberance, but it's very difficult to determine the timing when the market's going to go up or down. As a result, it's difficult for these funds to consistently beat the indexes. I suppose that's one rationale for combining these two ideas: the concept of stock market bubbles and, on the other hand, the literature showing very little evidence of persistence.

ROBERT SHILLER: Yes, that's right. I should point out that when I wrote *Irrational Exuberance*, I didn't really intend that investors should be trying to time the market all the time or making a big issue of it. My intent was merely to remark on the extraordinary time in which we were living and to call attention to the fact that there are definite times when investors ought to pay attention to overpricing or underpricing.

■ ■ ■

> I should point out that when I wrote *Irrational Exuberance,* I didn't really intend that investors should be trying to time the market all the time or making a big issue of it. My intent was merely to remark on the extraordinary time in which we were living and to call attention to the fact that there are definite times when investors ought to pay attention to overpricing or underpricing.

TONY KAO: In your article, you also spent some time discussing short-sale constraints. Could you comment on these constraints and their role as contributors to market inefficiency? Do you think the market would be efficient if these constraints didn't exist?

ROBERT SHILLER: Short-sale constraints, either the institutional problems or just the psychological problems with selling short, are an important reason why we see some of the most extreme anomalies in finance. There are cases where small firms become extraordinarily overpriced and very hard to short. In some sense, this is not really a sign of inefficiency according to the broad definition, since it becomes impossible for the smart money, or contrarian investors, to short the shares to take advantage of the inefficiency. However, in a wider sense, it's not just the impossibility of shorting but the inhibitions against shorting that produce smaller and perhaps less dramatic inefficiencies. Most people would prefer not to short a share that appears somewhat overpriced, given the fact that a short position has an unlimited loss potential and, in our investing culture, that's considered a rather risky thing to do. Also, margin calls are unpleasant and force unpleasant decisions, so most investors stay away from short positions altogether, never take them. So a stock can often be moderately overpriced and not shorted; that is, shorting is not enough to overcome the overpricing. That's an important factor that generates some of our apparent anomalies.

EDWARD BAKER: Has the social sciences side of the community actually tried to test the aversion to short selling?

ROBERT SHILLER: A number of papers have been written on the subject of determining whether the predictions about market inefficiency related to short-sale constraints hold up. For example, Chen, Hong, and Stein wrote a paper in which they showed that breadth of ownership positively predicts returns (Chen et al. 2002). They didn't actually measure short-sale restrictions, but they believed that concentrated ownership suggests that a few people may have bid the price up, and others are inhibited from correcting it. Anna Scherbina (2001) had another version showing that disagreement among analysts' opinions served as a measure of the relevance of short-sale constraints; that is, if there's a lot of disagreement, it means that some people are very strong on the stock, and presumably they bid the price up. Others, if they're reluctant to short the stock, let that happen. So her finding was that this disagreement also predicts returns. This is the best evidence of which I'm aware that suggests the importance of short-sale aversion, or restrictions, in actually predicting returns in the market.

TONY KAO: Do you think that hedge funds, which normally are not subject to short-sale constraints either because of lack of regulation or investors' preference, take full advantage of this, and how much does this contribute to their returns?

ROBERT SHILLER: I don't really know the answer to that question, but I can say that hedge funds are changing in composition all the time. We're seeing an explosion in the number of hedge funds, and the newer ones may not be as high quality as the older ones. Therefore, any conclusions drawn from studies of hedge funds in years past would not necessarily apply well today. Hedge funds appear to be becoming more sales-oriented than they were in the past, because there's a huge clamor to invest in them. They're also growing in size, which means it's harder for them to find the kind of niche investments they once found. So it's very difficult to predict where hedge funds are going in the future because the whole phenomenon is changing so greatly through time.

But let's say you want to pick a hedge fund in which to invest. Where I think the market efficiency theory goes wrong is that I really believe that people who are very intelligent—in a practical sense—and willing to work hard will probably, in the long run, earn extra returns. So one way an investor might use his or her intelligence and willingness to work hard would be to sort through all possible hedge funds. You can't just pick anything that calls itself a hedge fund—you have to look at the skills and talents of the people who are running it. Investors with better judgment ought to be able to select the better hedge funds. The people whom others point to as great or successful investors are considered such because they are smart. While that's viewed as inconsistent with market efficiency, in a broader sense market efficiency is still right because if you're average, you're likely to have average investment results. Just following some simple rule of thumb such as "Pick any hedge fund" is not going to make you rich.

EDWARD BAKER: I have another question related to hedge funds. Most investors with a diversified portfolio still have a bias toward long-only investments, mostly mutual funds. Do you think investors should be using hedge funds more than they do and get away from this long-only bias?

ROBERT SHILLER: Hedge funds are a very interesting investment vehicle, and yes, there should probably be more attention paid to short positions. One of the offerings that my company, Macro Securities Research, is trying to create is a security that does take short positions. We want to create securities that trade on the stock market, but that take short positions in the stock market or in other markets. There are already exchange-traded funds (ETFs), and you can short ETFs, but that's not the same thing as buying an ETF that's short, or a bear ETF. There are also bear funds, but we think this new security will offer some improvements on those. We'd like to make it easier for people to take short positions, not only in the stock market but in other markets such as real estate. Many investors are very overexposed to the real estate in a single city. This is a very common error—well, not exactly an error, since people are forced into it because there's no easy way to short real estate in their city. This is something we're working on, and I'd like to see it happen. So the answer to your question is yes, I think short positions should be an important part of one's overall investment strategy, much more commonly than they are now.

EDWARD BAKER: Our journal's main constituency is the investment consultant community, the people who advise others on how to better structure portfolios, at both the institutional and individual levels. What implications do you think behavioral finance has for them? Is it a useful area for consultants to explore?

ROBERT SHILLER: Yes, absolutely. Particularly for the individual investor, the role a consultant takes on is a little bit like a psychologist and a little bit like a social worker—you're giving people advice about their lives. I know it centers around their financial decisions, but an investment advisor has a very important public trust. So expanding the advisor's horizons to think about human psychology is fundamental. As a consultant, you may be giving very good advice, but it may not be taken if you don't understand the underlying human behavior. People can be very resistant to good advice, and you have to understand why.

■ ■ ■

> Particularly for the individual investor, the role a consultant takes on is a little bit like a psychologist and a little bit like a social worker—you're giving people advice about their lives. I know it centers around their financial decisions, but an investment advisor has a very important public trust. So expanding the advisor's horizons to think about human psychology is fundamental. As a consultant, you may be giving very good advice, but it may not be taken if you don't understand the underlying human behavior.

EDWARD BAKER: Do you think it's important that consultants learn how to protect investors from themselves, or is there another role they should be playing?

ROBERT SHILLER: Well, of course, consultants are protecting investors from other shenanigans out there too—fraud and market manipulations, among other things. Financial markets are inherently difficult to understand. You'd like to give analogies—to say that predicting the markets is like, say, predicting the seasons, something where we have a scientific basis for making predictions.

The problem with the markets is that they are just like people, and individual investors can easily get confused. A common error underlies herd behavior, and that's belief in the statement, "If most people are saying something, it's probably right." While that's probably true for everyday life, it's not true for investing, because when everyone is saying the same thing, it may be driving the market. That idea may be obvious to you and me, but it's one of the errors characteristic of individual investors. So they need someone who will stop them from running with the pack.

MATTHEW MOREY: Much of your work makes the point that, at certain times, investing for the long term may not necessarily be the best choice. Yet one of the things that frequently comes out in discussions with financial advisors is the importance of investing for the long haul, riding out the ups and downs of the market. How would you answer someone who says, "Stocks are best for the long run"?

ROBERT SHILLER: There's always some element of truth in all these different stories; it's just a question of where we're overstating the matter. One of the reasons people are urged to invest for the long run is to caution them about overtrading or churning. That's elementary good advice. You can use up your wealth in trading commissions if you trade too often. The problem is knowing when to draw the line and get out. The answer can be complex—that's another reason we need investment consultants.

MEIR STATMAN: Would you suggest that advisors, or investors themselves, use price/earnings (P/E) ratios or dividend yields, for example, to determine when it's time to get out of the market, even if it's infrequently? Or is that more likely to lead them astray than to lead them right?

ROBERT SHILLER: Well, a very high P/E ratio is a sign of trouble. So people should look at that, and obviously many investors do. But let's go back to 1999, when you had dot-com stocks trading at infinite P/E ratios—the various ratios were all out of line. This is an example of when an investment advisor can earn his or her fees by warning people away from those mistakes.

MEIR STATMAN: Or you could lose a client because you told him that in 1998, rather than 1999.

ROBERT SHILLER: It's much more comfortable being a tenured professor than an investment advisor. Being an advisor is a conflictual situation: You can be giving the right advice and have the client disagree with you or ignore you—or you can be giving the right advice and still get fired.

MATTHEW MOREY: That goes back to my earlier question. How can you decide the right time to get in and out of the market, rather than just staying in for the long haul? I think most investors get confused. They hear the story that the market's very overvalued, then they also hear that the market continues to go up.

ROBERT SHILLER: What it comes down to is that a buy-and-hold strategy may prove to be the right strategy, but thinking about it carefully is always helpful. For some people, buying a home in Los Angeles now, for example, would not be a wise decision because it is a risky situation, and they have to understand that they might be putting a huge part of their portfolio in a risky investment. It all depends on their life circumstances. Investing is complicated, and there are mistakes investors can make. It's not just failing to trade often enough, or trading too much.

People also tend not to diversify their portfolios. Putting all of your money into an expensive home is holding a very undiversified portfolio. If people take the time to think these things through with the help of an advisor, they might choose to live in a more modest home, for example, as a way of diversifying. We definitely need advisors who will spend time with people and help them think about their individual circumstances.

TONY KAO: Speaking of bubbles, you've talked about the idea of selling at a high point when everyone else is still buying or buying in at a low when everyone else is selling. However, in terms of selecting an investment or searching for an investment manager, very few people would invest in a mutual fund with declining returns or hire a manager with poor performance in anticipation of a turnaround. Can you explain this from a behavioral finance viewpoint?

ROBERT SHILLER: Well, most investors are not reading finance journals. They have more of a fly-by-the-seat-of-your-pants way of thinking, in which it seems very clear to them that you should pull out of losing funds or stocks and go into the winning ones. People are guided largely by intuition, and it's sometimes shocking the way they think. I've had people tell me that they have a large part of their portfolio invested in a high-P/E stock, and when I asked if they're worried, they say no, because they're "watching it"—and they're ready to pull out at any time.

EDWARD BAKER: In your article, you also mentioned some work that you've been involved with that shows a tendency for the prices of individual stocks to be related to their fundamental characteristics. Do you think this supports the view that a disciplined approach to long-term investing focused on fundamentals—an approach that ties fundamentals to prices—should pay off?

ROBERT SHILLER: I guess the answer is yes, in the long run. In a paper I wrote with Jeeman Jung (2005), we quoted Paul Samuelson's dictum that the markets are micro efficient but macro inefficient. We found that, to some extent, this is true. The stock market itself seems to be mainly driven by fashions and fads. However, when you look at individual stocks, it's a different story, because individual stocks are much more diverse, and some of them can be predicted to perform well over the long run. Their earnings will likely go up in the next decade, for example. Others can be predicted to perform poorly. People who look at a company and really think about it ought to be able to outguess others on how the company's course will run.

MEIR STATMAN: Can you explain the apparent dichotomy of having individual stocks that can be priced reasonably well relative to one another and a market, as a whole, that can deviate so far from its value?

ROBERT SHILLER: The answer is that individual stocks have much more volatile and predictable earnings. The earnings for the aggregate stock market are much more calm and not easy to predict very far out. That's the difference. I can say, for example, that the baby-boom generation will soon be retiring and ten years from now there will be increased demand for retirement homes, so that would be a good place to invest money, assuming other factors confirm the investment. That kind of reasoning appears to be able to get ahead of the market, if you do it in a subtle way. However, if you're thinking about predicting how the entire stock market will move, there's no basis for that sort of reasoning. Who knows what earnings are going to do in ten years? There just aren't the opportunities to use your intellect to predict aggregate stock market earnings. For one thing, they aren't variable enough; aggregate earnings have followed a fairly smooth trend for the past 100 years, growing at a real rate of about 2 percent a year.

MEIR STATMAN: It still seems like a puzzling idea because, after all, the market is simply the sum of all the stocks. So if you can get the stocks right, why can't you get the sum right?

ROBERT SHILLER: Well, first of all, people aren't getting the stocks right either, but the point is that the earnings for the whole market average out, so you're not left with much aggregate variation in earnings. All you're left with is the noise.

EDWARD BAKER: I'd like to ask a few questions about risk aversion. It seems to me that's one area where the traditional modeling approach tried to incorporate some behavioral elements. What does behavioral finance tell us about risk aversion? Can it help us gain better insights?

ROBERT SHILLER: One idea that was essentially enshrined with the invention of the capital asset pricing model was that different people have different risk tolerances, or risk aversions. It worked out very well in that mathematical model to assume that the only parameter, or behavioral element, along which people differ is in their tolerance for risk. This worked beautifully, giving us the famous efficient portfolio frontier and the tangency line. People simply array themselves along this line depending on their risk tolerances, and it makes a beautiful story. The problem is that risk aversion is hardly the only relevant parameter. Incidentally, many investment advisors would try first to elicit your risk tolerance to decide whether to put you in an aggressive growth portfolio or a conservative income portfolio. However, studies that tried to find consistent differences in risk tolerance across individuals, or at least within an age group, were unable to find differences that were highly consistent from one measure to another. It appears that people are more complex. It's not as simple as having timid people and bold people. Some people will be risk averse in one circumstance and not so averse in another. It's oversimplifying human nature to think we can put people into those two categories as the only psychological measure we use.

■ ■ ■

It appears that people are more complex. It's not as simple as having timid people and bold people. Some people will be risk averse in one circumstance and not so averse in another. It's oversimplifying human nature to think we can put people into those two categories as the only psychological measure we use.

People also differ in other ways. There was an interesting paper by Ameriks, Caplin, and Leahy (2002) about the propensity to plan. They found that one major difference across individuals is that some people like to plan their future, and others find planning unpleasant and simply avoid doing it. It's not that this latter group is more risk tolerant when it comes to their portfolios; it's that they're not even paying attention. Ameriks and his co-authors found that those who are planners tend to do very well in terms of having more money when it comes to retirement. These are the people who keep a file folder, look at their portfolios regularly and know where they're invested, keep up with financial news, and consider all the contingencies. So there's an important personality distinction. Those who are advising or consulting with individual investors have to recognize that these personality differences are really the difference between success and failure.

EDWARD BAKER: So have you concluded that risk aversion is a useless notion?

ROBERT SHILLER: No, it's not useless, but much of it is circumstantial. It depends on age, for one thing. Young people can take on better risk with their investment portfolios because it represents a smaller part of the entire portfolio with human capital added. Other life circumstances might also affect a person's risk tolerance. However, the concept that some personality types are consistently more risk tolerant than others is not as strong an idea as people commonly think.

EDWARD BAKER: We do see moments in time when investors seem to be more comfortable taking risk, and other moments when they're very uncomfortable. In times of heightened geopolitical risk, for example, we see money flowing into U.S. Treasuries, and then at other times, investors will be flocking to emerging markets.

ROBERT SHILLER: What you're talking about here is perceived risk, rather than risk preferences. There are times when people think we're living in a riskier world. After September 11th, for example, people's perceptions of risk went way up.

EDWARD BAKER: So you're saying that they're not more risk averse during those times—they just think there's more risk?

ROBERT SHILLER: That's right. After a stock market decline, people may perceive more risk than before when, in fact, the decline may have taken some of the risk out of the market. I haven't quantified this, but I believe risk perceptions probably move around more than risk preferences do.

MEIR STATMAN: Speaking of risk, can you comment on that old observation by Friedman and Savage that people who buy insurance also buy lottery tickets, despite the apparent inconsistency of that behavior?

ROBERT SHILLER: This again points to the complexity of human nature. The academic theory that people are maximizing expected utility doesn't really have much support from psychology. What economists want is a theoretical framework with which they can understand all of these economic phenomena, so there's a natural impulse for economic theorists to try to produce something elegant and rational. Friedman and Savage (1948) attempted to put these two phenomena—buying insurance, which is risk-averse behavior, and buying lottery tickets, which is risk-seeking—into the expected utility framework, but I don't think it worked. The simplest explanation for the reason people buy lottery tickets and at the same time buy insurance involves prospect theory. Evidence shows that in making economic decisions, people are easily influenced by the context and ambience that accompany the decision problem. People have a tendency to exaggerate very small probabilities if their attention is drawn to them. Even though the probability

Right Brown of winning the lottery may be smaller than the probability of being struck by lightning, people don't see it that way because the threat of lightning is just not salient to them. On the other hand, the lottery ticket is presented in such a way that the small probability of winning becomes salient and feeds people's imaginations. I think this is closer to the correct answer to why people buy both insurance and lottery tickets. At the stage in his career when Friedman first made his observation, his mission was to set the course for economic theory. I admire Milton Friedman very much, but I've come to believe that his efforts to encourage economists to proceed with expected utility models was probably misleading rather than constructive.

EDWARD BAKER: Any final thoughts about what you'll be doing in the future, any work that you can share with us?

ROBERT SHILLER: I'm currently working on a second edition of *Irrational Exuberance* that will come out in 2005, five years after the first book, in which I look at the stock market volatility of the 1980s and 1990s with the insights gained over five additional years.

■ ■ ■

What's driving the economy as a whole, what's moving the unemployment rate, GDP, etc., is substantially irrational as well. Understanding the psychological foundation of human behavior in financial markets can facilitate the formulation of macroeconomic policy and the development of new financial institutions.

EDWARD BAKER: Have you changed your views at all over that time?

ROBERT SHILLER: Well, yes, I don't think the stock market is as overpriced. It's still overpriced, but not nearly as dramatically as it was in 2000. Earnings are up, and prices are down. A lot of the irrational exuberance has shifted to the real estate market, at least in certain cities. The second edition of the book is an attempt to add a little more perspective. It's five years later, so I view things a little differently. However, the first edition was basically about behavioral finance and the insights we had about the market at that time, and much of that hasn't changed. I'm also working on a book with George Ackerlof [winner of the 2001 Nobel Memorial Prize in Economic Sciences] entitled *Behavioral Macroeconomics*, which will be a book of readings. The field of macroeconomics has been less affected by psychology than the field of finance has, but it really deserves just as much input. What's driving the economy as a whole, what's moving the unemployment rate, GDP (gross domestic product), etc., is substantially irrational as well. Understanding the psychological foundation of human behavior in financial markets can facilitate the formulation of macroeconomic policy and the development of new financial institutions.

EDWARD BAKER: Since consumer demand is the major component of U.S. economic activity, that alone suggests that psychology should have a large role in explaining macroeconomic phenomena.

ROBERT SHILLER: The problem with economics is that it's very difficult to compartmentalize things. Finance is fundamentally related to macroeconomics, so understanding a speculative bubble in the stock market involves feedback not just from financial variables, but from macroeconomic variables as well. Ultimately, it feeds into people's views of themselves and their relationships with others—it's a social phenomenon that requires all the different aspects of social science. I view behavioral finance as one part of an integration of all the social sciences. People who are interested in behavioral finance tend to be aware of the compartmentalization of our disciplines and of the costs that entails. I don't think of behavioral finance as a niche movement; I think of it as populated by people who want to be aware of and understand the broader picture. As such, behavioral finance needs to be integrated into the social sciences at large.

■ ■ ■

REFERENCES

Ackerlof, George A., and Robert J. Shiller. 2009. *Animal Spirits: How Human Psychology Drives the Economy, and Why It Matters for Global Capitalism.* Princeton, NJ: Princeton University Press.

Ameriks, John, Andrew Caplin, and John V. Leahy. 2002. Wealth Accumulation and the Propensity to Plan. NBER Working Paper No. W8920.

Chen, Joseph, Harrison Hong, and Jeremy C. Stein. 2002. Breadth of Ownership and Stock Returns. *Journal of Financial Economics* 66, no. 2–3: 171–205.

Friedman, Milton, and Leonard J. Savage. 1948. The Utility Analysis of Choices Involving Risk. *Journal of Political Economy* 56, no. 4 (August): 279–304.

Jung, Jeeman, and Robert J. Shiller. 2005. One Simple Test of Samuelson's Dictum for the Stock Market. *Economic Inquiry* 45, no. 2: 221–228.

Scherbina, Anna. 2001. Stock Prices and Differences in Opinion: Empirical Evidence That Prices Reflect Optimism. Working paper, Northwestern University. http://papers.ssrn.com/sol3/papers.cfm?abstract_id=267665.

Shiller, Robert J. 2000. *Irrational Exuberance.* Princeton, NJ: Princeton University Press.

———. 2003. From Efficient Market Theory to Behavioral Finance. *Journal of Economic Perspectives* 17, no. 1 (winter): 83–104.

———. 2003. *The New Financial Order: Risk in the 21st Century.* Princeton, NJ: Princeton University Press.

———. 2012. *Finance and the Good Society.* Princeton, NJ: Princeton University Press.

Statman, Meir, and Hersh Shefrin. 1993. Behavioral Aspects of the Design and Marketing of Financial Products. *Financial Management* 22, no. 2 (summer): 123–134.

This interview was published in its entirety in *Journal of Investment Consulting* 7, no. 1, Summer 2004.

CHAPTER 14

RICHARD THALER: FOUNDING FATHER OF BEHAVIORAL ECONOMICS

RICHARD H. THALER, PHD

Charles R. Walgreen Distinguished Service Professor of Behavioral Science and Economics at the University of Chicago Booth School of Business; one of the founding fathers of behavioral finance; co-author, *Nudge: Improving Decisions on Health, Wealth, and Happiness,* among other books and numerous articles in academic journals.

Richard Thaler is considered the founding father of behavioral economics, a theory of decision making that is the nexus of economics and psychology. Early on, Thaler recognized the value of expanding his conceptual framework, which led him to collaborate with Daniel Kahneman and Amos Tversky. Thaler defines his career as that of a troublemaker. For example, he began with the assumption that investors do not always act rationally and then set out to learn why. This led to the publication of *Nudge,* a book about choices. With co-author Cass Sunstein, Thaler explored how people make choices and what processes and structures might lead to better choices. In *Nudge,* Thaler and Sunstein advocate strategies that do not force anyone to do anything, yet effectively promote good choices.

■ ■ ■

MARGARET TOWLE: Thank you for participating in our Masters Series. We would like to start with a question we ask all of our Masters. What were the major factors that helped shape your career and bring you to where you are today? Please talk about your major achievements, as well as what you view as your greatest challenges.

RICHARD THALER: I'm a professor, I've never had a real job, and my career has been one as a professional troublemaker. That's something that came naturally to me as a kid, and I was lucky enough to figure out a way to earn a living doing that. The people who had the biggest influence on me were Danny Kahneman[1] and Amos Tversky,[2] two psychologists whom I was lucky enough to spend a year with in 1977 and 1978 when I was starting to take the idea of behavioral economics seriously. Along the way, I've had many collaborators who did all the work.

MARGARET TOWLE: What do you consider your greatest challenges, either academically or in some of the other work you have done?

RICHARD THALER: I think the greatest challenge was what my colleague Colin Camerer[3] once called the sufficiency bias. That term is a bit obscure, so let me explain it. If you present some anomaly or fact, and somebody can construct a rational explanation for that fact, regardless of how implausible it might be, that explanation is considered sufficient to render the anomaly irrelevant or unimportant. Another way of putting it is that economists give rational explanations the benefit of being the null hypothesis that has to be rejected. So throughout my work, it's been necessary to (1) discover some empirical fact, (2) offer some behavioral explanation for the fact that's consistent with empirical findings in psychology, and then (3) rule out all other explanations for that fact—and that's a challenge.

MARGARET TOWLE: Given your vantage point as an academic, what do you see as the major trends in the area of behavioral finance today?

RICHARD THALER: The field of behavioral finance has grown so quickly that I am no longer on top of everything that is coming out, so let me use the trick my students usually use when confronted with a difficult question, and that's to answer a different question. I think it's fair to say that the area of the financial industry in which behavioral finance has had its greatest impact has been in the design of defined contribution retirement schemes. I think those plans, like 401(k) plans, were headed in a bad direction. When the plans got started, they typically included fewer than ten options, but the number of options started growing rapidly. When I joined the University of Chicago faculty, we had two providers, one of which was Vanguard. I think we had every fund Vanguard offered as an option, aside from the tax-free municipal bond funds, which they had the foresight to remove; otherwise, some people would have taken them. It's a really bad idea to offer people more than a hundred options in a plan; nobody can deal with that. So I think the ideas that came out of behavioral research—automatic enrollment and automatic escalation, or "save more tomorrow" as Shlomo Benartzi[4] and I called it, plus sensibly created and reasonably priced default investment vehicles like target date funds—have transformed that industry. If these three things are in place, along with a sensible match, you're pretty much assuring that participants have at least a decent chance at a B+ retirement portfolio. If we could get rid of company stock, we would get up to A–, but that's been a stubborn relic.

MEIR STATMAN: I have a question related to what you just said. We know that the design elements being introduced into defined contribution plans are enormously successful, but have they left behind some people who could not be nudged into saving? Many of these people are the ones we care about most—that is, low-income workers who switch plans and employers frequently and just cash out. What can we do to help them?

RICHARD THALER: Well, designing these types of plans is all about tradeoffs. In the book *Cass Sunstein and I wrote, *Nudge*, we devised policies that don't force anybody to do anything. We're criticized for that on the left and the right, which makes us think we're doing things about right. People on the left say nudging isn't enough; you should just force people to save. Actually, most universities do that, including mine, and that's a point of view. Social Security is designed that way. But if you do that, it will hurt some people who have good reasons for not joining a retirement plan. The first couple of years I was an assistant professor, I did not contribute because I had so much student debt I decided to pay that off first. There could be many sensible reasons for not joining, at least not immediately. If you force people in, you'll catch the ones who would otherwise be lost and you'll hurt others. Automatic enrollment often results in more than 90 percent of eligible workers being enrolled, and we don't know what percentage of that missing 10 percent has good reasons for not joining. The bigger problem is not the people who automatic enrollment fails to pick up; the bigger problem is that a large proportion of the workforce does not have a plan available. We need to create some sort of national individual retirement account [IRA] or something like the auto IRA or President Barack Obama's recently proposed "*my*RA." Various versions of this idea have been floating around for a long time. Under the *my*RA approach, employers would be encouraged to enroll their employees in this plan automatically, but the employers would not be responsible for administering or contributing to the accounts. I think the latest proposal is that an employee would invest in something like an inflation-protected Treasury instrument until the account balance gets big enough that it makes sense to shift the investment into something else. We can argue about the best design for a plan like this, but creating a viable retirement savings option for the large number of people who have no retirement savings plan seems to me our biggest challenge.

■ ■ ■

We know that the design elements being introduced into defined contribution plans are enormously successful, but have they left behind some people who could not be nudged into saving? Many of these people are the ones we care about most—that is, low-income workers who switch plans and employers frequently and just cash out. What can we do to help them?

MICHAEL DIESCHBOURG: There's some work on hedonomics being done by Christopher K. Hsee, professor of behavioral science and marketing at the University of Chicago Booth School of Business. This research focuses on maximizing happiness with limited wealth. People need a better idea of what they need to really enjoy retirement, so I was wondering if some work should be done not only on nudging workers to save for retirement but also on nudging them to determine the level of wealth they need to retire happily versus just trying to reach a financial goal. In other words, can people optimize their level of income in order to maximize happiness with a limited wealth goal?

RICHARD THALER: Certainly, the next big issue the retirement industry needs to confront is the decumulation phase. If we get the retirement saving plans up to a B+, the decumulation phase gets a gentleman's C, and that's being generous. Typically, employers hand workers a check and say goodbye and good luck. This is unfortunate because decumulation is a much bigger problem than accumulation. Just trying to solve the problem conceptually is difficult. First of all, you'd have to update your plans every time you live another year and get another annual physical, and the annuities market is far from efficient. Then there are good products and bad products, and it's hard for individuals to sort them out.

So what would you really want? You'd want some kind of annuity option in your retirement plan. The way the system works now is that employers act as a fiduciary who designs a plan and picks a suitable set of investment vehicles. That's the easy part. Retirees could do pretty well by simply going to a low-fee mutual fund company and picking a target date fund on their own. But no one is acting as a fiduciary on the decumulation phase, and finding a suitable decumulation strategy in the marketplace is much harder. I know of at least one corporate pension plan that has an annuity option, but the U.S. Department of Labor has been unable to figure out a sensible way of giving plan sponsors a safe harbor for putting an annuity option into the plan. They wrote one, but everybody realizes it's inadequate. The plan sponsor basically would have to express confidence that the provider will be able to make the payments over the foreseeable time horizon. Well, that could be forty years, so who could safely say that about any insurance company? Once upon a time, we might have thought a person could just say, the insurance company has a triple-A rating, so that'll be a safe harbor. But rating agencies have deservedly lost our respect, so right now we're stymied. I've talked to people in the Department of Labor who generally understand the problem and would like to do something about it but haven't been able to figure out what they could do. The corporate pension plan I mentioned, United Technologies, has an innovative and thoughtfully designed plan, but it's complicated. It's safe to say its employees don't understand it; it's probably understood only by the people who designed it. I think there's a lot of work to do on this front, but I'm not sure what the answer is.

LUDWIG CHINCARINI: I think many people resist behavioral finance because it involves many challenges—for example, limited models of prediction. Even when there's overvaluation, few models predict or tell you when an asset is overvalued. Many corporate clients might want to do what seems like a common-sense strategy that many people know about, but because there is no specific prediction from these models, they would rather stick with rational models. What is your response to this, and how does behavioral finance move to something such as a capital asset pricing model (CAPM) or some other model that is capable of predictions?

RICHARD THALER: I'm happy to put behavioral finance against a CAPM in terms of predictions. The CAPM says the only thing that matters is beta. My golf buddy, Gene Fama,[5] has shown that the only thing that doesn't matter is beta. If we use prediction as the measure of a model, traditional finance makes precisely wrong predictions. Behavioral finance is trying to improve on that record, which is not hard. Thirty years ago, Werner De Bondt[6] and I wrote a paper in which we predicted an anomaly, and I don't know whether anybody else in finance has done that before or since. The process of trying to figure out Werner's programming error, which didn't exist, led Fama and French[7] to acknowledge that there's a value premium. This realization eventually led to the three-factor model and now there's a five-factor model, and in the five-factor model there's absolutely no pretense that these factors represent risk. So I think everybody's doing behavioral finance now—except maybe Fama's son-in-law, John Cochrane.[8]

■ ■ ■

If we use prediction as the measure of a model, traditional finance makes precisely wrong predictions. Behavioral finance is trying to improve on that record, which is not hard.

RONALD KAHN: As we've discussed, there's no question that behavioral finance has had a great impact on defined contribution plans, but to Ludwig's point, I think the idea of value goes back before behavioral finance. I also think behavioral finance has done a great job of providing further explanations for things that asset managers already knew. I don't believe any practitioner would say it wasn't until Fama and French that we understood that size and value were important. I'm wondering to what extent behavioral finance really has identified new investment ideas as opposed to explaining ideas we already knew.

RICHARD THALER: Let me answer that in two ways. The first is to note that I think we've now come full circle. The early efficient market hypothesis said nothing matters, and everything you read in Graham and Dodd[9] was wrong and useless. Then the first round of revisions said, well, actually value might be worthwhile, but it's risk. The latest models include things like investment and profitability. So I think we've gone back, and we should just have people read Graham and Dodd and stop. Has behavioral finance led to insights into how to invest? As some of you know, I'm a principal in a money management firm, Fuller and Thaler Asset Management, in San Mateo, California. We use behavioral finance to invest, and it seems to work for us, so I think it's possible to do that. The basic idea is you start with a bias, a judgmental bias that you think leads to mispricing, and then you create a disciplined way of forming portfolios informed by that bias and you make sure your portfolio managers are not subject to the same biases as everybody else by limiting the kinds of things you ask them to do. I agree with you that in the academic literature the distinction between behavioral finance and the rest of empirical finance is pretty blurred, and that's all for the good. I wrote an article quite a long time ago called "The End of Behavioral Finance," in which I predicted that at some point behavioral finance would no longer exist because all of finance would be as behavioral as it should be. I wrote something similar about economics more generally, and I think we're getting there. So at some point, I no longer will be able to call myself a troublemaker.

EDWARD BAKER: I think behavioral finance also has a potential application in the investment consulting business. In your book *Nudge*, you talk about choice architecture as a means of motivating individuals to make better choices. It seems to me that consultants could design a way of interacting with clients that nudges them to make good investment decisions so that consultants would become choice architects rather than providers of advice. What are your thoughts about this?

RICHARD THALER: I think any financial advisor is a choice architect, even the bad ones. The bad ones are just bad choice architects. Unless the client just says here's my money, do what you want—which I don't think is a very common occurrence—being a financial advisor is one part portfolio manager and one part clinical psychologist. I'm not sure which part is more important, but the choice architecture aspect resides in framing decisions for clients in a way that enables them to understand the tradeoffs and make sensible decisions. This is related to the point that was mentioned earlier. You want to design a portfolio that will make the members of a household as happy as possible, but the problem is that people aren't very good at anticipating how they're going to react to various market outcomes. We've seen that 401(k) investors have been remarkably good at buying high and selling low. For example, people sold off equity funds and missed the enormous bull market that started in 2009. I don't think that money started flowing back into equities until 2013. So people are going to do the wrong thing, and in bull markets they're going to ask their financial advisors, "Why don't you have me invested all in tech stocks?" Then when the market goes down, they're going to ask, "How come I'm losing so much money?" The real goal of a financial advisor is to help each client understand what's possible and what isn't. And that has to be accomplished at the same time the financial advisor convinces clients that the advisor is really smart and can help them achieve their goals.

EDWARD BAKER: Can choice architecture be made into a systematic science?

RICHARD THALER: Yes, I think it can. Although Cass and I invented this term, people have been doing choice architecture forever. Coining the term sort of made us experts at this approach, but it's not like we had never done it. Since the book came out, I've gotten involved in numerous attempts to apply these ideas in various domains for various governments, but I wouldn't say we now have a scientific system or a recipe. Each problem is unique. We can use a certain set of tools, but a financial advisor is a little like a chef. There's no formula to tell you how to create a great dish. You can learn what techniques and flavors work, but it's not like you can read a book and become a three-star Michelin chef. We have a certain amount of knowledge, but there's no master recipe book yet.

■ ■ ■

> We can use a certain set of tools, but a financial advisor is a little like a chef. There's no formula to tell you how to create a great dish. You can learn what techniques and flavors work, but it's not like you can read a book and become a three-star Michelin chef. We have a certain amount of knowledge, but there's no master recipe book yet.

MARK ANSON: When I went to business school some twenty years ago, there was a standard way to gain a better understanding of the financial markets: We got a graduate degree at a well-known business school. Nowadays, with the growing acceptance of behavioral finance, would it be better to get a graduate degree in psychology rather than finance or economics in order to better understand the financial markets?

RICHARD THALER: No, because most psychologists don't know anything about financial markets. Back when we were first considering behavioral finance, a famous social psychologist, Stanley Schachter,[10] actually wrote a couple of behavioral finance papers, submitted them to the journals, got yelled at, and decided to quit. I think he's the last psychologist who made a serious attempt to do that. There are huge barriers to entering the study of financial markets, so if you want to learn about behavioral finance, the right place to do that is a business school. But you're going to have to listen with a critical ear in many of the courses you take because most corporate finance courses start with the CAPM. I have no idea why, but we're teaching things we know are false. The idea that companies should do capital budgeting based on beta seems to me a pretty ridiculous idea. If I were teaching a finance class, I would certainly teach the CAPM. In my worldview, the CAPM would be true in a world in which everyone was rational. So I would teach it as a sort of idealized model, just as I would teach the efficient market hypothesis. In some other universe, the efficient market hypothesis and the CAPM both would be true, but it would be a universe without humans.

MATTHEW MOREY: I teach finance, and I wonder why professors are generally so reluctant to teach behavioral finance in standard introductory finance courses. Almost all of the introductory finance books are still built on rational models and include very little about behavioral finance. Why is that, in your view?

RICHARD THALER: Inertia—one of the most powerful of behavioral factors.

EDWARD BAKER: Is more emphasis on applications what's missing for behavioral finance fans? Choice architecture is an obvious application. If that idea were developed more completely, perhaps schools would find behavioral finance more appealing.

RICHARD THALER: I think that's true. Some interesting stuff is going on in corporate behavioral finance, but the traditional model has a forty-year head start, so there's not quite a fully coherent body of literature. In fact, that's probably never going to come about because if you want one simple, parsimonious economic model, you're not going to do better than the rational model. It just doesn't predict behavior very well. So what we have now is the rational model as the starting place and then a long list of departures. People keep asking me when we're going to come up with the behavioral CAPM. I remember being asked that question in 1987, so people have been asking this for almost thirty years. There were a few attempts to write such models in the 1990s, but I would say they were not completely satisfactory. Psychology does not have a theory of psychology; what it has is a long list of phenomena and theories that go with each entry. Maybe that's the way economics is going. I don't know. We're still new at this.

MEIR STATMAN: I'd like us to address the notion of market efficiency. We have two notions of market efficiency, one is that price is always equal to intrinsic value and the other is that you cannot beat the market. Of course, if the price is right, you cannot beat the market, but if you cannot beat the market, that doesn't necessarily mean the price is right. How do you see this debate playing out?

■ ■ ■

People keep asking me when we're going to come up with the behavioral CAPM. I remember being asked that question in 1987, so people have been asking this for almost thirty years. There were a few attempts to write such models in the 1990s, but I would say they were not completely satisfactory. Psychology does not have a theory of psychology; what it has is a long list of phenomena and theories that go with each entry. Maybe that's the way economics is going.

RICHARD THALER: I agree with you, and I always stress that the efficient market hypothesis contains those two components. The bulk of the literature has been devoted to the idea that you can't beat the market—I call that the no-free-lunch part of the hypothesis—and I would say that is the truer part. I say this because, as Mike Jensen[11] first pointed out in his thesis, most active managers fail to beat the index. That's still true. Beating the market is hard, and being in this business has not altered my view of that. An asset manager who beats the market two out of three years is a very good manager. However, I think the idea that the price is right is the more important part of the hypothesis. I think it's the more important part because the interesting, intellectual question is how good a job do financial markets do in allocating resources? If prices can get way off, they're not doing a great job, which is not to say somebody has a better way. But look at the technology bubble of the late 1990s: The NASDAQ went to 5,000 and then fell by two thirds, and fourteen years later we're still not back to 5,000 even in nominal terms. Fischer Black[12] once wrote that he thought prices were right within a factor of two. Fischer died in 1995, but I think if he had lived five more years he would have made that a factor of three.

Then we went through the housing bubble. Consider just those two bubbles, technology and housing, and the resources that went into them. During the technology bubble, MBA students left school to go to California and become billionaires, and most of them came back a couple of years later to finish their degrees. A lot of resources were misdirected. The thing to keep in mind about the technology bubble is that the Internet did not turn out to be a disappointment—just the opposite. In 2000, no one could possibly have imagined that we would all be carrying powerful computers in our pockets. The Internet has exceeded our wildest expectations, and still the prices were way off. In his famous mea culpa speech, Alan Greenspan admitted he was shocked that people weren't paying enough attention to counterparty risk and, more basically, he had not believed that prices could diverge very much from intrinsic value.[13] That's why he wasn't worried about the technology bubble or the housing bubble. He believed policy makers, central bankers, and finance ministers did not need to worry about that.

The first step is acknowledging the possibility that the price is not always right. I would favor a policy—say, with respect to real estate—that when local markets look frothy, using some sensible measure like price-to-rental ratios, it would make sense for Fannie and Freddie, if they still exist, or some equivalent agency to increase lending requirements. If that had happened during the first part of the 2000s, it certainly would have tamped down the bubble in places like Arizona, Las Vegas, and South Florida and saved people a lot of grief. It might even have prevented the financial crisis.

EDWARD BAKER: Part of the problem is that this idea of fair value is a bit of a chimera and perhaps is subject to the biases and other behavioral elements you described.

RICHARD THALER: It's true that we don't know what intrinsic value is. All I'm arguing is that we acknowledge the possibility that prices can diverge from intrinsic value. When I spoke to groups of practitioners in the late 1990s, I would talk about a portfolio of five Internet stocks and ask, "If I give you $1,000 of that portfolio, what would you say—using whatever definition you think is appropriate—is the intrinsic value?" The median response was fifty cents on the dollar. My second question was, "What is your prediction as to the return on that portfolio over the next six months?" Median response: up 20 percent. That, to me, sounds like a bubble.

MARGARET TOWLE: Is there anything we haven't discussed that you would like to add?

RICHARD THALER: Just let me reiterate that I'm not in favor of stopping teaching things like the CAPM or the efficient market hypothesis. Without these benchmarks, including the Modigliani-Miller theorem[14] and other basic models, we can't really understand how financial markets are supposed to work. The only danger in teaching these models is if students believe that they are good descriptions of the world we live in.

■ ■ ■

ENDNOTES

[1] Daniel Kahneman is a senior scholar and professor of psychology and public affairs emeritus at the Woodrow Wilson School of Public and International Affairs at Princeton University and the author of the popular book *Thinking, Fast and Slow*. He received the Nobel Memorial Prize in Economic Sciences in 2002 for his collaborative work with Amos Tversky.

[2] Amos Tversky (1937–1996) was a cognitive and mathematical psychologist whose long-term collaborations with Daniel Kahneman focused on how people manage risk and uncertainty. Together, the two men developed prospect theory. Tversky died in 1996. When Kahneman was awarded the Nobel Memorial Prize in Economic Sciences after Tversky's death, he said he considered it a joint prize.

[3] Colin F. Camerer (1959–) is the Robert Kirby Professor of Behavioral Finance and Economics at the California Institute of Technology, where he teaches cognitive psychology and economics.

[4] Shlomo Benartzi is professor and co-chair of the Behavioral Decision-Making Group at the UCLA Anderson School of Management. His special interests are household finance and the behavior of retirement savings plan participants. In collaboration with Richard Thaler, he developed the concept of Save More Tomorrow (SMarT).

[5] Eugene F. Fama is the Robert R. McCormick Distinguished Service Professor of Finance at the University of Chicago Booth School of Business. He received the 2013 Nobel Memorial Prize in Economic Sciences, along with Lars Peter Hansen of the University of Chicago and Robert J. Shiller of Yale University, for their work on explaining asset prices and how financial markets function.

[6] Werner F. M. De Bondt is the Driehaus Professor of Behavioral Finance and director of the Richard H. Driehaus Center for Behavioral Finance at DePaul University. Considered one of the founders of behavioral finance, he studies the psychology of financial decision making.

[7] Eugene F. Fama and Kenneth R. French have written a series of articles casting doubt on the validity of the capital asset pricing model. The Fama–French three-factor model describes two factors above and beyond a stock's market beta that can explain differences in stock returns: market capitalization and value. Fama and French also offer evidence that their three-factor model explains various patterns of average returns, often labeled "anomalies" in past work.

[8] John H. Cochrane (1957–) is the AQR Capital Management Distinguished Service Professor of Finance at the University of Chicago Booth School of Business.

[9] In their 1934 book *Security Analysis*, Columbia Business School professors David Dodd and Benjamin Graham came up with a method for valuing stocks, laying the intellectual foundation for what eventually would be called value investing.

[10] Stanley Schachter (1922–1997), who before his death was the Robert Johnston Niven Professor of Social Psychology at Columbia University, is perhaps best known for developing the two-factor theory of emotion in collaboration with Jerome E. Singer (1934–2010).

[11] Michael Cole Jensen (1939–) is the Jesse Isidor Straus Professor of Business Administration, Emeritus, at Harvard Business School. He is known for developing a method for assessing fund manager performance, the so-called Jensen's alpha, which measures the performance of an investment in relation to a benchmark.

[12] Fischer Black (1938–1995) was a U.S. economist associated with the University of Chicago, the MIT Sloan School of Management, and Goldman Sachs. In 1973, Black and Myron Scholes published their option-pricing formula, which became known as the Black–Scholes model. This model, which represented a major contribution to the efficiency of the options and stock markets, remains a widely used financial tool.

[13] Alan Greenspan's October 2013 testimony before a U.S. congressional committee has been called his "mea culpa" speech.

[14] The Modigliani-Miller theorem states that a firm's market value is determined by its earning power and the risk of its underlying assets and is independent of the way it finances its investments or distributes dividends.

REFERENCES

De Bondt, Werner F. M., and Richard Thaler. 1985. Does the Stock Market Overreact? *Journal of Finance* 40, no. 3. Papers and Proceedings of the Forty-Third Annual Meeting American Finance Association, Dallas, Texas, December 28–30, 1984 (July): 793–805.

Hsee, Christopher K., Reid Hastie, and Jingqiu Chen. 2008. Hedonomics: Bridging Decision Research with Happiness Research. *Perspectives on Psychological Science* 3, no. 3: 224–243.

Thaler, Richard H. 1999. The End of Behavioral Finance. *Perspectives*. Association for Investment Management and Research (November/December). http://faculty.chicagobooth.edu/richard.thaler/research/pdf/end.pdf.

Thaler, Richard H., and Cass R. Sunstein. 2008. *Nudge: Improving Decisions about Health, Wealth, and Happiness*. New Haven, CT: Yale University Press.

This interview was published in its entirety in *Journal of Investment Consulting* 16, no. 1, 2015.

CHAPTER 15

ED THORP: KING OF GAMBLERS

EDWARD O. THORP, PHD

President, Edward O. Thorp & Associates; Former Professor of Mathematics and Finance at University of California, Irvine; taught at University of California, Los Angeles and New Mexico State University; author, *Beat the Dealer* and co-author of *Beat the Market*, as well as numerous articles in academic journals.

Ed Thorp is a strategic heavyweight with a robust conceptual framework. Academically, his studies evolved from chemistry to physics to mathematics. Like many of the Masters, however, he was interested in applying his theories to the real world. This led him first to gambling and then to the stock market. Instead of keeping his competitive strategies to himself, Thorp wrote two books, *Beat the Dealer* and *Beat the Market* (with Sheen Kassouf). Appearing on the popular game show *To Tell the Truth*, Thorp stumped the panel with his prowess as a card-counting gambler. *Beat the Market* helped launch the use of derivatives, transforming global markets. Always looking ahead, Thorp has arranged to have his body cryogenically frozen when he dies, in anticipation that someday he may even beat death.

■ ■ ■

MARGARET TOWLE: Dr. Thorp, I just want to start out by thanking you for taking the time to talk with us. You are probably familiar with our publication and our emphasis on taking theoretical ideas and discussing their practical applications. I think that is especially appropriate in light of what you've done throughout your career in terms of using mathematical models, while always keeping in mind the inherent challenges and problems of applying them practically. That approach is most obvious in your casino experiences. So let's begin by asking you about the major factors that helped to shape your career, your major achievements, and your biggest mistakes or disappointments. You have such a great background in terms of your academic experience but also in terms of truly applying that experience in the real world. Could you give us some insights based on your experiences?

EDWARD THORP: The way I think about the world was probably shaped by my early experiences. When I was a child of three, my father took me in hand and decided to see how much he could teach me. That went very well for him for a couple of years, until he got too busy to keep it up. However, that was enough to get me started teaching myself. I learned to read well during the ages of three to five and to do elementary math, and I just took off from there. I got into doing science on my own as a junior high and high school student. Basically, I didn't have anyone to teach me, because the schools I went to weren't particularly good. I thrived on just having time to myself and thinking things through for myself.

MARGARET TOWLE: What area of the country was that, as far as where you grew up?

EDWARD THORP: We moved to Lomita, California, near Los Angeles when I was about ten-and-a-half, so I grew up in southern California. I went to a little high school called Narbonne, which I think was ranked thirty-one out of thirty-two in the Los Angeles school system. I had the luxury of being neglected, so I could just do what I wanted when I wanted and learn what I wanted whenever I felt like it. That got me into an independent, self-teaching mode and also into a way of thinking about things in which I didn't accept what I was told. I didn't reject what others told me, but I simply wanted to think it through for myself. I came to somewhat of a compromise in life where I didn't try to reinvent the wheel just because I thought I could. If there was something to be learned from other people, I would learn that as well as I could, but I didn't hesitate to go out on my own and investigate an idea or a problem that came to me. That's the sort of orientation that shaped my career.

One thing I felt early on was that when I do something theoretical, which I enjoy, then that theoretical thing ought to be tested in the real world to show that it really is something worthwhile, rather than just a pretty construct that won't be of any further value. I tend to work on problems that are goal-oriented, such as finding a winning strategy for a gambling game or finding a market inefficiency or devising a way of analyzing something in the market that will give me an edge. Then the fun is building models and series and seeing if they actually work. That's what I've been doing.

MARGARET TOWLE: To expand upon that a little bit, given your background in a blend of academia, blackjack gambling, and hedge fund management, can you talk about the differences and similarities in those? From what I've read, you had quite a fantastic record in hedge fund management. What do you see as the similarities between gambling and hedge funds? What are the skills that might apply to both of those, in terms of similarities and differences?

EDWARD THORP: Academically, I evolved from chemistry to physics to mathematics. I received my PhD in mathematics and then went out into the university world to teach. As it happened, I'd always had an interest in applications from all of my science play in my high school years. One idea I'd had during those days was the physical predicting of roulette. That idea had stuck with me, so as I was getting my PhD, I was working on that problem, just on the side for fun. That gave me an outlook toward gambling games that later paid off in the market. Although conventional wisdom held that you couldn't beat these games, the outlook was that that wisdom was not necessarily true and, in fact, was probably wrong. Gambling games, which were perceived to be efficient—in the financial-world sense of the word, might not be. In fact, I was convinced that wasn't the case in roulette. So I came to this orientation that the conventional wisdom wasn't right. That led me not only to build a wearable computer[1] for roulette in conjunction with Claude Shannon[2] of the Massachusetts Institute of Technology, but also to investigate card-counting in blackjack. I happened to see an article on blackjack strategy published in a statistical journal that was fairly close to even. After I used it just for fun, I came back and figured out a way to construct a winning strategy for the game. That told me you could, in fact, beat gambling games, and I got into exploring that idea in much more depth. When I actually played blackjack, I learned how to manage money. The so-called Kelly criterion[3] was the type of thing I used for bankroll management, and I learned about that from Claude Shannon, who had worked with J. L. Kelly at Bell Labs some time earlier. He had actually refereed Kelly's fundamental paper (Kelly 1956).

That gets me to the point about the relationship between gambling and investing, that is, what you learn from one helps with the other. Gambling games are, for the most part, an area where you can calculate the odds, the probabilities, in detail and get them rather exact. There are some exceptions, like sports betting and so forth, that are more like social or financial markets. But you can actually come into a gambling game with known probabilities and get answers. You have the advantage, like you have in the physical sciences, of so-called repeatable experiments. You can simulate a gambling game a million times if you want because you know the probabilities. It's much more difficult in the securities markets because we just have one history from which we have to infer what's going on, and the probabilities that we have are not exact—they're just estimates. We're in a world that's controlled by people, which evolves in complex ways that we don't fully understand. So you don't have the same simple rules you have in the physical sciences and in the calculations that are behind gambling games. Nonetheless, the things you learn about gambling games carry over, in large part, to the investment world.

MARGARET TOWLE: Could you elaborate a little more about the hedge fund side? I read where one interviewer said he thought that, despite your quantitative orientation, you had quite good "street smarts," or a common sense feel for this area. It seems that could relate specifically to the role of fundamental research. Do you see a role for that in hedge funds?

EDWARD THORP: Let me address several things here. First, going back to street smarts, that's an interesting thing, because I had no street smarts when I entered the gambling world—street dumbs maybe. I simply was naïve about it, I didn't know what to expect, and so I was cautious because of that. I had to feel my way and go through this very strange, tricky world. If you've seen the movie *Casino*, which was about Las Vegas in the 1970s—well, when I played in the casinos in the 1960s, things were worse. They were worse yet in the '40s and '50s. That's when people like Bugsy Siegel[4] were being shot up. Things began to improve when the legitimate corporate people started coming in, starting with Howard Hughes[5] early on and then other people behind him. I picked up some street smarts by being in the gambling world, and that proved to be very helpful when I moved over to the investing world.

What I typically did was use the skills and knowledge I had—in this case, my background from the gambling world and my belief in the likelihood that the markets were not efficient. I want to say more about efficient markets a little later. I had a lot of mathematical tools, especially some probability and statistics tools that I had used in the gambling world. Those seemed to carry over very nicely to the investment world. So I tended to look at problems from that point of view, unlike somebody like Warren Buffett, who might have gone out and kicked tires on a company when he was a young man and judged whether that company was a bargain to buy into. I looked for situations where the risk was relatively low compared with the return, and I came across the idea of hedging. That's what got me started. Back in 1965, I read a warrant[6] pamphlet, the RHM warrant survey,[7] and that got me thinking about warrants and options. I saw that you could "mathematicize" it, and I met Sheen Kassouf,[8] with whom I later wrote the book *Beat the Market*, when we were both new professors at the University of California, Irvine back in 1965. That led me to think more about warrant formulas. Then in 1967, I said to myself, "What if the world were risk-neutral? What warrant formula would you have?" I wrote down what later became known as the Black-Scholes model[9] and started using that to invest. I saw that I had a powerful tool that would give me an edge that no one else seemed to have. I began investing for people around the university, and then in 1968 I ran into Warren Buffett, who was a friend of the dean of the graduate school, Ralph Gerard,[10] who was a Buffett investor. Buffett was shutting down [his investment partnership], and Gerard wanted Buffett to have a look at me and see whether I'd be a good place to invest money. Buffett and I hit it off, and Gerard ended up investing with me. This little pool of investors became part of the hedge fund that I started in 1969 with a fellow named Jay Regan[11] back East. The hedge fund was originally called Convertible Hedge Associates and later renamed Princeton/Newport Partners in 1974. We thought that was a better name. I don't remember why now. That ran from 1969 until 1988 when we ran into a misfortune with which you're probably familiar.

■ ■ ■

First, going back to street smarts, that's an interesting thing, because I had no street smarts when I entered the gambling world— street dumbs maybe. I simply was naïve about it, I didn't know what to expect, and so I was cautious because of that. I had to feel my way and go through this very strange, tricky world.

EDWARD BAKER: I was very interested in your comment that you tried to apply what you learned in gambling to investing, and one thing in gambling is that you have relatively fixed distributions. That isn't so clear in the financial markets. Do you think it is true that the distributions are fixed? Is it just a problem of finding the right distribution, or do we need more dynamic techniques that allow for changing distributions?

EDWARD THORP: No, I don't think they're fixed. I think that we only get estimates of the distributions and that we can only be somewhat sure of the estimates. That makes the problem in the financial world much more difficult, I think, because you have these uncertainties in the distributions.

GEOFFREY GERBER: You mentioned starting your firm in the late 1960s. Sitting here today, you have more than forty years of perspective on quantitative systems applied to the stock market. My question really has two parts: First, how have you safeguarded your quantitative system from failing miserably or hitting a long stretch of bad luck? Second, what's your biggest concern at present with the U.S. equity market? Is it inflation or changes in regulation or more financial debacles or something else?

EDWARD THORP: Regarding the first question, with blackjack, it was a matter of finding something that people believed wasn't true. I thought it was mathematically very interesting, so as an academic, I felt an obligation to publicize my findings so that people would begin to think differently about some of these games. Then there was a lot of skepticism and mockery from the gambling community, so I felt an obligation to prove that what I'd done actually worked. That's why I went out to Las Vegas and played blackjack and wrote a book about it.

■ ■ ■

> I thought that this formula had to be the same as what I was running on my computers then, so I plugged it in and drew a graph. However, the graph didn't agree with the graph that I had drawn from my formula, and I realized that I had three formulas, not one.

Moving on to the investment world, when I began Princeton/Newport Partners in 1969, I had this options formula, this tool that nobody else had, and I felt an obligation to the investors to basically be quiet about it. The tool was just an internal formula that was known to me and a few other people that I employed. Time passed, and Black and Scholes (1973) published this formula. I remember getting a pre-publication copy in the mail with a letter from Fischer Black saying that he and Scholes were admirers of my work and that they had taken the delta hedging idea of my book *Beat the Market* one step further by assuming there was no arbitrage and that this paper presented what they came up with. I thought that this formula had to be the same as what I was running on my computers then, so I plugged it in and drew a graph. However, the graph didn't agree with the graph that I had drawn from my formula, and I realized that I had three formulas, not one. One of the formulas was the Black-Scholes model; another assumed that short-sale proceeds on the stock side—if you were short stock and long warrants—could not be used by the investor or at least wouldn't accumulate interest; and the third assumed if warrants or options were short and stock was long, then the short-sale proceeds on the warrants or options couldn't be used. With the CBOE [Chicago Board Options Exchange] opening in 1973, you could now use short sales, so the central Black-Scholes formula—the middle of the three formulas I had—was the one that applied at that time. However, prior to that, I wasn't able to use short-sale proceeds, so I needed my other two formulas also. I published all three formulas about two or three months later. I was scheduled to give a talk at the International Statistical Institute conference in Vienna, and I needed something to talk about, so—almost the same day that I received the Black-Scholes paper—I just wrote up my three formulas and sent them in at that point, knowing that this was no secret any more (Thorp 1973).

Then there was essentially a race between me internally at Princeton/Newport Partners and my little research group and the academic world. The academic world was exploring the options formula and applying it in many different ways, but it was taking them a while. One of the big hang-ups was the so-called American put formula. There's a differentiation in the options formula between European options, which are exercisable at expiration, and options that are exercisable prior to expiration, sometimes in complex ways as it turned out in later years. The original distinction was European versus American options, which could be exercised at any time. The American options had boundary conditions that were more complex than they were for the European options, and they generally could not be solved by analytic methods with a complete formula. Sometimes they could, but more often than not they could not. The European option, on the other hand, could be solved by a formula. The CBOE was planning to bring out American puts in 1974. One afternoon I sat down and, in about an hour, I programmed the solution to the American put problem. We ran off options curves and they looked right and we tested them. So we were ready to go. Then I was having dinner with Black in late 1974 or early 1975, prior to a Center for Research in Security Prices (CRSP)[12] meeting. At that time, CRSP had meetings every six months, where people talked about these kinds of issues, and Black had invited me to Chicago to give one of the talks. He began to ask me about the American put problem. I had brought the curves to show him because I had already solved it, and I was ready to explain how it worked. Then he began to explain to me how hard it was and why so far no one had figured it out. I realized that if I revealed the solution to the problem, then the competitive edge that my partnership had with American puts would disappear almost immediately. I put my papers back in my briefcase and simply listened.

Our misfortune in this particular instance was that the American put problem got solved around 1977 in academic papers, and the CBOE delayed using them until about that time. So we lost that competitive edge. There was a race of this sort internally between the academic world and Princeton/Newport Partners all through the 1970s into the 1980s. We stayed enough ahead that we had a significant edge in a number of areas. Convertible bonds, for example—we had a better model than anybody else until probably the late 1980s, maybe even 1990. When Princeton/Newport shut down and I took a break in 1989 and 1990, I called Black at Goldman Sachs and told him that we had this convertible bond model and that we knew he was looking to build one, so he might want to buy ours. He flew out to see it, and he liked it, but he didn't buy it because it was programmed in a language that would have caused him to do extensive reprogramming. Even at that time, he acknowledged that it was well ahead of what he had seen. It was an interesting time for me because I spent a lot of time and energy trying to stay ahead of the published academic frontier. Of course, the unpublished frontier is further along because there's a time delay between creation and the appearance in print.

GEOFFREY GERBER: If we could, I'd like to go back for a minute to the second part of my earlier question, that is, what's your biggest concern with the U.S. equity market today?

EDWARD THORP: Let me start at a lower level than the level I want to get to. I think that one of the big issues today is that the playing field in the financial world is not level. If big institutions behave in a risky way and threaten to bring down the whole financial community and throw the entire country into a depression, they don't seem to have to pay a price commensurate with what they've done. Instead, the public ends up bailing them out. We're in a situation where the "too big to fail" institutions seem to have an option on the future rather than taking the full upside/downside risk that they should be assuming. They have privatized profits and socialized risk, in one formulation. That's a concern for me, and I don't see that has been changed by what we've gone through in the last few years. The fact that we don't have this level playing field, that people who are powerful and politically connected can manage things for themselves in a way that's much more advantageous than the run-of-the-mill rich or the run-of-the-mill public can, is an issue. It's led to a major transfer of wealth from the rest of the country to a very small group at the top. I happen to be fortunate in being one of the relatively wealthy people at the top, but I haven't used political connections or any extra edge of that type, any nonleveling of the playing field, to get there. I got there just by thinking. This polarization of wealth and increasing inequality in the country bothers me, not just because of itself but because of the way it's happened. It's happened because there's not a level playing field, and there's a lack of concern about the bottom in the country, which troubles me a lot, and a lack of concern about investing in things that are useful, like science, education, infrastructure, and so forth, things that we need to build an economic machine that will be more productive. I think a lot of the GNP (gross national product) is getting wasted. People don't seem to think about this or care about it. They're more focused on more immediate details. That's my overarching concern.

EDWARD BAKER: I have a somewhat different question. Going back to some of your other comments, I presume that the no-arbitrage principle is very important to the way you approach opportunities. Do you see that as a principle in the market that's changed a lot over time? Do you see it getting worse now with some of the regulatory issues coming up and frictional costs unfolding the way they are? What are your experiences there?

EDWARD THORP: Your point about frictional costs and lack of regulation—in particular, lack of transparency—is a good one. It leads to inequities in pricing. The same product sells at different prices in different places because you don't have enough transparency in the markets. If derivatives—convertibles, CDOs (collateralized debt obligations), and so forth—were traded on an exchange like options are, then everybody would see what the prices are, they would all be trading at the same prices, and there would be transparency as well as protection, because the exchange would stand between the counterparties. That would be good. I think that the people who trade these derivatives heavily at larger institutions don't want this situation to change because they can charge much higher fees if there is no transparency. It reminds me a little of the real estate market and the way it was earlier. That market is slowly becoming more transparent, but they've been quite good at nontransparency too, with great disparity in the commission structure depending on who the players are. So, anyway, I'm concerned about a lack of transparency in the markets and a lack of accountability and a lack of protection for the various counterparties.

MARGARET TOWLE: In the *Wall Street Journal* interview you did together with Bill Gross of PIMCO,[13] you commented—not so much on how people react—but about the huge amount of money that has flowed into hedge funds, seemingly overwhelming available investment opportunities, and you made reference to the overbetting phenomenon or gamblers' ruin. In your opinion, are there still opportunities, or pockets of inefficiencies, in this market that could be exploited using mathematical models?

EDWARD THORP: What's generally happened over the last four decades is that there were very few hedge funds around when we started back in 1969—a couple hundred, maybe. Also, there weren't any market-neutral or derivatives-based hedge funds at that time until Princeton/ Newport Partners became the first one. Then more and more people began to enter this area, over the next two decades, with the derivatives revolution. Quantitative investing became very profitable and very successful. We got to a point in the 1990s when, if you hung out a shingle saying "Hedge fund opening here," a line would form at your door almost immediately, and all kinds of investors would join up if they heard about good profits being made in earlier years. So the same opportunity set was being chased by much more money. I also think that many of the new hedge fund managers were perhaps of less quality and competence than the ones who had already been around for a while. Not only did they have less experience, but we were tapping into a broader base of candidates, so we were getting ones that weren't as good. Hedge funds began to migrate from a place where, collectively, they had a significant edge to more of an asset-gathering group. I think that now there are significant edges in hedge funds here and there, but it's not nearly as easy to find good ones in which to invest as it used to be, and I don't think the edge is as large. Hedge funds have headed toward being just another large asset class.

GEOFFREY GERBER: You mentioned the abundance not just in terms of hedge funds but even in terms of long-only managers. What are your thoughts on the crowding out theory?[14] As all of these quant managers started growing, did you have reason to change your model? Did it cause you to change how you implemented your market-neutral strategy?

EDWARD THORP: Basically, I had two large periods of hedge fund management. One was Princeton/ Newport Partners from 1969 through the end of 1988, during which I generally was using derivatives to hedge and capture excess return. One of the strategies that we developed during that period was something now known as statistical arbitrage.[15] We actually first found it in our shop in either December 1979 or January 1980. It was right around the end of the year. We were working on a project, and one of the researchers came and asked us to look at what he had done, which was running the portfolio of the most up stocks in the last month versus the most down stocks. He had run it over the past 18 years or so, using a CRSP database that went back to 1962 at that time, I think. In any case, there was a very statistically significant separation between the two portfolios. In fact, if you were long the recently most down stocks and short the recently most up stocks, you would have captured an annualized 20-percent return. It wasn't really regular. It had probably a standard deviation of 20 percent or 25 percent.

GEOFFREY GERBER: And huge turnover as well.

EDWARD THORP: Yes, huge turnover. So costs were a big issue. But even with the costs that we were paying, we could get fairly close to that. However, we were already making that much with convertible hedging, so we said, "Well, convertible hedging has much less risk, so we'll put this strategy aside as an interesting idea." Then Gerry Bamberger[16] at Morgan Stanley discovered this principle in 1982. He later felt that he had been marginalized and that the credit due him had been taken over by a person who had come in from the outside to run the quantitative group there. So Bamberger left Morgan Stanley, and he answered an ad that we had put out looking for people with strategies that might have an edge. So we co-ventured with him, and that worked quite well. We ran that strategy until the end of Princeton/Newport Partners. The original strategy began to weaken in 1987, so I devised a different version that then also did very well. When Princeton/Newport shut down in 1988, I took some time out and did Japanese warrant hedging and not much else. Then in 1992, a large Fortune 100 pension and profit-sharing plan that had been one of Princeton/Newport's investors heard how well statistical arbitrage was doing and we started a statistical arbitrage fund for them. We ran that until 2002, and we found that in later years—2000–2002—there seemed to be a lot more participants and the edge seemed to be diminishing. It had fallen from returns in the 20-percent range down into the low teens. I decided it wasn't worth doing and I might as well just take time out and enjoy myself, so we wound that down. I think times got a little tougher for statistical arbitrage after that.

GEOFFREY GERBER: Yes, they did. So you stopped in 2002?

EDWARD THORP: Yes. I basically then turned into a family office and just ran our family money, allocating it to hedge funds and to other places after that. We also do some securities research. We spent a fair amount of time looking at commodity trend following,[17] for example. That looked reasonably good when you examined the past, but then strategies that worked well in the past did not do nearly as well when you did them in real time. So it seemed like it was very hard to get rid of the data mining issue there.

GEOFFREY GERBER: And that would have been a reversal from reversal to momentum.

EDWARD THORP: Yes, exactly.

MARGARET TOWLE: In that regard, it does sound like you are working on some interesting projects. What are some of the areas, or the next problem, that you plan on tackling?

EDWARD THORP: Most recently I've been thinking about "black swan"[18] insurance. Just to use the terminology from Nassim Taleb's famous book, there are two worlds you can think about. One he called the world of "Mediocristan" in which standard statistics—the kind of statistics you see in the physical sciences, things that behave fairly reasonably—apply. The log-normal world of Black-Scholes is Mediocristan. Then there's the world of "Extremistan," where you get fat tails[19] and black swans and huge upside or downside moves periodically—the crash of 1987, the 2008–2009 period, and so forth. The question I've been thinking about is a simple one: Suppose that you can construct a portfolio that has three things in it—Treasury bills, a stock index, and options on that stock index—can you use the options to get a better payoff structure than if you didn't use options in that mix? Traditional investing, that is, a long index with any excess money going into Treasury bills just for super simplicity, would be modified by adding options. They could be way out of the money, they could be in the money, or whatever, and you have the constraint that you can't lose everything. So you can't put it all in options because if the market went down enough, you would lose all that you had invested. You just buy an option at Black-

Scholes prices, let the clock run for one time period, see what happens, and do it again. Then you analyze how the short-term and long-term payoff characteristics behave. I'm in the middle of looking at that now to see if we can get anything better by using options. It's been very interesting so far, but we're not done.

■ ■ ■

Suppose that you can construct a portfolio that has three things in it—Treasury bills, a stock index, and options on that stock index—can you use the options to get a better payoff structure than if you didn't use options in that mix?

MARGARET TOWLE: That does sound interesting. We would like to explore a few larger issues related to the role of an investment advisor or investment consultant for institutional clients. Many of our readers are part of this profession so we would like to get your perspective on how you see that role. We talked earlier about some of the mistakes investors might make. What do you see as the role of the investment advisor or consultant in helping investors avoid these mistakes, and how does that differ between institutional clients and individual clients?

EDWARD THORP: I sit on the board of a university endowment, a university foundation, and this comes up periodically at our meetings. We get advice from outside advisors, and it seems to me there are two issues. The first is to figure out what risk-return characteristics best suit the client, and that's going to vary from client to client. The second is to see whether there are any excess risk-adjusted returns that really are available. That's usually rather questionable from what I've seen. Most of the strategies that are proposed don't have demonstrable excess return in them. There are stories, but the stories usually aren't good enough. So I think one role of the investment advisor would be to very carefully screen out asset-gatherers who are masquerading as alpha-gatherers.

MARGARET TOWLE: That's good advice.

EDWARD THORP: It's a tough one, though, because there are a lot of conflicts of interest that arise, or that may arise, depending on who's paying whom what.

EDWARD BAKER: And once you identify such an investment manager, how would you characterize the objectives in their investment guidelines?

EDWARD THORP: I know the board that I sit on has investment guidelines that allocate in a certain range to various categories, such as real estate, private equity, bonds, domestic equity, international equity, and so forth. They move these guidelines around. They spend a lot of time adjusting the mixes. That's a traditional way to do it. You won't get in trouble doing it that way. I'm not sure that the time and energy spent get us very much, though. They'll debate whether to have 20 percent or 25 percent in domestic equity, and the finance committee will spend a lot of time offering opinions about this. Maybe they'll decide to move the guideline from 20 percent to 25 percent, but no matter what happens, it will only have an incremental effect on returns that is so small that it's hardly noticeable and appears to me to be almost random.

My view is that this should be a simplified process. Basically, people should be putting money into index funds when they can't demonstrate that an investment with similar characteristics is better. For instance, suppose that they go to a long equity manager. In order to give him money, I think they should have to be able to demonstrate that the index that most closely matches him—small stock, intermediate stock, growth, value—is not as good. It's tricky to do that with just historical information, because if you have 100 managers out there and none of them is any better than the index—let's say they're all the same, just to be charitable—then there will be a random fluctuation around the index return, and you tend to select the managers who did better. However, if in fact they had the same expected returns going forward, you would have accomplished nothing. Actually, what seems to happen, from what I can see, is that the underperformance roughly matches the fees. I would say that the burden of proof is on the non-index manager. There are inefficiencies in the market, but they're not easy to demonstrate, and I think that needs to be done before one shifts money in that direction.

MARGARET TOWLE: I think the industry does seem to be moving away from those traditional asset classes and categories to more factor-based exposures in allocating a portfolio. If we look at the so-called Yale model[20] or other models for endowments, there seems to be at least an argument that skill-based strategies—that is, more alpha rather than beta—would be appropriate for that. So your example of a long-only manager seems perfectly reasonable, given what we've seen about that as far as inefficiency, especially in the large capitalization area. What do you think about skill-based strategies, not even necessarily long/short, but a strategy such as a global macro where the manager is processing information and has a world view using a variety of instruments across many asset classes? Would that fit anywhere into your conceptual framework as far as endowments?

EDWARD THORP: Sure, it makes sense to me if you're outside the traditional markets where participants can force efficiency or extract profits if they don't get the markets to move toward efficiency. If you're in a situation like that, and many of the things you mentioned are like that, then it makes perfect sense that there are going to be opportunities out there. Then the real issue is demonstrating in any specific case that you've found something that qualifies. That was one of the original arguments for hedge funds, too. They could go where you couldn't have gone before or where you couldn't go on your own. There were inefficiencies there because not everybody could get at them to trade them away.

GEOFFREY GERBER: As a quant myself, I'd like to ask a question based on Scott Patterson's book, *The Quants: How a New Breed of Math Whizzes Conquered Wall Street and Nearly Destroyed It.* I know that book refers to you as "the godfather of the quants." As the godfather, what do you see as the future of quantitative investing, especially in light of the difficulties quants have faced over the past few years?

EDWARD THORP: I think that the opportunities for quantitative investing are likely to get better, simply because markets are becoming larger and more interconnected and the tools the quants have continue to improve. So that's one side of it. The other side is that there can be a disconnect between the models that the quants build and the real world, and that disconnect can lead to serious trouble, for example, the mortgage pool models or the Long-Term Capital Management[21] approach to doing things with super-high leverage, assuming the world is Mediocristan rather than something else. So we have those two sides of it, and I think there will be tension there as this evolves into the future.

MARGARET TOWLE: Are there any areas that we haven't asked you about that you think are relevant or that you'd like to discuss?

EDWARD THORP: One brief comment on market efficiency: It seems to me that to talk about markets being efficient or inefficient is not quite the right way to look at it. It's a combination of what's going on in the markets and the participants in the marketplace. Let me elaborate a little bit. Imagine a casino world where nobody knows about card-counting in blackjack. So everybody's playing along, and they're all losing 2 percent because they're using a strategy that on average loses that much. It's not the best strategy, and they don't think about the cards that fall. It doesn't seem to make any particular difference or, if it does, they don't know how to use that information. Then one person figures out how to count the cards that have been used and how to get an edge. Did the blackjack market suddenly become inefficient at that point, or was it inefficient before anybody figured this out? If the person who figures out how to count cards does nothing, is the market still efficient, or not? Or does that person actually have to walk in and play in order to make the market inefficient?

■ ■ ■

> One brief comment on market efficiency: It seems to me that to talk about markets being efficient or inefficient is not quite the right way to look at it. It's a combination of what's going on in the markets and the participants in the marketplace.

It seems to me that market efficiency or inefficiency is a joint property of the market itself, what's going on in it, and what the participants know and are able to do. If you look at any one person, that person will have some knowledge of markets and may have some knowledge of efficiency or inefficiency in markets, and that knowledge may be correct or incorrect. However, that is going to vary from person to person. For example, Warren Buffett has knowledge about the fundamentals of a lot of companies, among many other things. So in that area, the markets are inefficient from his point of view, but there are a hundred million people out there who don't have that knowledge, and they should behave as if the markets are efficient because, from their point of view, they don't have any edge at all. Again, I think it's a joint property of the participants and the markets and ought to be looked at that way. If a person says that he can beat this market because it's inefficient, that's not a good statement in itself. That person needs to be able to demonstrate that he has knowledge that gives him an edge in such a way that it can't be refuted by somebody acting as a devil's advocate. Basically, if you think there is inefficiency, you've got to use the devil's advocate test on it.

MEIR STATMAN: The way I like to phrase it is, "The market may be crazy, but that doesn't make you a psychiatrist."

EDWARD THORP: I like that.

■ ■ ■

ENDNOTES

[1] The first wearable computer was built in 1961 by Edward Thorp and Claude Shannon and used to predict roulette wheels. The system consisted of a pocket-sized analog computer, microswitches (worn in shoes) that indicated the speed of the wheel, and miniature speakers. The system was tested successfully in Las Vegas in June 1961, but hardware issues with the speaker wires prevented the system from being used beyond the first test runs. The device was first disclosed in the revised edition of Dr. Thorp's book *Beat the Dealer* (1962) and later discussed in detail in Thorp (1969).

[2] Claude Shannon (1916–2001), known as "the father of information theory" (the science behind the Internet and all digital media), was an American mathematician, electronics engineer, and cryptographer. His 1948 paper titled "A Mathematical Theory of Communication" formed the basis for the field of information theory. He also is credited with originating both digital computer and digital circuit design theory. Shannon was a member of the Massachusetts Institute of Technology faculty from 1956 to 1978.

[3] The Kelly criterion is a formula used in gambling to establish the optimal size of a series of bets and, by extension, to determine equity allocation and diversification in investing. It is named for John L. Kelly, Jr. (1923–1965), the scientist who formulated the criterion while working on long-distance telephone signal noise issues at AT&T's Bell Labs in the 1950s.

[4] Benjamin "Bugsy" Siegel (1906–1947), an American gangster, was one of the driving forces behind the development of Las Vegas and built the city's first major casino/hotel, the Flamingo, in 1946. As the result of a dispute over construction funds, Siegel was the target of a mob hit in 1947.

[5] Howard R. Hughes, Jr. (1905–1976) was an American aviator, industrialist, film producer, and philanthropist. Beginning in 1966, he purchased several casino/hotels, local television stations, and other major businesses in Las Vegas, with the expressed purpose of creating a glamorous image for the city.

[6] Warrants are derivative securities that entitle the holder to purchase the underlying securities (usually equities) of the issuing company at a specific price within a certain timeframe. Warrants are guaranteed by the issuing company, and the lifetime of a typical warrant is measured in years.

[7] The *RHM Survey of Warrants, Options, and Low-Price Stocks* was a hardcopy newsletter published by Sidney Fried of RHM Press in the 1950s through the 1970s.

[8] Sheen Kassouf (1929–2006) was an economist known for his research in financial mathematics. Kassouf was a founding faculty member and professor of economics at the University of California, Irvine.

[9] In 1973, Fischer Black (1938–1995) and Myron Scholes (1941–) published their option pricing theory, designed to calculate the value of an option by considering the stock price, strike price, expiration date, risk-free return, and the standard deviation of the stock's return. Later that year, Robert Merton expanded the theory and coined the term "Black-Scholes model."

[10] Ralph W. Gerard (1900–1974) was a neurophysiologist and behavioral scientist known for his work on the nervous system and psychopharmacology. In the latter part of his career, he focused on education and became the first dean of the graduate division at the newly formed University of California, Irvine, where he served from 1965 until his retirement in 1970.

[11] James (Jay) Regan served as managing general partner of Convertible Hedge Associates and Princeton/Newport Partners from 1969 to 1988. He is currently a general partner in Harcourt Enterprises.

[12] The Center for Research in Security Prices (CRSP) was established in 1960 with the initial mission of constructing an equity database that would include the prices, dividends, and rates of return of all stocks listed and trading on the New York Stock Exchange since 1926.

[13] To read the interview in its entirety, see Patterson (2008).

[14] The crowding out effect, within the context of quantitative managers, refers to the phenomenon that quantitative models driving a strategy's success are easy to replicate, which make opportunities to capture inefficiencies short lived. Thus, the phenomenon of many quantitative managers using the same models results in a crowding out of market opportunities.

[15] Statistical arbitrage is an equity trading strategy that uses mathematical modeling techniques to identify profit situations arising from pricing inefficiencies between securities.

[16] Gerald (Gerry) Bamberger, a computer science graduate from Columbia University, worked at Morgan Stanley & Co. in the early eighties. He left the firm in 1985.

[17] Commodity trend following is an investment strategy based on technical analysis of market prices rather than fundamental analysis.

[18] The black swan theory describes rare, unpredictable, and high-impact events. (The term comes from the fact that it was commonly assumed that all swans were white until black swans were discovered in Australia in the seventeenth century.). In his book, *The Black Swan: The Impact of the Highly Improbable*, Nassim Nicholas Taleb applied the term to events such as the rise of the Internet and the September 11, 2001, attacks on the United States.

[19] In a normal bell-shaped distribution of portfolio returns, the majority of returns can be found in the "bell," which centers around the weighted average return for the entire market. The ends, or tails, of the curve represent returns that are either extremely bad (left) or extremely good (right). Larger-than-normal tails are called "fat tails," indicating more data on the extremes than expected. Fat tails indicate that extreme market moves were more likely than would be predicted by normal distributions.

[20] David Swensen, the chief investment officer of Yale, developed the Yale model, (also known as the endowment model). The model relies on the tenets of modern portfolio theory for portfolio construction, with high allocation to alternative investments, (especially private markets), high allocation to equities, low allocation to fixed income and avoids market timing among asset classes.

[21] Long-Term Capital Management was a hedge fund established in 1994 that reached $7 billion under management by the end of 1997. The highly leveraged fund was designed to profit from combining academics' quantitative models with traders' market judgment and execution capabilities. In August 1998, following the Russian financial crisis and an ensuing flight to quality, the fund lost substantial amounts of capital and was on the brink of default. The threat of a systemic crisis in the global financial system led the U.S. Federal Reserve to orchestrate a $3.5 billion bailout by major U.S. banks and investment houses in September 1998. The fund closed in 2000.

REFERENCES

Black, Fischer, and Myron Scholes. 1973. The Pricing of Options and Corporate Liabilities. *Journal of Political Economy* 81, no. 3 (May/June): 637–654.

Einhorn, David, and Aaron Brown. 2008. Private Profits and Socialized Risk. *GARP Risk Review* (June/July): 10–26.

Kelly, J. L. Jr. 1956. A New Interpretation of Information Rate. *Bell System Technical Journal* 35: 917–926.

Patterson, Scott D. 2008. Old Pros Size Up the Game: Thorp and PIMCO's Gross Open Up on Dangers of Over-Betting, How to Play the Bond Market. *Wall Street Journal* (March 22): A9. http://online.wsj.com/news/articles/SB120614130030156085.

———. 2010. *The Quants: How a New Breed of Math Whizzes Conquered Wall Street and Nearly Destroyed It.* NY: Crown Business.

Poundstone, William. 2005. *Fortune's Formula: The Untold Story of the Scientific Betting System That Beat the Casinos and Wall Street.* New York, NY: Hill and Wang.

Shannon, Claude E. 1948. A Mathematical Theory of Communication. *Bell System Technical Journal* 27 (October): 379–423, 623–656.

Taleb, Nassim Nicholas. 2007. *The Black Swan: The Impact of the Highly Improbable.* New York: Random House.

Thorp, Edward O. 1960. Fortune's Formula: The Game of Blackjack. *Notices of the American Mathematical Society* (December): 935–936.

———. 1962. *Beat the Dealer: A Winning Strategy for the Game of Twenty-One.* New York: Random House.

———. 1969. Optimal Gambling Systems for Favorable Games. *Review of the International Statistical Institute* 37, no. 3: 273–293.

———. 1973. Extensions of the Black-Scholes Option Model. Contributed Papers, 39th Session of the International Statistical Institute, Vienna, Austria, August 1973, 1,029–1,036.

Thorp, Edward O., and Sheen T. Kassouf. 1967. *Beat the Market: A Scientific Stock Market System.* New York: Random House.

Thorp, Edward O., Leonard C. Maclean, and William T. Ziemba (editors). 2010. *The Kelly Capital Growth Investment Criterion: Theory and Practice.* Hackensack, NJ: World Scientific Publishing Company.

This interview was published in its entirety in *Journal of Investment Consulting* 12, no. 1, 2011.

INDEX

■ ■ ■

A

academic finance, 65, 132

accountability, 60, 63, 194

Ackerlof, George, 176

active investing, 32

active management, 14, 15, 16, 32, 33, 36, 90, 99, 100, 101, 102, 103, 185

Adelphia, 12, 21

administrative markets, 58, 60

admired companies, 103

adversarial collaboration, 47–48, 53n9

advertising, 48

advisors. *See also* consultants

    as choice architects, 182–183

    value of, 159–160

agency dilemma, 66n11

agency society, 13, 22

aggregate stock market earnings, 173–174

AIG, 138, 148

alpha, 5, 6, 7, 59, 74, 106, 161, 198

American put formula, 193

Ameriks, John, 174, 175

annuities/annuity options, 72, 112, 114, 131, 132, 138, 165–166, 181

anomalies, 36–37, 99, 155–157, 169, 181

Anson, Mark, 80n3

AQR, 83

arbitrage pricing theories, 141

Arrow, Kenneth J., 135n17, 159

Arrow type plan, 131

Asness, Cliff, 83, 87

asset allocation, 3, 6, 72, 74, 90, 92, 106, 124, 129, 147, 159

asset allocation model, 84

asset bubbles, 142

asset management, 83, 87, 92, 93

asset pricing, 27, 29, 34, 37, 103, 131, 155, 157

asset pricing model, 27, 34, 35, 36, 103, 131, 158. *See also* capital asset pricing model (CAPM)

asset pricing theory, 27

Australia, 75, 107

automatic enrollment, 179, 180

availability heuristic, 50, 53n10

B

Bamberger, Gerald (Gerry), 196, 201n16

Bank of New York, 69, 80n2

Barberis, Nicholas, 52, 54n17

Barra, Inc., 163

Barra models for equities, 163

Barra/S&P indexes, 163

Batterymarch Financial Management, Inc., 56, 58, 65, 66n2

The Battle for the Soul of Capitalism (Bogle), 20

Bayesian, 84, 93n6, 109

Bear Stearns, 145

Beat the Market (Thorp and Kassouf), 191, 192

behavioral finance/behavioral economics, 28–29, 30, 33, 52–53, 57, 60, 61, 91, 105, 157–158, 166, 167, 171, 173, 174, 177, 179, 181–182, 184

Behavioral Macroeconomics (Shiller and Ackerlof), 176

Benartzi, Shlomo, 179, 186n4

benchmarks, 126, 161, 162, 186

Bernanke, Ben, 12

Bernstein, Peter, 1–10

Bernstein-Macaulay, Inc., 10n1

beta, 5, 6, 74, 106, 107, 108, 142, 143, 154, 155, 181, 198

bias

    loss aversion bias/loss aversion, 46, 47, 52

    sufficiency bias, 179

big data, 121, 134n8

Black, Fischer, 60, 66n12, 83, 84, 93n4, 120, 132, 152n3, 159, 161, 185, 187n12, 192, 193, 200n9

Black Monday, 115n10

black swan theory, 109, 115n11, 196, 201n18

Black-Litterman model, 84–85, 93n5

Black-Scholes model, 4, 66n12, 111, 112, 113, 120, 132, 139, 141, 152n3, 191, 192, 196, 200n9

Bodie, Zvi, 157

Bogle, John C. (Jack), 11–25, 58, 66n9

Boltzman, Ludwig, 54n15

bottom-up approach, 59, 60

bounded rationality, 53, 54n19

Bowles, Erskine, 66n15

Box, George E. P., 135n19

Brandeis, Louis, 12, 25n1

Brignoli, Richard, 111, 115n15

Brignoli Models Inc., 115n15

Brinson, Gary, 115n5, 156

Brinson asset class view, 108

Bubba principle, 57

bubbles, 96, 97, 99, 142, 173, 177, 185

Buffett, Warren, 19, 21, 22, 24, 50, 190, 191, 199

Bundesbank, 66n14

buy-and-hold strategy, 172

C

California Public Employees' Retirement System (CalPERS), 6, 72, 80n3, 101

call-selling strategies, 138

call-writing strategies, 138, 139

Camerer, Colin F., 179, 186n3

Campbell, John, 96

capital asset pricing model (CAPM), 13, 27, 36, 37, 85, 112, 113, 131, 134n16, 143, 153n8, 154–156, 158, 159, 160, 174, 181, 184, 186

Capital Ideas Evolving (Bernstein), 2

Capital Ideas: The Improbable Origins of Modern Wall Street (Bernstein), 2

Caplin, Andrew, 174

CAPM/mean-variance paradigm, 155

Carhart, Mark, 83

"The Case for Mutual Fund Management" (Bogle), 14

CCA (contingent claims analysis), 127, 128, 134n14

Center for Research in Security Prices (CRSP), 35, 193, 201n12

central clearing corporation/clearinghouse, 139–141

Chartered Financial Analysts (CFA), 59

Chen, Jingqiu, 169

Chicago Board Options Exchange (CBOE), 192, 193

chief executive officer (CEO) compensation, 63, 67n16

Chile, 75

China, 62–63, 64

choice architecture, 182–183, 184

Cisco, 97–98

clients. *See also* investors

  customized solutions for, 148

  education of, 73–74, 111

  as pushing toward advisors forecasting future, 108–109

  responsibility of, 147

closed-end funds, 98, 99

CMH (cost matters hypothesis), 16

Cochrane, John H., 181, 187n8

collateralized waterfalls, 71

Columbia University, 118

commodities, 30–31, 89

commodity trend following, 196, 201n17

complexity, 60, 61–62, 71, 147, 175

Compustate, 35

confidence, 42, 43, 44, 45

consultants, role of, 8–9, 59, 92, 147–149, 171–173, 197. *See also* advisors

contingent claims analysis (CCA), 127, 128, 134n14

convertible bond model, 193

Convertible Hedge Associations, 191

Cornfeld, Bernard, 17, 25n4

corporate governance practices, 9, 21–23, 59–60, 63

corruption, 9

cost matters hypothesis (CMH), 16

cost of living adjustments (COLAs), 77

costs, as diminishing investors' share of pie, 24

covariance matrixes, 88

Cowles Foundation for Research in Economics, 105, 115n4

Cox, Christopher, 22

credit model, 120

crises, 3, 48, 68, 85–86, 88, 89, 91, 93n7, 107, 121, 127, 128, 132, 138–140, 144, 146, 149, 150, 151, 186

crowding, 85, 86

crowding out theory, 195

crowding out theory/effect, 201n14

CRSP (Center for Research in Security Prices), 35, 193, 201n12

D

dark pools, 57, 66n8

De Bondt, Werner F. M., 167, 181, 187n6

De Santis, Giorgio, 83

Debreu, Gerard, 159

debt model, 120

decay rates, 88

decision theory, 51

decumulation phase (of retirement), 180–181

defaulters, 123, 134n10

defined benefit (DB) business/plans, 7–8, 76, 122, 124, 125, 126, 127, 129, 131

defined contribution (DC) plans, 7, 75, 76, 122, 124, 125, 128, 129, 131, 179

derivatives, 5, 119, 132, 150, 194, 195

Dijk, Erik van, 113

Dimensional Fund Advisors, 128

Dimensional Managed DC (Managed DC), 128–129, 134n15

disclosure, 59–60

distribution

    fixed distributions, 191

    Gaussian distribution, 109

    nonnormal distributions, 31

    probability distribution, 109, 110, 113, 164

    stable distributions, 31

    Student's t-distribution, 109

diversification, 8, 13, 89, 102, 105, 106, 108, 157

Dodd, David, 182, 187n9

Donaldson, William, 22

Dow Jones Wilshire 5000 Total Market Index, 15

downside protection, 85

downside risk measures, 164

E

economic crises. *See* crises

Econs, 51, 53n11

efficient frontier, 105, 114, 115n2, 160

efficient market hypothesis (EMH), 13, 16, 182, 184, 185, 186

efficient market theory, 27, 28, 29, 39n5, 152, 168, 170

Einstein, Albert, 52, 54n15

emotion, role of, 46, 47, 50, 51

emotional happiness, 45

empirical asset pricing model, 112

endowments, 76, 90, 101, 146, 168, 198

"The End of Behavioral Finance" (Thaler), 182

Enron, 21, 103

environmental, social, and corporate governance investing (ESG), 91, 93n10

equal weighting, 114

equilibrium theory, 159

Equitable, 138

equity mutual funds, 18–19

Estonia, 74, 75

ethics

    of fees for advice, 9

    importance of, according to LeBaron, 57

Europe, 73, 132

evolutionary finance, 57

exchange-traded funds (ETFs), 17–18, 90, 170

exotic beta portfolio/strategy, 84, 88

expected utility theory, 52, 53n14, 119, 134n5, 175, 176

extreme value theory, 144

F

factors. *See also* Fama-French three-factor model; five-factor model; multifactor models; one-factor model

    momentum factor, 35, 36, 88

    sensitivity factors, 128

    size factor, 36

    value/growth factor, 36

failed agency society, 13

fairness, of fees, 47

Fama, Eugene F. (Gene), 26–39, 96, 97, 112, 113, 155, 181, 182, 186n5

Fama-French three-factor model, 34–35, 36, 39n10, 155, 181, 187n7

farm assets, 56–57

fat tails, 31, 32, 39n8, 109, 144, 153n9, 196, 201n19

federal fiduciary duty standard, 22

Federal Reserve, 82, 83, 91–92, 121, 127, 150

feedback loops, 98

fees

    for advice, 9, 47

    involved in index funds, 49

fiduciary duty, 12, 20, 22, 128, 129–130, 181

fiduciary philosophy, 13

finance theory, 121, 131, 151

financial crises. *See* crises

financial economics, 127, 164, 165

Financial Engines, 10n4, 109, 157

financial innovation, 148, 165

financial institutions, bailing out of, 139, 144–145, 146, 194

financial models, future of, 113

Fink, Laurence D. (Larry), 71, 81n7

First Index Investment Trust, 14

Fisher, Irving, 29, 39n6

five-factor model, 181

fixed distributions, 191

fixed income, 70–71, 75, 83, 85, 88, 90, 109, 112, 120, 126

flexibility, 144–145, 146, 147, 148, 149

flexible probabilities, 88

foundations, 76, 90

Foundations of Finance (Fama), 29

401(k)s, 74, 75, 102, 107, 109, 161, 164, 179, 183

framing, 54n18

French, Kenneth (Ken), 28, 29, 33, 34, 90, 113, 155, 181, 182

Friedman, Milton, 136, 152n1, 175, 176

front running, 66n7

Fuld, Richard S., Jr., 151, 153n15
Fuller and Thaler Asset Management, 182
fully discretionary accounts, 60
functionalism, 119, 134n4
fundamental indexing, 38–39

G

gambling games, 189–190, 191, 192
game theory, 115n12
GARCH process, 165
GASB (Governmental Accounting Standards Board), 126
Gaussian distribution, 109
General Motors, 12
Gerard, Ralph W., 191, 200n10
Gerstner, Lou, 21
Gibson, Roger, 109, 115n8
Ginnie Maes (GNMA) (Government National
　　Mortgage Association), 71, 81n5
global equilibrium, 84
goals-based investing, 120–121, 122–125, 129
gold, 62
Goldman Sachs, 83, 86, 87, 88, 89
government regulation, 139–141, 144
Governmental Accounting Standards Board (GASB), 126
Graham, Benjamin, 182, 187n9
Gray, Dale, 127, 134n12
Greenspan, Alan, 12, 96, 149, 153n13, 185, 187n13
Gross, William (Bill), 194
Grossman/Stiglitz paradox, 101
group psychology, 44
growth investing, 58, 60
Guided Choice, 109

H

Hansen, Lars Peter, 83, 93n3
Harvard University, 118
hedge funds
　　Fama on, 31–32
　　influence of, 95, 96
　　LeBaron on, 64
　　Leibowitz on, 74
　　monitoring costs of, 147
　　original argument for, 198
　　role of, 101, 190–191
　　Scholes on future of, 142
　　Shiller on, 170
　　Thorp on, 195

hedging, Bogle on, 18
hedonomics, 180
Heisenberg, Werner, 152n7
Heisenberg uncertainty principle of finance, 143
herding/herd behavior, 44, 45, 172
heuristics of judgment, 43, 53n5
high-frequency trading (HFT), 57, 66n6
holdout sample, 27
holistic managers, 62
Hong, Harrison, 169
housing bubble, 185–186
Hsee, Christopher K., 180
Hughes, Howard, Jr., 190, 200n5
humility, 1, 6

I

Ibbotson, Roger, 115n6
Ibbotson data, 108, 113
idiosyncratic risk, 106, 108, 142
illiquidity, 76, 101, 103, 113, 138–139, 144
immediate annuity, 112, 166
immunization, 69, 71, 72, 73
index funds/indexing/index management, 14, 15, 16–17,
　　18, 20, 22, 23, 49, 91, 98, 99, 100, 147, 198
individual retirement accounts (IRAs), 75, 102, 180
inflation
　　current lack of, 91
　　in retirement, 79–80
inflation-indexed bonds, 81n8
information ratio, 162
informed traders, 34
initial public offerings (IPOs), 3
innovation, financial, 148, 165
insider trading, 59
institutional ownership/investors, 20, 23, 63, 90, 95
intermediaries, role of, 141, 142, 143, 144, 145, 147, 148
international investing, 38
Internet, role of, 58
Internet bubble, 96, 97, 99, 185
Interstate Commerce Commission, 4
intrinsic value, 21, 28, 29, 184, 185, 186
intuition/intuitive thinking, 42, 43, 114, 173
investing
　　active investing, 32
　　environmental, social, and corporate governance
　　　　investing (ESG), 91

investing *(continued)*
  goals-based investing, 120–121, 122–125, 129
  growth investing, 58, 60
  international investing, 38
  liability-driven investing, 72
  passive investing, 32
  quantitative investing, 195, 198–199
  sustainable investing, 91
  value investing, 58, 60
  venture capital investing, 101, 146, 158
investment advisory profession, 5
Investment Companies (Wiesenberger Financial Services), 105, 115n1
investment guidelines, 197–198
investment shorts, 64
investor model, 145
investors. *See also* clients
  education of, 24, 73–74
  mistakes made by, 172–173
  responsibility of, 147
IPOs (initial public offerings), 3
IRAs (individual retirement accounts), 75, 102, 180
Irrational Exuberance (Shiller), 168, 169, 176
irrationality, 6, 29, 30, 33, 34, 36, 51, 96, 97, 98, 99, 157, 176
Ivest Fund, 17

J

Jacobs, Bruce, 113
James, Estelle, 74
January effect, 99
Jensen, Michael Cole (Mike), 185, 187n11
John Magee paper, 58, 66n10
Jung, Jeeman, 173

K

Kahneman, Daniel, 41–54, 167, 178, 186n1
Kassouf, Sheen, 191, 200n8
Kelly, J. L., 190
Kelly criterion, 190, 200n3
Kepos Capital, 83, 84, 85, 86, 87, 88, 90
Keynes, John Maynard, 52, 54n16
Klein, Gary, 43, 53n6
Kondratieff, Nikolai, 66n4
Kondratieff long-wave winter, 66n5
Kondratieff waves, 57, 61, 66n4
Koopmans, Tjalling C., 105, 115n3
Kritzman, Mark, 113

L

Lancaster, Kelvin, 153n12
law of small numbers, 42, 53n4
Lay, Ken, 103
Leahy, John V., 174
LeBaron, Dean, 55–65
Lehman Brothers, 139, 140, 143, 145, 146, 151, 152n5
Leibowitz, Martin L. (Marty), 68–80
Leland O'Brien Rubinstein Associates, 111
level playing field, lack of, 194
leverage, 86, 96, 107, 109, 110, 111, 126, 127, 144–145, 150–151, 199
Levy, Haim, 110
Levy, Ken, 113
liability calculations, 77
liability-driven investing, 72
libertarianism, 59, 66n11
life satisfaction, 45
life-cycle funds (life-stage funds), 7, 10n3, 160, 161
Lifecycle Hypothesis, 122, 131
life-style funds, 160
linear programming, 105
Lintner, John, 27, 116n17
Lipsey, Richard, 153n12
liquidity, 2, 34, 76, 86, 88, 101, 103, 113, 126, 142, 143, 144, 146, 147, 149
Litterman, Robert B. (Bob), 82–93, 159
Lo, Andrew, 22
lobbying, 59
long-only investments, 170
long-only manager, 195, 198
Long-Term Capital Management (LTCM), 120, 134n7, 137, 152n4, 199, 201n21
loss aversion bias/loss aversion, 46, 47, 52

M

MacBeth, James, 37
machines, role of, 58
macro models, 121, 127
Macro Securities Research, 170
macro statistical arbitrage, 87
macroconsistency, 158, 159
macroeconomics, 60, 120, 149, 176, 177
macrofinancial risk, 127
macro-inefficiency, 7, 173
Magee, John, 66n10
Malkiel, Burton G. (Burt), 95–103

Managed DC (Dimensional Managed DC), 128–129, 134n15

managers, average tenure of in fund industry, 15

Mandelbrot, Benoît, 31, 39n7

market efficiency, 36, 96, 99, 100, 101, 112, 141, 146, 157, 168, 170, 184, 199–200

market inefficiency, 33, 36, 98, 99, 101, 103, 157, 159, 168, 169, 190, 199–200

market mistakes, 98, 99

market model, 143

market regulation, 52–53

market risk/reward theory, 154

market timing, 90, 96, 106, 169

Markowitz, Harry M., 4, 6, 13, 37, 39n11, 104–114, 159, 160

Massachusetts Institute of Technology (MIT), 26, 82, 83, 118, 119

mathematics, role of, 52

mean variance, 6

mean variance risk-return paradigm, 107

mean-variance analysis, 105–108

mean-variance approximation, 110

mean-variance portfolio theory, 105

mean-variance theory, 119, 134n6

mental accounts, 46, 47

Merton, Robert C., 118–133, 152n3, 157, 200n9

Merton, Robert K., 119, 134n3

micro-efficiency, 7, 173

Microsoft, 12

Miller, Merton, 26, 27, 28, 36, 39n1, 136, 152n2

miracle of compounding returns, 16

mistakes
  by investors, 172–173
  of market, 98, 99

MIT (Massachusetts Institute of Technology), 26, 82, 83, 118, 119

models
  asset allocation model, 84
  asset pricing model. *See* asset pricing model
  Black-Scholes model. *See* Black-Scholes model
  capital asset pricing model (CAPM). *See* capital asset pricing model (CAPM)
  convertible bond model, 193
  credit model, 120
  debt model, 120
  empirical asset pricing model, 112
  Fama-French three-factor model, 34–35, 36, 155, 181
  financial models, future of, 113
  five-factor model, 181

models *(continued)*
  investor model, 145
  macro models, 121, 127
  market model, 143
  Merton on, 132–133
  multibeta model, 155
  multifactor models, 27
  one-factor model, 85, 106, 108
  option pricing theory/model, 120, 137–138, 152n3, 200n9
  of prediction, 181
  QP (quadratic programming) model, 163
  random walks/random walk model, 26, 27
  rational agent hypothesis/model, 51, 53
  rational model, 181, 184
  Sharpe-Lintner-Mossin Capital Asset Pricing Model, 113. *See also* capital asset pricing model (CAPM)
  Thaler on, 186
  theoretical equilibrium model, 116n17
  trader model, 145
  Yale model, 198

Modigliani, Franco, 119, 134n2

Modigliani-Miller theorem, 186, 187n14

Modigliani's Lifecycle Hypothesis, 122, 131

momentum factor, 35, 36, 88

money market funds, 138, 139

Monks, Bob, 21

Monte Carlo simulation/analysis, 108, 109, 110, 112, 114, 115n7, 127, 134n13

Morgan Stanley, 196

Morgenstern, Oskar, 110, 115n12

Mossin, Jan, 116n17

multibeta model, 155

multifactor models, 27

multi-lens framework, 60

multiperiod equilibrium, 165

mutual funds, 11–12, 22, 23–24, 99–100, 168

Mygren, Simon, 113

*my*RA, 180

N

narrow framing, 52, 54n18

Neff, John, 15

network effect, 93n12, 114

neuro-economics, 50

new economy funds, 19

the new normal, 78–79

next-generation retirement system design/implementation, 120

no-arbitrage principle, 194

noise traders, 34

nonnormal distributions, 31

A Non-Random Walk Down Wall Street (Lo), 22

Nudge (Thaler and Sunstein), 179, 182

numéraire, 131, 132, 135n18

O

Omega, 142–143

one-factor model, 85, 106, 108

optimism, 44, 50

optimization, 107, 114, 121, 123, 158, 159, 161

option pricing theory/model, 120, 137–138, 152n3, 200n9

optionality, 145, 146, 151

options formula, 192, 193

Orange County, California bankruptcy, 69, 80n1

overconfidence, 43, 48, 49, 50

over-the-counter (OTC) market, 89, 139–141

ownership society, loss of, 20, 22

P

Pacific Investment Management Company (PIMCO), 78

Page, Sebastien, 113

passive investing, 32

Patterson, Scott, 198

pension funds, 44, 45, 56, 69–74, 77, 101, 106, 115n5, 125, 146, 163

pension plans, 74, 77, 78, 90, 125, 126, 127, 165, 181

Pension Protection Act of 2006, 123, 134n9

Pension Relief Act of 2010, 126, 134n11

perceived risk, 175

performance, measurement of, 162

performance persistence, 99

personal finance, 165

PIMCO (Pacific Investment Management Company), 78

policy portfolio, 6, 158, 159

portable alpha, 5, 6, 10, 39

portfolio insurance, 98, 111, 115n14

"Portfolio Selection" (Markowitz), 105

portfolio theory, 4, 13, 104, 105, 106, 109, 112, 124

"Portfolio Theory versus Financial Engineering, and Their Roles in Financial Crises" (Markowitz), 107

prediction markets, 61, 66n13

price theory, 28

price/earnings (P/E) ratios, 172

A Primer on Money, Banking, and Gold (Bernstein), 2

Princeton University, 41, 95

Princeton/Newport Partners, 191, 192, 193, 195, 196

principal-agent problem, 60, 66n11

principles-based regulatory framework, 3

private equity investments, 76

probability distribution, 109, 110, 113, 164

prospect theory, 52, 53n13, 175

puts and calls, 111, 112

putty clay, 153n10

Q

QP (quadratic programming) model, 163

quant crisis, 85–86, 87, 93n7

quant equity space, 86, 87

quant managers, 195, 198

quantitative investing, 195, 198–199

The Quants: How a New Breed of Math Whizzes Conquered Wall Street and Nearly Destroyed It (Patterson), 198

Qubes, 18

R

random walks/random walk model, 26, 27

A Random Walk Down Wall Street (Malkiel), 95, 96, 98, 99

Ranieri, Lewis S. (Lew), 71, 81n6

rational agent hypothesis/model, 51, 53, 53n12

rational expectations, 83, 93n1

rational model, 181, 184

rational valuation, 97

rationality, 51. *See also* bounded rationality

ratios

    information ratio, 162

    price/earnings (P/E) ratios, 172

    reward-to-variability ratio, 161, 162

    Sharpe ratio, 90, 161–162, 164

Regan, James (Jay), 191, 201n11

regression analysis of time series (RATS), 82

regret, 46

regulation, 37, 52–53, 132, 139–141, 144

Reinhart, Carmen M., 79

relative asset pricing theory, 131

research, issues that need to be addressed, 165–166

retirement

    funding for as complex problem, 130

    goal setting for, 122

    how we think about, 165–166

retirement *(continued)*
  next-generation retirement system design/implementation, 120
return-generating process, 165
reverse optimization, 159
reward-to-variability ratio, 161, 162
RHM Survey of Warrants, Options, and Low-Price Stocks, 191, 200n7
risk
  idiosyncratic risk, 106, 108, 142
  macrofinancial risk, 127
  misassessment of, 149–150
  perceived risk, 175
  systemic risk, 92, 121, 142
risk aversion, 160, 174, 175
risk management, 6, 18, 83, 85–87, 88–89, 92, 141, 148, 151
risk premia, 84, 85, 88, 90
risk tolerance, 45, 147, 149, 160, 174, 175
risk-free assets, 125, 131, 132
risk-parity approach, 84–85
risk-return story, 35
risk-return tradeoff, 107
risk-transfer services, 142
Roberts, Harry, 26, 39n2
Rogoff, Kenneth S., 79
Rosenfeld, Andrew, 45, 53n7
Rubinstein, Mark, 111
rules-based regulatory framework, 3
Russell, Frank, 163

S

S&P Depositary Receipts (SPDR), 18
Salomon Brothers, 68, 69, 70
Samuelson, Paul, 7, 14, 22, 118, 119, 134n1, 173
Sarbanes-Oxley Act, 3–4, 10n2, 37
Sargent, Thomas J. (Tom), 83, 93n2
Savage, Leonard J., 110, 115n13, 175
scalping, 57, 66n7
scandals, 12, 23, 63, 69
Schachter, Stanley, 184, 187n10
Scherbina, Anna, 170
Scholes, Myron S., 66n12, 120, 132, 136–152, 152n3, 192, 200n9
second best, theory of, 149
Securities and Exchange Commission (SEC), 4, 148
Security Analysis (Dodd and Graham), 187n9

semivariance, 110
sensitivity factors, 128
shadow-banking system, 142
Shannon, Claude, 189, 190, 200n2
shareholder/owner approach, 12
shark repellents, 57, 66n3
Sharpe, William F. (Bill), 5, 7, 13, 27, 109, 112, 116n17, 143, 154–166
Sharpe ratio, 90, 93n9, 161–162, 164
Sharpe-Lintner-Mossin Capital Asset Pricing Model, 113. *See also* capital asset pricing model (CAPM)
Shiller, Robert J. (Bob), 96, 98, 167–177
shocks, 107, 122, 127, 142, 143, 144, 145, 146, 149, 150, 151, 185
short positions, 169, 170–171
short selling, 10, 169
short-sale constraints, 169–170
short-sale rule, 116n18
Siegel, Benjamin (Bugsy), 190, 200n4
Sims, Christopher (Chris), 83
Simscript, 105
Simscript II, 105
simulations, 155. *See also* Monte Carlo simulation/analysis
size factor, 36
small numbers, law of, 42, 53n4
Smith, Adam, 21
Social Security, 53, 74, 75, 80, 124, 129, 147, 165, 179
socially responsible stocks/social responsibility, 19–20, 27, 28, 29, 103
SPDR (S&P Depositary Receipts), 18
specialization, 19, 65
speed limits, 144
stable distributions, 31
Standard & Poor's 500 Stock Composite Index, 14, 15, 106, 109, 111
Stanford University, 82, 83, 136, 154
statistical arbitrage, 57, 87, 195, 196, 201n15
Stein, Jeremy C., 169
stock picks, Malkiel on, 98
stop-loss limits, 46, 53n8
strategic asset allocation, 106
Student's *t*-distribution, 109, 115n9
Student's *t*-tests, 115n9
substitution versus flows, theory of, 141
sufficiency bias, 179
Sunstein, Cass, 179, 183
Surowiecki, James, 157

surprise, as inevitable, 8

sustainable investing, 91

Swensen, David, 22, 23, 201n20

Switzerland, 63

System 1, 42, 43, 44, 45, 48, 51, 53n3

System 2, 42, 44, 45, 48, 51, 53n3

systemic risk, 92, 121, 142

systemic risk regulator, 142, 152n6

T

tactical asset allocation, 106

Taleb, Nassim Nicholas, 115n11, 196, 201n18

target date funds, 10n3, 120, 130, 179, 181

target rate of return, 90

taste, matters of, 19, 27–28, 29, 30, 32, 33, 35, 36, 147–148

technology bubble, 185

Thain, John, 87

Thaler, Richard (Dick), 41, 51, 53n1, 167, 178–186

theoretical equilibrium model, 116n17

theories

    asset pricing theory, 27

    black swan theory, 109, 196

    crowding out theory/effect, 195, 201n14

    decision theory, 51

    efficient market theory, 27, 28, 29, 39n5, 152, 168, 170

    equilibrium theory, 159

    expected utility theory, 52, 53n14, 119, 134n5, 175, 176

    extreme value theory, 144

    finance theory, 121, 131, 151

    market risk/reward theory, 154

    mean-variance portfolio theory, 105

    mean-variance theory, 119, 134n6

    option pricing theory/model, 120, 137–138, 152n3, 200n9

    portfolio theory, 4, 13, 104, 105, 106, 109, 112, 124

    price theory, 28

    prospect theory, 52, 175

    relative asset pricing theory, 131

    theory of risk-return, 27

    theory of second best, 149, 153n12

    theory of substitution versus flows, 141

Theory of Games and Economic Behavior (von Neumann and Morgenstern), 115n12

The Theory of Finance (Fama and Miller), 31

The Theory of Investment Value (Williams), 104

Thinking, Fast and Slow (Kahneman), 42, 43, 51

Thorp, Edward O. (Ed), 188–200

three pillar system, 74–75

three-factor model, 181. *See also* Fama-French three-factor model

TIAA–CREF, 75

time series, 149, 153n14

timing, investors as having innate sense of bad timing, 19

top-down strategy, 113

Towers Watson, 75

trader model, 145

trading, lack of understanding about, 34

transparency, 4, 194

Treasury inflation-protected securities (TIPS), 63, 125

Treynor, Jack L., 161

"Trusting the Stock Market" (Guiso et al.), 37

Tversky, Amos, 41, 42, 46, 51, 52, 53n2, 167, 178, 186n2

2 and 20, 33, 39n9

tyranny of compounding costs, 16

U

Unconventional Success (Swensen), 23

United Kingdom, 3, 77, 125

University of British Columbia, 42

University of California, Irvine, 191

University of California, San Diego, 104

University of Chicago, 26, 104, 105, 136, 179

University of Minnesota, 82, 83

uptick rule, 113, 116n18

U.S. Department of Labor, 181

U.S. Treasury bonds, 63

Usmen, Nilufer, 109

"Utility of Wealth" (Markowitz), 105

V

value investing, 58, 60

value/growth factor, 36

Vancil, Richard F. (Dick), 56, 66n1

Vanguard 500 Index Fund, 14

Vanguard Index Participation Equity Receipts (VIPER), 18

The Vanguard Group, 12, 13, 14–15, 17, 18, 23, 179

variance, use of, 7

variance swap, 89, 93n8

venture capital investing, 101, 146, 158

volatility, 7, 60, 71, 84, 85, 88, 89, 108, 127, 141, 143, 146, 148, 149, 150, 167, 176

Volcker, Paul A., Jr., 91, 93n11

von Neumann, John, 110, 115n12

W

warrant formulas, 191
warrants, 137, 191, 192, 200n6
waterfall, 71, 81n4
wearable computer, 189, 200n1
Weill, Sanford (Sandy), 2
well-being, 5, 45, 49, 50
Wellington Fund, 11, 17
Wellington Management Company, 14, 15, 17
Wiesenberger Financial Services, 14, 25n3, 105
Williams, John Burr, 104–105
Windsor Fund, 15
Winston, Ken, 163
Wisdom of Crowds (Surowiecki), 157
Wolfowitz, Paul, 9
World Bank, 9
WorldCom, 21

Y

Yale model, 198
Yale University, 95, 167
Your Money and Your Brain (Zweig), 114

Z

Zweig, Jason, 114